Global Inequality and Human Needs

Preface

In the wake of the terrorist attacks of September 11, 2001, many Americans were jarred into forming a more global perspective. For some, the consequences of American political and economic policies could no longer be compartmentalized, held separate from the daily routines of family, work, and consuming goods in a global marketplace. Some Americans acknowledged that, although the perpetrators were guilty of a horrific crime, the American way of life and its foreign policies during the preceding decades had played a role in generating the anger that fueled support for extremists rather than for moderates. Of course, for many other Americans, the attacks were simply the acts of an inscrutable and evil enemy. For them, President Bush's rhetoric of the Evil Empire resonated, similar as it is to the long tradition of Cold War political posturing. The president's threat to use first-strike nuclear weapons against enemies goes yet further as saber-rattling in the face of global uncertainty.

The threat of terrorist attacks became a public health threat, whether from violent explosions or from chemical or biological agents. Will the threat promote a revitalization of the U.S. public health infrastructure, which provides health prevention and education, inoculations, health screenings, and treatments? Dealing with health care, education, and poverty should be, in my opinion, high on the national agenda—especially now. These are our best defenses against ignorance and evil, and the building blocks of a democratic society with a high standard of living.

The impetus for this book came from three experiences. The first involved working for several years as a researcher in AIDS prevention, alongside professionals trained in public health, psychology, and medicine. I was disappointed to see how little sociological insights had penetrated their conceptual approaches. However, it was heartening that I and other sociologists and anthropologists could make a meaningful contribution to prevention efforts that were rooted in the everyday routines and social life of at-risk individuals. Combining public health and sociological work was rewarding, and I hope that this book also contributes in that direction.

A second impetus came from teaching a course on world affairs to senior sociology majors and finding that few books highlighted the human costs (in mental and physical health) of social class and global inequalities. This book focuses on health and illness as primarily social phenomena. It identifies several principles for better understanding the distribution of health as a resource—and its relationship to the distribution of other resources.

A third impetus came from being asked for several years to teach a course about human stress which had been geared to middle-class concerns of time pressures and stress management. As a macrosociologist, I began building an analysis of human stress that recognized social class and gender differences, as well as global differences in standard of living, level of violence, and extent of inequality. As I began to read in the area of social inequality and health, as well as the detailed reports of the World Health Organization and World Bank, along with weekly world events in the *Economist*, a larger picture of human stress emerged—one that is structured by economic, political, and social institutions and events.

My goal is to bring together some of these disparate areas (health statistics, world events, global economy, class relations) in ways that make conceptual and empirical sense, and to point to some of the patterns underlying the seeming uniqueness of case examples. For this reason, two chapters (Chapters 2 and 3) are devoted to theory, and most chapters have a heavy dose of conceptual interpretation, linking cases to broader patterns.

Perhaps this book raises as many questions as it answers. My hope is to generate interest and curiosity in the subject and to provide tools for us to carry on as global citizens. The morning paper and network news don't provide enough information for us to do this; alternative sources of news and information are essential. This is a time when U.S. well-being is equated with economic growth and consumer spending. There is no other way, according to the chair of the Federal Reserve, Lou Dobbs's *Moneyline*, and others representing the economic, political, and media status quo. And yet there are other ways in which the standard of living can be improved and inequality reduced. Equity-enhancing strategies could improve the quality of social life and do less damage to the environment and to less-privileged populations at home and abroad. I have provided policy examples that help to make this point.

Acknowledgments

Several colleagues helped with this project. Tony Waters generously read most chapters (a couple of them twice) and gave invaluable feedback. He provided the social status–versus–wealth example of Mother Teresa compared to a Colombian drug lord (Chapter 2). My friend and colleague of over twenty-five years, Katherine Mooney, read the entire manuscript and made many helpful comments and suggestions. My friends and colleagues Cynthia Siemsen and Janja Lalich each read a chapter and provided a fresh perspective when I was growing weary. I am grateful for the attention these individuals gave to this project at times when their own lives were busy and demanding.

Several students also played a role in this project. I thank Meka Klungtvet-Morano for her precision and consistency in helping me to research, track, and proofread a long list of references. During various stages of the process, several students sought out sources for me; help came from Gracious Palmer, Corrina Bettencourt, Robin Winston, and Jennifer Billesbach-Harris. Giovanna Bacigalupi helped with the glossary and finding documents.

My friends and colleagues in the Gumption Collective (Nandi Crosby, Andy Dick, Liahna Gordon, Dan Pence, and Cynthia Siemsen) provided support and encouragement during the final stages. My dean, Jeanne Thomas, and department chair,

Kathleen Kaiser, provided financial support for student assistance during the last months of the project.

I thank Jeff Lasser and Andrea Christie at Allyn and Bacon for their assistance and support. And thanks to the following reviewers who provided helpful suggestions: Barbara H. Chasin, Montclair State University; Cheryl Howard, University of Texas, El Paso; Jonathan F. Lewis, Benedictine University; and David G. Peck, Shippensburg University.

Tom and Sean Murphy, my husband and son, deserve special thanks for their patience and wacky senses of humor. I dedicate this book to them. Tom read and commented on chapters even when his own programming work was overdue, and Sean counted words in a quote and looked up page numbers. During this project he was transformed from a middle-sized child into a six-foot thirteen-year-old. So my child and this book came of age together.

I am responsible for any errors or oversights in the following chapters. I have done my best to attribute the many scholars whose work is represented here. I thank them and hope that this book will offer new insights and make students more familiar with their research. Readers' comments and suggestions are welcome at lwermuth@csuchico.edu.

Thinking Socially About Health

The health system . . . has the responsibility to try to reduce inequalities by preferentially improving the health of the worse-off. . . . The objective of good health is really twofold: the best attainable average level—goodness—and the smallest feasible differences among individuals and groups—fairness.

—World Health Organization, *The World Health Report 2000*

Afghanistan's string of recent wars already has produced the largest number of refugees in the world—some 3.6 million. Some 900,000 Afghans are internally displaced—the result of a drought and continued fighting between the Taliban and its opponents. The numbers are numbing. But, like those who died in the Sept. 11 attacks, each one represents a story, and a tragedy.

—"Embracing Afghan Refugees," *Christian Science Monitor*, September 19, 2001

For centuries, gravestones have revealed that the wealthy live longer than the poor. A more recent realization is that social inequality—not just poverty—is harmful to people's health. Societies are becoming less equal: Inequality within countries is increasing sharply, and inequality among countries is increasing as well. According to the United Nations, in 1960 the 20 percent of people living in the richest countries had thirty times the income of the poorest 20 percent. By 1997 that figure had risen to seventy-four times. Just as income and wealth differences between the more and the less privileged are growing, so is the gap between those who become ill and die young, and those who live long, healthy lives. This may be called "the health and longevity gap" between the wealthy and the poor. Pockets of poverty, even in developed countries, put citizens' mental and physical health in jeopardy. Ethnic, social class, and territorial disputes; civil unrest; war; and genocide continue to traumatize civilians and claim thousands of lives.

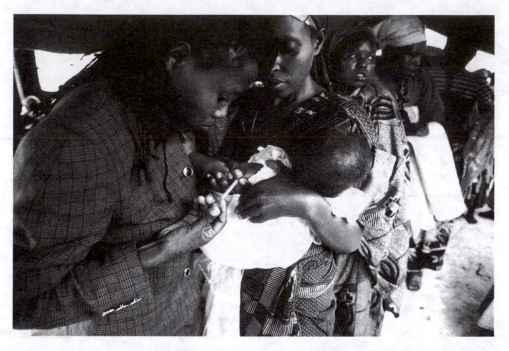

A clinic in Rwanda sponsored by UNICEF provides vaccinations to infants. Local clinics save lives with preventive and primary health care.

A countertrend is that, overall, longevity continues to inch upward in poor as well as wealthy countries. In poor countries, this is in large part due to technological advances that save lives. For example, rehydration techniques prevent infants from dying from diarrhea, and inoculations guard them against life-threatening illnesses. However, these improvements are by no means universal; thousands of infants and children still die of preventable ailments. In wealthy countries, with increasingly high standards of living, longevity inches upward with improvements in the standard of living, despite the increasing disparity between the health of the affluent and the poor.

This book explores health differences among social groups and between societies. This first chapter introduces models for thinking about health socially and proposes a political economy approach to examining health inequalities. We consider the following questions:

- What are the social influences on health and disease?
- Why do some social groups become ill and die prematurely more often than others?
- Are there social policies that can protect individuals from harmful influences?

What Is a Healthy Society?

In a healthy society, people have a better chance of living a long life. People have fewer years impaired by chronic illness, emotional problems, or disability. "Healthy society" is a relative concept, of course, because optimal health varies historically. What would be considered an average life expectancy in 1900 (forty something) would be considered short by today's standards, with life expectancies in the seventies in most developed societies. Population "gains" in health include increased life expectancy, less childhood and early adulthood disease, and fewer years of disability.

Thinking Socially About Health

Public health experts are used to thinking about health in individualistic terms, a value that reflects cultural views in developed societies. Most of us think about health as resulting from some combination of our physical constitution, our behaviors, and turns of nature. We think of illness in biological terms, such as cancerous cells multiplying into a tumor or viruses attacking a fatigued body. Public health messages and the popular media encourage us to take care of our health through sound eating and exercise habits, and they urge us to avoid the harmful effects of smoking, drinking, and driving under the influence. We learn on the news about environmental risks and screening tests for genetically linked diseases. More foreign is the idea that our country, occupation, income, neighborhood, and marital status could influence our likelihood of becoming ill and dying prematurely. And yet, when told that wealthy people live longer than poor people, we are not surprised. We realize that the resources available to those with a high standard of living have payoffs in health and well-being.

Public health officials take a broader view when they look at how disease travels. Public health workers intervene to reduce smoking and drunk driving accidents, to control high blood pressure, and to prevent and treat influenza, syphilis, tuberculosis, and HIV infection. These efforts have prolonged and saved lives. Public health researchers have also tried community-based health interventions. Such projects promote healthy behaviors, such as avoiding smoking and using seatbelts and car seats. Other examples include community campaigns aimed at preventing teen pregnancy and sexually transmitted diseases. In each of these cases, the campaign is successful if behavioral norms are changed. However, interventions have not been able to address the underlying problems of poverty or high levels of social inequality that contribute to unhealthy behaviors; that is, the social aspects of health.

The social aspects of health and disease are poorly evaluated in official U.S. health data, which do not include measures of poverty. The chief agency for tracking disease in the United States, the Centers for Disease Control and Prevention, generally has not collected social class indicators. In place of social class, "race" is used to measure social group differences. Unfortunately, racial categories tell us little in the absence of the social class variables (income, education, and occupation). Because "race" is primarily a social category rather than a biological one, racial categories create an erroneous impression of biologically based differences. Ethnicity does explain some of the differences in disease and death rates, but these differences can be discovered only by controlling for social class, age, gender, and country of birth. This contributes to confusion about race-based explanations for disease differences. For a better understanding of how to improve health outcomes and reduce illness among those most affected, the relative weight of these variables must be analyzed. When social class is controlled for, most of the variations among ethnic groups disappear.

Researchers advise that we need better data in order to study the social inequalities in health. They often compare ours with British and European data, which include measures of social class.

Despite these well-known associations, we are hampered in our efforts to track, understand, and reduce socioeconomic inequalities in health for two reasons. First, U.S. vital statistics, disease registries, and medical care utilization statistics, unlike those in many European countries, report only basic data about the health of the nation in terms of race, sex, and age, even when the socioeconomic data may be available. Yet the data reported often form the basis for policy. Second, the measures used are often inconsistent and inadequate for capturing the full range of socioeconomic disparity. For example, our focus on the poor and the nonpoor obscures a whole range of socioeconomic differences that affect health (Moss & Krieger 1995, 302–303).

Professional journals are now publishing a flurry of studies that include socioeconomic status, as measured by income, education, or occupation in the United States, and researchers are pointing to the dramatic health differences of privileged versus disadvantaged social groups. Authors are articulating the need for policies that reduce inequalities (Kaplan & Lynch 1997; Wilkinson 1994, 1996, 1997; Williams & Collins 1995; Rogers et al. 2000). However, government has been slow to take up the charge, with the result that U.S. health disparities continue to be poorly measured. This is a convenient state of affairs for those wishing to avoid creating policies that address the underlying causes of health disparities.

Social Networks, Social Isolation, and Health

A by-product of an individualistic notion of health is that human *social* needs are overlooked, despite clear evidence that isolation is harmful to mental and physical health (House et al. 1988). Observers have known for some time that social factors affect health. A century ago, sociologist Emile Durkheim (1897/1966) observed that socially isolated people are more likely to commit suicide. In the United States, evidence from the mid-twentieth century indicated that unmarried and more socially isolated people were known to have higher rates of tuberculosis, accidents, and psychiatric disorders (Dohrenwend & Dohrenwend 1969; Holmes 1956; Kohn & Clausen 1955; Tillman & Hobbs 1949). Following Durkheim, researchers surmised that supportive relationships anchor and buffer us from life's stresses and strains. For example, marriage is a health buffer in the contemporary United States: Deaths from all causes are consistently higher for unmarried than for married adults. Especially men's health benefits from marriage, with fewer suicides and illnesses, more successful recovery from surgery, and longer life expectancy than for unmarried men. For all societies, a reasonable hypothesis is that, where there are supportive social ties, there are health benefits to the population.

An individualistic approach to health also obscures its cultural and institutional underpinnings. Keeping infants, children, and adults well; nursing ill people back to health; and providing life-giving care to the chronically ill are essentially *social* endeavors, embedded in personal and institutional relationships. For example, families are central to maintaining health. Adults watch over the health of their children, partners, and often aging parents as well. In many countries, school personnel monitor symptoms of illness among children and deliver health screening and inoculation services. Nonprofit community organizations provide supportive services for ill, disabled, and dependent persons. An array of programs helps to keep people socially connected and healthy. In addition, medical practice has the potential to care for the social as well as the biological needs of patients. Many health care providers practice compassionate medicine, personally contributing to the health of their patients.

The AIDS Epidemic

The HIV/AIDS epidemic, which began in the early 1980s, slowly moved the U.S. medical world out of its paradigm of viewing the individual as *the* unit of analysis. After a few years of tracking the human immunodeficiency virus, it became clear that, if transmission was to be slowed, the social relationships in which risk behaviors occurred needed to be understood. The San Francisco gay men's community was initially hesitant in its own preventive efforts but then launched a community-based campaign that brought remarkable reductions in risk behaviors. It quickly became a model for community-based AIDS prevention. This grassroots movement altered norms of behavior within supportive communities and generated networks of care and support for those with HIV disease.

These were not easy tasks. The ups and downs of monitoring symptoms took away the predictability of daily life. As one caregiver described his friend, "He was so sick when he first got out of the hospital that I had to do everything for him. Now, I need to start encouraging him to do more things for himself, but it's hard for both of us to go through these changes" (quoted in Wardlaw 2000, 124). Another caregiver described the unpredictability of the dying process.

> I thought I had time to say what I needed to, but he died before I got the chance. What really caught me off guard was his inability to communicate. I didn't get to finish talking to him about so many things, so when he fell into a coma, I felt the loss more than when he finally died. (quoted in Wardlaw 2000, 125)

From early in the 1980s through 1995, 513,486 AIDS diagnoses were reported in the United States, and 13,291 cases were reported in Canada through March 1996 (Centers for Disease Control and Prevention 2000). Infections among children and injection drug users have declined since the mid-1990s. In North America there has been an overall slowing in new cases. However, relative increases in infection have occurred from heterosexual contact (especially in New York, Miami, and Washington, D.C.), among women compared to men, and among African-Americans and Latinos compared to white groups. Among incarcerated people in the United States, the rate of infection is seven times higher than among the nonincarcerated population.

Globally, more than 60 million people have been infected with the AIDS virus (UNAIDS 2001). By January 1992 half a million children had been infected, either in the womb, during birth, or (less often) through breastfeeding (Mann et al. 1992). At the end of 2001, an estimated 40 million people were living with HIV; in many less-developed countries, the majority of new infections occurred in young adults, with young women especially vulnerable (UNAIDS 2001). Rates in Asia increased rapidly during the latter half of the 1990s but are highest in Sub-Saharan Africa, where HIV/AIDS is now the leading cause of death. Worldwide, it is the fourth leading cause of death.

Researchers and public health officials were slower to mobilize community-based approaches. Movement toward a more social paradigm developed in stages. Initially, the "health belief model" kept research focused on *individuals*. The basis of countless studies, the health belief model focused on each individual's ideas about disease vulnerability and prevention as predictive of behavior. A second stage was recognition of *social networks* and *peer cultures* as key to individuals' sexual and drug use practices. Gaining contact with "insiders," public health staff trained community outreach workers to cajole and persuade high-risk individuals to change their drug use and sexual practices in order to reduce HIV transmission.

A third stage came as epidemiologists and AIDS prevention workers were faced with the glaringly high proportion of HIV/AIDS cases among African Americans, Latinos, and other economically disadvantaged groups. For example, it was estimated that half of the drug injectors in New York City were infected in the mid-1980s. In the absence of social class data, race became a focus in AIDS rates. As a result, differences between whites and people of color, rather than differences of social class, were highlighted. The medical and research establishment was nearly silent on HIV–social class associations and, specifically, on poverty as an AIDS risk. Attention to these issues came with the leadership of Dr. Jonathan Mann of the World Health Organization (WHO), later director of Harvard's School of Public Health. He began to speak out about marginalized and poor peoples of the globe as being the most vulnerable to HIV infection. In this way, Dr. Mann globally linked the vulnerabilities of gay youth with those of drug users and sex workers. He also pointed to locations where inadequate nutrition and health care enhanced the spread of diseases, including HIV. The World Bank project to document "Voices of the Poor" included these comments on the AIDS epidemic in African countries:

A person with AIDS suffers a lot because there will be no communication whatsoever because people will get afraid of him and he will end up without friends. (from South Africa, quoted in Narayan 2000, 246)

AIDS widows . . . have been chased with their children from their villages. They end up in the city, arriving with nothing, knowing almost no one, and looking for work. They . . . have been accused of witchcraft and chased from their villages after an unexplainable death. [This] new type of young, homeless women are accused of the deaths of their young, seemingly fit, husbands. . . . [T]hey are probably in danger of being infected themselves. (from Burkina Faso, quoted in Narayan 2000, 247)

The U.S. Centers for Disease Control and Prevention was slow to change. Consequently, in the most advanced disease-tracking operation in the world, with the largest national data set, it was not possible to examine the class dynamics of the AIDS epidemic. However, to the agency's credit, in the mid-1980s its Community Research Branch encouraged studies of social networks and was willing to support unconventional ways to reach "high-risk, vulnerable" populations. These studies provided increasing evidence that social class and community culture were key variables in understanding routes of infection. It also became evident that less-privileged social groups received later diagnosis of HIV disease and less access to experimental treatments. They also died sooner after diagnosis. Increasingly mindful of social class, age, and gender in the epidemiology of AIDS, many psychosocially oriented researchers began to add some of these variables to their studies.

Poverty, Social Inequality, and Health

Poverty is a serious health problem in the United States, the richest country in the world. Poverty strains marital and family relationships, and for individuals without families, being poor often turns into homelessness. In poor households there are scarce resources for protecting members from life's stresses. In addition, substance abuse and violence are health problems that are symptomatic of the malaise and alienation of poverty. The proportion of deaths caused by poverty among adults in the United States—18 percent in 1991—has increased in recent decades and now is comparable to that attributed to cigarette smoking (Hahn et al. 1995). One response might be that smoking is something that an individual can do something about, but poverty is not. However, policies influence the degree of poverty in societies, and in democratic societies, citizens can influence policies in a variety of ways. Poverty is not a fixed condition, and in affluent societies, we can think of poverty as a set of preventable health problems.

Poverty is harmful to health in two ways. First, basic human needs for food, shelter, and drinkable water are insufficiently met. And, second, poverty alongside of affluence contributes to a lack of trust and cohesiveness within a social group. This social inequality and lack of social trust create poorer health than would otherwise be expected in populations.

If the health problems of the poor are ignored, economic growth is likely to result in an even greater divide between the health of the rich and the poor. Two general trends compete. The first is increased wealth leading to a better standard of living and improved population health. Above and beyond the threshold of meeting basic human needs, affluence can enhance the comforts of material life and increase longevity. A second, countervailing trend impedes health improvements when economic rewards are distributed very unevenly. Increasing social inequality can result in deteriorating social relationships and greater alienation among social groups. Poorer health overall is the result.

For example, the Congo (formerly Zaire) is rich in natural resources, but the citizens' standard of living, education, and health were left poor and underdeveloped during Mobutu Sese Seko's three and a half decades in power. Mobutu's government made arrangements for European and U.S. corporations to mine precious metals and export them out of the country. Very little real economic development occurred, as Mobutu's family and small band of supporters got extremely rich while running an empty, "shell" government.

Another example may be found in the expansion of the California economy during the 1980s. Wealth increased, but so did inequality. Social policy did not step in to protect the poor and uninsured against health problems. During this decade, thousands more Californians, mostly children, were left without health insurance. In contrast to the Zaire example, economic development did progress, but the benefits of the expansion were felt mostly by the upper and upper-middle classes. The administration of Governor Pete Wilson was opposed to expansion of welfare state policies; consequently, a decline in prenatal and preventive child health care ensued.

Researchers use the term *excess mortality* to describe higher death rates than would be expected in a population, given its demographic characteristics and standard of living. This is what occurs where there is greater economic inequality, whether measured across counties, states, or countries. Social inequality damages individual health in numerous ways. Messages of individual failure combine with the real deprivations of downward mobility and poverty to increase stress, disease, and accidents. Under more extreme conditions, war, rape, and genocide cause trauma and death.

A comparison of Sweden and the United States is apt here. Sweden has a far more equitable distribution of income than the United States. The Gini Index is a measure of inequality in which the lower the score, the greater the income equality; Sweden's is 25, whereas that for the United States is 41 (World Bank 2001, Table 5). This index does not account for the enormous differences in wealth (as opposed to yearly income) between affluent groups, but it does show yearly income differences. Inequality is reflected in social policies as well. By the 1970s Sweden was a model welfare state, with a broad range of programs providing more security to more people than could be found in any other country (Twaddle 1999). By contrast, the United States offers a patchwork of social programs, often with inconsistencies among states and cracks through which unemployed and low-income people may fall. The United States spends more per capita on health care than any other country, but inequality is reflected in the slightly lower life spans of Americans compared with Swedes. Sweden has a life expectancy of over seventy-nine, seventy-seven for men and eighty-two for women; the United States has a life expectancy of seventy-seven, seventy-four for men and eighty for women (World Bank 2001, Table 2).

On the positive side, greater social equality can increase social trust and participation in community organizations, developing a kind of social wealth that contributes to the health of all members of the community. Social equality and affluence tend to result in societies' better health and longevity. The association between relative social equality and disease and death rates brings into focus *the social group as a meaningful unit of analysis in research and health policy.*

How Does Social Inequality Bring About Differences in Health?

We know that life without clean water, adequate food, and decent housing is bad for health and shortens life; this is *absolute poverty. Relative poverty*, in which individuals are constantly faced with others' more privileged lives, is also harmful. Relative poverty is a more social and psychological kind of hardship than absolute material poverty. How does each "get into" individuals' bodies? The mechanisms of individuals' material poverty are more straightforward: Malnutrition and life in tropical climates, without adequate protection from mosquitoes and other dangerous aspects of the environment, harm the body in direct ways. And, when health care and vaccines are not available, disease and death come early. It is more complex to trace the mechanisms through which social inequality damages those at lower ends of the hierarchy. However, there are several models that lead the way. We examine them in the remainder of this chapter.

The Health Gradient

The "health gradient" (see Figure 1.1) is a descriptive model. It is a straight line representing the linear association between low to high socioeconomic status (SES) and the corresponding high to low risk for disease and death (morbidity and mortality in Figure 1.1) (Adler et al. 1993; Adler et al. 1997). We might ask: Is it really that simple? Studies show that socioeconomic status "is a persistent and pervasive predictor of variations in health outcomes" (Williams & Collins 1995, 350). Measured in many different ways and in different places, higher levels of income, education, and occupation are associated with lower death rates. This is true in countries such as India and Malawi, where elites have higher standards of living and lower death rates than the poor, even though the "elite" may have an income less than that of a "poor" person in the United States. For example, a parent of two children in the United States who earns $7 an hour makes less than $15,000 a year—at or below the poverty line. This same amount in an underdeveloped country might place an individual among the middle class.

Developed countries such as Japan, Spain, and Great Britain, where *relative poverty* occurs, also have a health gradient. In the United States, for example, death

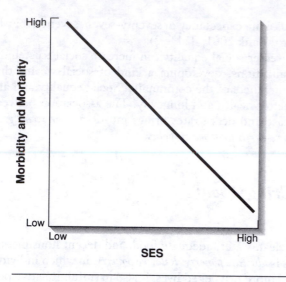

FIGURE 1.1   *Representation of the Relationship Between SES and Health Outcomes*

Source: Norman B. Anderson & Cheryl A. Armstead, Toward understanding the association of socio-economic status and health: A new challenge for the biopsychosocial approach, *Psychosomatic Medicine* 57 (1995): 213–225.

rates of those with a total annual family income under $5,000 (in 1980 dollars), regardless of gender or ethnicity, are double or more than double those with incomes greater than $50,000 (Rogot et al. 1992). Relatively affluent individuals can expect to live well into their seventies in the United States, with little disability; women, having a biological health advantage, can expect to live several years longer than men at all levels of the gradient. But, in the poorest parts of the globe, this gender gap in longevity is narrowed by the effects of poverty on women's lives, including higher rates of malnutrition, death in childbirth, and violence against women. In Malawi, for example, life expectancy is equally short at forty-two years for men and women; by contrast, life expectancies for men and women in Mexico are sixty-nine and seventy-five, respectively (data from 1998, World Bank 2001, Table 2).

The relationship between top and bottom levels of the health gradient make sense: Poor people have more daily and chronic stress, poor jobs or unemployment, bad housing, and limited health care. Above poverty levels, life chances improve greatly because basic human needs are more fully met. Living conditions improve as one moves up the social hierarchy, and these improvements have payoffs in health and longer life. However, above a certain level of affluence, we would expect an evening out of chances for health and longevity. There's only so much health that wealth can buy, right? But statistics show that individuals higher up the social ladder do continue to gain health benefits from their privileged position, because they have slightly better health and longer lives than those just below them. The mechanisms for this advantage are not fully understood.

A Biopsychosocial Approach

The biopsychosocial approach recognizes a smorgasbord of factors affecting health, including genetic and physiological makeup, demographic characteristics, socio-economic status, social environment, and individual behavior. Researchers have tried to figure out what some of the connections are between these various influences. For example, racism, social isolation, and hostility are harmful to health. On the positive side, having a sense of control over one's life is associated with behaviors related to good health, such as sound eating, sleeping, and driving habits.

Psychologist Norman Anderson (1989; Anderson & Armstead 1995) studies the higher rates of hypertension among African Americans. Hypertension is excessive blood pressure on the walls of the arteries, which puts the whole circulatory system under strain. Hypertension can lead to serious problems, including kidney disease and failure, cardiovascular disease, and stroke. Anderson suggests that racism and lower socioeconomic status play an important role in both *elevated baseline blood pressure* (higher blood pressure at equilibrium or resting levels) and *acute episodes* of high blood pressure (higher blood pressure at times of high stress). Anderson wants to understand why some African Americans experience harsh living conditions but do *not* develop hypertension. Do some individuals have more effective coping styles and belief systems that protect them from developing hypertension? Does this hold true even when they live in an unsafe neighborhood? If so, their coping skills could be taught to others in campaigns to prevent hypertension.

Anderson and Armstead (1995) have identified factors linking socioeconomic status and health (Figure 1.2). Their model incorporates socioeconomic as well as individual attitudinal and behavioral factors. All categories can directly and indirectly affect health outcomes. The variables listed in Figure 1.2 show us the "big picture" of influences on health outcomes, but they do not provide a clear roadmap for how these factors are interconnected and causally related. Two examples serve as illustrations of ways in which socioeconomic status and health may be connected in real life.

The Health of Maquiladora Workers.   In 1965, to encourage corporations to set up subsidiaries for production of exports, Mexico set up policies for an industrial zone along its border with the United States. Companies are able to import parts and materials duty free and to pay export taxes only on the value added to their products. In 1994 the North American Free Trade Agreement (NAFTA) brought explosive growth to these industrial-zone plants, known as *maquiladoras*. Poorly paid work in the Mexican economy, combined with inflation and the displacement of farmers, create pressure on workers to seek jobs in the *maquiladoras* (Brenner et al. 1999, 272). Working and environmental conditions in these industrial zones affect workers' health in a variety of ways. First, a poor standard of living is set by low wages. An analysis of wages following passage of NAFTA found that workers in Mexico's six border states suffered real wage declines since the implementation of NAFTA; indeed, only in Nuevo León (which has relatively few *maquiladora* workers) did workers fully recoup declines in wages lost since the end of 1994. During the first three quarters of 1998, *maquiladora* workers earned on average 59.7 pesos per day (approx-

1 Socio- demographic	2 Socio- economic Status	3 Social, Environmental, Medical	4 Psychological and Behavioral	5 Physiological	6 Outcomes
Age Ethnicity Gender Location	Education Income Occupation Family wealth Perceived SES Economic mobility Childhood SES Material possessions Trading/ bartering practices National income distribution	Residential characteristics Occupational environment Social support Social/ professional hierarchy Access to health care	Psychological distress Personality factors Health-promoting behaviors Health-damaging behaviors	Cardiovascular Immune Muscular Endocrine Height Weight	**Health and Illness**

FIGURE 1.2 *Possible Factors Linking SES and Health*

Source: Norman B. Anderson & Cheryl A. Armstead, Toward understanding the association of socio-economic status and health: A new challenge for the biopsychosocial approach, *Psychosomatic Medicine* 57 (1995): 213–225.

imately $6 U.S.) (Brenner et al. 1999, 273). Such low wages directly affected basic human needs. One employee of Matnéticos de Mexico (a Sony subsidiary) described her situation:

> In 1984, I earned 300 pesos [per week], and with that money I was able to buy the weekly *mandado* [groceries] at a cost of 50 pesos, pay a woman to take care of my children, and still have money left over. Now, after accumulating 10 years of seniority, I earn 408 pesos [per week]. It is not enough. I have to pay rent, gas, electricity, and my weekly *mandado* alone costs 200 pesos. If I have enough for meat, I buy it; otherwise I don't. (quoted in Brenner et al. 1999, 274)

In addition to the effects of low wages on workers' standard of living and therefore health, working conditions can directly affect health. A number of studies link *maquiladora* working and living conditions to poor health. There is evidence of polluted air, water, and soil (Brenner et al. 1999, 279). A 1995 study of 497 workers in Nogales, Sonora, found that almost one-fifth reported having no nurse or doctor at the work site, and almost one-third reported that their plant offered no information

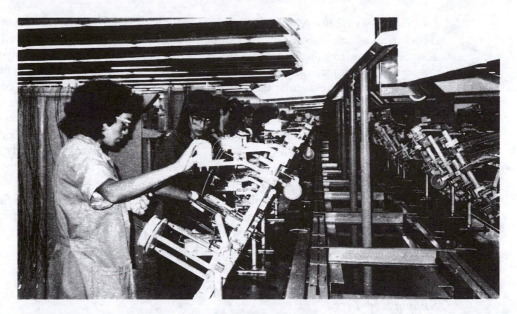

Women work at a General Motors assembly plant in northern Mexico. Hundreds of these maquilado-ras *(factories) line Mexico's border with the United States, paying substantially lower wages.*

about occupational risks. Where no risk information was made available, a work-related disease or illness was more than two and a half times as likely to be reported. Those with a nurse or doctor present were less than one-third as likely to report a work-related accident occurring in the previous six months (Balcazar et al. 1995; cited in Brenner et al. 1999, 274). Workers sustained injuries at almost twice the rate of U.S. industrial workers, and the workers in the study in Nogales were in jobs with below-average risk of injury.

Another study of 267 workers from fifty *maquiladoras* examined exposure to chemical, physical, and ergonomic hazards (Pérez-Stable 1991). Nearly half of the workers reported skin contact with chemicals during part or all of their shifts; 43 percent reported direct exposure to chemical dusts; 46 percent reported direct exposure to gases or vapors; and 38 percent reported exposure to airborne organic compounds. Results revealed strong and significant correlations between reported exposure to airborne chemicals and nausea or vomiting, stomach pain, urinary problems, and shortness of breath. Another risk came from doing repetitive, machine-paced movements. Symptoms of pain, numbness, or tingling in the hands were significantly associated with the amount of strenuous manual work, repetitive work, or work in uncomfortable positions. Twenty percent of workers in the study reported having these symptoms during the prior year. The relatively young ages of *maquiladora* workers highlight the significance of the one-in-five prevalence of these symptoms. In addition, cancers and deaths from congenital anomalies in the Mexican border zone are higher than overall Mexican rates and substantially higher than in the U.S. border zone (Brenner et al. 1999, 285).

Driving in Traffic.   A surprising example of the impact of modern living on health comes from an unpleasant aspect of affluence and mobility. In affluent as well as less-developed countries, driving in congested urban areas tries people's patience and, if the stress is chronic, can damage health. Higher stress levels are associated with higher rates of cardiovascular disease, a leading cause of death in developed countries. No matter how plain or fancy their cars, all drivers must find ways to cope with the frustrations of driving in traffic. Personality type and coping styles come into play in our responses to delays and the unexpected and annoying actions of other drivers. If a quick emergency reaction is called for, heart rate increases and the body releases stress hormones. When the crisis passes, a healthy person's bodily functions usually return to a baseline level without physical harm. However, a person who chronically drives aggressively, gets angry with other drivers, and expresses that anger is not likely to return promptly to a state of equilibrium. He or she will stay in an aggravated state for longer periods of time, adding stress and strain to body and mind. This aggravation lowers immunity and lines the arteries with plaque, contributing to arteriosclerosis and eventually to heart attack and death.

Supportive Ties

What maquiladoras and traffic have in common is that they are products of the group, not of individual behavior. Our *social* health has a major impact on our *mental* and *physical* health. Having friends and family to talk with and call on for help is good medicine. How is this so? Social networks provide practical help as well as emotional support. Family or friends might give us a ride when the car breaks down or help with repairs. When we talk to a friend or get a hug, our blood pressure and stress levels are lowered. If we suddenly lose our job and a family member takes us in, our health is protected from the harsh effects of isolation and homelessness. We also feel calmer if we know there are people there to help us. These kinds of support are directly good for our bodies. We may take them for granted, but our relationships are good medicine.

Social epidemiologist Lisa Berkman's study of survival during the six months following heart attack illustrates the benefits of supportive ties. Patients with one or two supportive individuals in their lives were significantly more likely to stay alive than those with no supportive individuals (Berkman 1995). This relationship endured when the researchers controlled for the effects of age, gender, and severity of the heart attack on individuals' likelihood of survival. People who are alone and socially isolated are more vulnerable to poor health, and they die at two to three times the rate of people who are socially well integrated (Kawachi & Kennedy 1997). In today's world of far-flung extended families, the elderly often live at a distance from their children and relatives. Elderly women are especially likely to live alone, to subsist on a fixed income, and to have lost spouses and friends. Their friendships with other women often sustain them in their elder years.

Self-efficacy is a sense of being in control of one's life (Bandura 1977) over seemingly arbitrary forces, including the weather, economic recession, and layoff. In numerous studies, self-efficacy is associated with healthier behaviors and attitudes, in situations ranging from heart attack survival to pregnancy prevention and smoking cessation. Not surprisingly, people with social support are more likely to feel this sense of control over their lives and are more motivated to behave in health-promoting ways.

Whereas social support and a sense of control have positive buffering effects on health, antisocial dispositions and behaviors have the opposite effect. For example, hostile individuals are at greater risk of heart disease and premature death. A study of doctors trained at the University of North Carolina found that those who scored high in hostility during their training were four to five times more likely to have heart problems over the following twenty-five years than their classmates with low hostility scores (Williams 1989). Medical researcher Redford Williams identifies three aspects of hostility: (1) cynical *attitude*, (2) chronic *thoughts and feelings* of anger and hostility, and (3) frequent *expression* of anger and hostility. Although professionals are capable of giving themselves heart disease with their hostile attitudes, the poor and homeless really have a lot more to be angry about. It is reasonable to hypothesize that hostility is more pronounced among the poor, unemployed, homeless, and otherwise marginalized members of societies. Hostility may develop into chronic anger or a variety of other physical and mental illnesses (Dohrenwend & Dohrenwend 1969).

The biopsychosocial approach has driven important research on health. However, the relationships between socioeconomic position, behavior, and health outcomes are not fully understood. What are the mechanisms through which social circumstances affect people's health? Sociologists have made significant contributions to this area of discovery.

An Inclusive Paradigm of Socioeconomic Status and Health

From their review of studies examining influences on health, sociologist James House and his colleagues (1988) conclude, "Social relationships have a predictive, arguably causal, association with health" (544). House's colleague and fellow sociologist David Williams offers a paradigm of socioeconomic status and health, inviting researchers to carry out studies to illuminate the various relationships among the factors he identifies and specific health outcomes.

Williams's paradigm (Figure 1.3) recognizes the interconnections among an individual's biology, demographic factors, and socioeconomic status. These are the basic factors that shape health. Next, psychosocial factors, such as health practices, social ties, perceptions of control, and stress, come into play. For example, the quality of the job influences job stress levels and also one's social status; quality includes pay, benefits, interesting as opposed to monotonous tasks, and safe rather than hazardous conditions. For example, let's compare a telecommunications representative with a doctor. The telecommunications worker takes calls from customers having trouble with their service, takes care of those problems, and then must turn the call into a "sales opportunity," pitching products and services. Computers and supervisors closely monitor time spent, interactions on calls, and sales to customers. The pay and status of the job are modest. By contrast, doctors, especially in the United States, are highly regarded, well trained, and handsomely paid. Although they are more constrained than in the past by corporate and governmental controls, doctors continue to

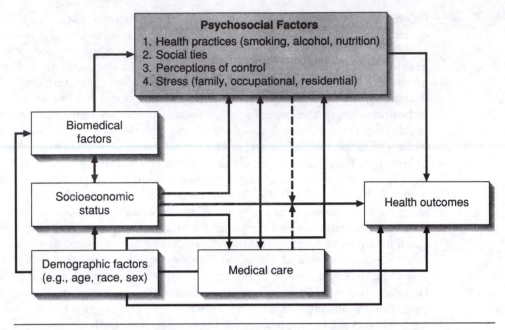

FIGURE 1.3 *A Paradigm for Research on Socioeconomic Status and Health*

Source: D. R. Williams, Socioeconomic differentials in health: A review and redirection, *Social Psychology Quarterly 53*, no. 2 (1990): 81–99. Copyright 1990, American Sociological Association.

make important decisions about their patients' care and their own practice. Doctors' occupational conditions are likely to produce a greater sense of control over their lives and greater self-esteem than do those of customer service representatives. Their daily stress occurs within a society that respects and pays them well, and they are likely to have family and friends who provide social support. These factors influence the behavioral patterns of workers and, over time, their health.

A social network of family and friends may help to buffer the effects of a stressful job. A customer service representative under pressure at work to boost her sales may unwind at the end of the day by enjoying her children and getting her mind off work pressures. However, she most likely works a "double day," with an evening of chores, supervising homework, and managing a household. A male doctor is likely to have a wife who manages these duties, and she is likely to employ a number of helpers, including gardeners, housekeepers, and handymen. Female doctors and other women who combine professional work with motherhood must find a way to juggle these two rewarding, yet demanding, occupations. Thus a job and income may buffer the effects of a stressful home life. For some parents, pressed by the daily needs of their children and home responsibilities, a more ordered work routine may provide a welcome change.

The stratification of health is evident in several variables within Williams's paradigm. The "Socioeconomic Status" box situates the individual in the social hierarchy by occupation, income, and education. For example, we know that unemployment is bad for health, especially for working-age men, for whom work is an important part of their status. Men with lower educational levels are more likely to experience periods of temporary and long-term unemployment. "Psychosocial Factors" also are heavily influenced by one's class position; being unemployed or working in an unsatisfying job can lead to depression, which in turn can increase smoking or drinking. Lower-income and less-educated men drink and smoke more than their higher-paid, better-educated counterparts. Smoking, drinking, and drug use release stress temporarily, but *add* stress to the physical recovery process. Heavy drinking often causes stress in relationships as well, reducing social support at home. Another way that one's job affects health is through health and retirement benefits. People employed in higher-status jobs (such as teachers, lawyers, nurses, and engineers) are more likely to have medical insurance and to receive regular medical checkups. This allows problems to be treated early, allowing for conditions such as high blood pressure, breast cancer, and diabetes to be successfully managed or cured.

Illegal risk-taking behaviors have further negative consequences. Arrest can result from driving while intoxicated or from possession of an illegal substance. However, affluent individuals are less likely to be caught, arrested, or prosecuted for such deviant acts. In addition, their drugs are more likely to be legal. Higher-status citizens have greater privacy and generally receive more lenient treatment by authorities. They can afford to hire lawyers, therapists, or other experts to defend them and lend professional legitimacy to their problems. In short, class privilege shields individuals from some of the stressful consequences of risk-taking behaviors.

Occupational Quality and Health Outcomes

Sociologist K. A. S. Wickrama and colleagues' model (1997) places occupational quality in the pivotal role of shaping the individual's degree of social integration, marital integration, and sense of control (Figure 1.4). A person's social position is linked to health-risk behaviors, and the configuration as a whole shapes physical health. How much money an individual makes and the social status of a given job play central roles in shaping an array of personal, family, and social outcomes, and, consequently, health. Because it focuses on paid work in the labor force, this model is best suited to employed adults. Moreover, it is better suited to men than to women. In their roles as wives and homemakers, women may draw many of the benefits (or costs) that the model associates with employment. Working part time may provide women with some of the rewards and stimulation of work outside the home. Time at home as a mother and partner may be rewarding in maintaining primary, meaningful relationships. The model is not especially well suited to full-time homemakers, teens and unmarried young adults, college students, people who are not married, and the elderly and retired.

Social, Psychological, and Physical Pathways
to Health Outcomes

The model developed by epidemiologists Eric Brunner and Michael Marmot (1999, 20) illustrates some of the pathways by which physical, psychological, and social conditions result in mental and physical health outcomes (Figure 1.5). The model

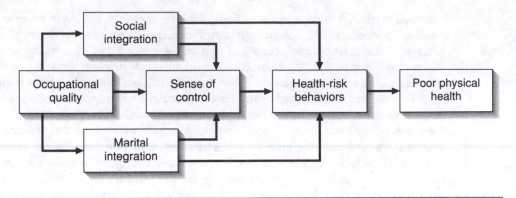

FIGURE 1.4   *The General Theoretical Model of Relationships Between Occupational Quality and Poor Physical Health*

Source: K. A. S. Wickrama, Frederick O. Lorenz, Rand D. Conger, & Glen H. Elder, Linking occupational conditions to physical health through material, social and interpersonal processes, *Journal of Health and Social Behavior,* 38, no. 4 (1997): 363–375. Copyright 1997, American Sociological Association.

includes life course effects by recognizing early life events and living conditions throughout the life course.

Lack of "Social Capital" as the Explanation for Social Inequality's Effect on Health Outcomes

Bruce Kennedy, Ichiro Kawachi, and D. Prothrow-Stith (1996), at Harvard's School of Public Health, compared the U.S. states and found that the degree of income inequality was correlated with states' mortality rates. The degree of income inequality is also correlated with the rate of infant mortality, homicide, and death from cardiovascular disease and cancers. This association holds whether a state is more or less affluent. In other words, inequality in and of itself reduces the health and well-being of populations.

How does inequality make its way into people's health? Kawachi and Kennedy (1997) suggest that inequality diminishes "social capital," a kind of communal wealth that comes from community cohesion and trust. A safer and healthier social community results, composed of individuals who contribute to and reap health rewards. Healthy communities are composed of individuals who are well integrated, with social networks and high levels of participation in all kinds of organizations, including teams, religious organizations, and voluntary associations. Conversely, the lack of social trust and cohesion resulting from high social inequality leads to alienation. A striking example occurred in 1964 when Kitty Genovese was stabbed to death in front of her apartment building in the Queens borough of New York City. Neighbors heard the attack, but no one called the police or an ambulance. No one intervened to help her. There was opportunity for the police to intervene, as the attacker reportedly walked off but then came back to stab the victim again when he realized she was not

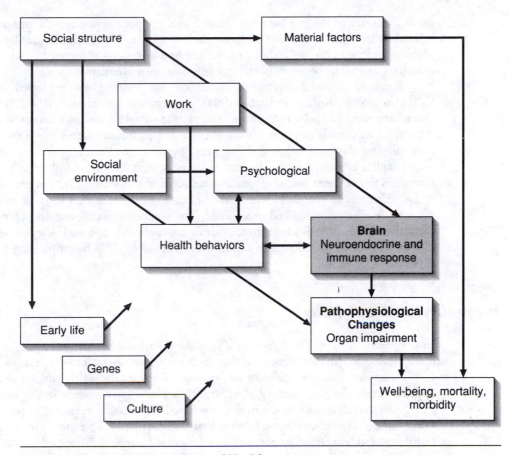

FIGURE 1.5 *Social Determinants of Health*

Source: Eric Brunner & Michael Marmot, Social organizations, stress, and health. In Michael Marmot & Richard G. Wilkinson (Eds.), *Social Determinants of Health* (Oxford, UK: Oxford University Press, 1999), 17–43. By permission of Oxford University Press.

dead. The event was reported widely in the press, and there was collective horror at just how callous the neighbors had been. In terms of the social cohesion model, New York City's residents were suffering from a terrible shortage of *social capital*.

In the Kawachi study, the authors operationalize social capital in two ways: as (1) voluntary participation in organizations and (2) self-reported trust in others. These are interpreted as indicative of a healthy degree of social cohesion, involving active social relationships in which individuals cooperate to meet shared goals. Cohesion and trust in turn produce a kind of social wealth. This collective goodwill buffers social relations and moderates individuals' behaviors and stress levels. This model is consistent with evidence that social support contributes to health and longevity in a variety of ways, including through instrumental help, information, and emotional support. Social capital enhances trust, civility, and involvement. Kawachi and colleagues conclude, "the size of the gap between the rich and the poor is powerfully and negatively related to level of investment in social capital" (1997, 1495). Consequently, there is global reason for concern today, because income inequality is increasing within many countries as well as between Northern and Southern Hemispheres.

Kawachi's "social capital" is based on the concept as developed by James Coleman (1988), Robert Putnam (1993), and Francis Fukuyama (1995). These authors have studied social integration and regard social capital as a community asset. This approach tends to assume homogeneity and common interests in a community, downplaying class and cultural differences. By contrast, Pierre Bourdieu's notion of social capital is rooted in social class analysis; it examines how individuals use their resources to compete. Social capital is a resource of individuals, "the aggregate of the actual or potential resources which are linked to possession of a durable network of more or less institutionalized relationships of mutual acquaintance and recognition" (Bourdieu 1986, 248). Both of these notions are applicable to a sociology of health and illness. This book includes class and resources in the analysis by employing a political economy approach.

Inequality Internationally

In *Unhealthy Societies: The Afflictions of Inequality*, Richard Wilkinson, a socioeconomic epidemiologist, further develops the inequality and social cohesion thesis (1996; 1997). He identifies the social causes of improvements in health and longevity over approximately the past century. A central thesis is: Improvements in the standard of living and overall quality of life in the developed world had a dramatic impact on lowering rates of infectious diseases. With that transformation, the causes of death (especially heart disease) for upper and lower social classes flip-flopped. Two striking examples are cardiovascular disease and obesity, which became more prominent among low-income groups during the latter half of the twentieth century. Ironically, cardiovascular disease had been regarded as "the businessman's disease" earlier in the century in Britain and the United States, in reference to ambitious businessmen who worked nonstop until their hearts failed. In another switch in lifestyle and social status, being extremely slim became fashionable during the latter 1960s, just as low-income people could afford sufficient food to become plump (Bourdieu 1984). Overweight is related to a variety of health problems.

Developed affluent countries, including the United States and Great Britain, for the most part experienced their "epidemiologic transitions" during the first half of the twentieth century. However, the positive health effects of a higher overall income and standard of living varied considerably during the twentieth century according to how equitably resources were spread among populations. For example, in more equitable societies such as Japan, dramatic improvements in longevity occurred later in the century. Between 1965 and 1986, Japanese life expectancy increased by seven and a half years for men and eight years for women (Wilkinson 1996, 18). Comparing the income distributions of Japan and the United States, we see that, as of 1993, the 10 percent of the Japanese population receiving the lowest income earned 4.8 percent of income, and the highest 10 percent earned 21.7 percent (World Bank 2001, Table 5). In comparison, the U.S. figures for 1997 indicate that 1.8 percent went to the lowest 10 percent, and 30.5 percent went to the top 10 percent. Among developed countries, incremental improvements in the quality of material and social life are responsible for continued, though more modest, improvements in longevity. Wilkinson's thesis suggests that, controlling for other factors, health and longevity improvements are highest where there is greater social equality.

Very poor countries today have yet to pass through this epidemiologic transformation, in which the standard of living improves and infectious diseases decline. In fact, many underdeveloped countries today fall into the "premodern" epidemiological category, which means that life expectancy is relatively shorter and more people become seriously ill from infectious diseases such as influenza, malaria, and tuberculosis. Based on World Bank figures for the 1990s, several societies include many citizens living on $2 a day or less. These include, for example, Mali (61 percent living on less than $2 a day), Zambia (61 percent), Nigeria (59 percent), Central African Republic (58 percent), Madagascar (51 percent), India (41 percent), Honduras (37 percent), Pakistan (35 percent), and Botswana (31 percent) (World Bank 2001, Table 4).

The Political Economy of Health: Adding Global and Power Dimensions to Social Influences on Health

"Political economy" embraces considerations of global political and economic forces, the state, government, social classes, public administration, policy making, and the distribution of resources between and among populations. What do these have to do with health? Political economy adds the dimension of power as institutionalized and wielded by a variety of social groups, organizations, and agencies. These institutional arrangements affect individuals' lives and health in many ways. A political economy analysis involves a world economy in which transnational corporations compete and move their business around the globe in order to maximize profits, finding inexpensive labor and resources and avoiding environmental restrictions. These movements affect labor markets, wages, and the living conditions of workers around the globe. This perspective builds on a theoretical tradition in sociological theory, including Karl Marx's analysis of social classes and capitalism and Immanuel Wallerstein's world systems theory.

Economic development often brings about improvements in infrastructure and living conditions that benefit all sectors of the population. For example, improvements in water supply, agricultural production, nutrition, housing, and education can move societies through the epidemiological transition to better meet basic human needs. As nutrition and sanitation improve, infectious diseases decrease and the death rate drops. Following World War II, several countries (for example, Japan and South Korea) made their way through the epidemiological transition, with resulting improvements in health and longevity. Currently, many developing countries, including Indonesia and China, are in the process of making the epidemiologic transition, despite continued struggles with infectious diseases. A few countries are experiencing a backward slide in health due to the AIDS epidemic (Botswana and Zimbabwe), and still others are kept in chaos by war and violence (Sierra Leon and Afghanistan).

In general, more affluent countries have better health. Improvements in health from economic growth are not automatic, however. For example, increases in gross national product (GNP) above and beyond meeting basic human needs produce smaller improvements in longevity (Wilkinson 1996). "This suggests that once countries have reached some threshold level of income (around $5,000 per capita in 1990), life expectancy plateaus" (Wilkinson 1996, 34). Further increases in a country's GNP are more weakly associated with increases in life expectancy.

Are there times when economic growth *detracts* from a population's health? If economic growth widens income inequality and decreases the care of basic human needs, then health improvements will not be as dramatic. Highly equal societies, such as Japan and Sweden, have the highest levels of health and longevity. France, Spain, and Australia are also in the category of highest life expectancies (World Bank 2001, Table 5). Life expectancy in the less-equal United States ranks twenty-fourth according to the World Bank, behind the countries listed above and also behind several others. Table 1.1 lists several developed countries, using the Gini Index as a measure of inequality (the higher the number, the greater the inequality). Alongside this measure of inequality are life expectancies. All of these developed countries have high life expectancies, but note the slightly lower life expectancies toward the bottom of the list. An exception is Denmark, with high equality but female longevity that is not as high as other countries in the table. These are not perfectly comparable figures, because the measures of inequality occurred in different years, and a multitude of factors is involved in life expectancies (diversity of the population, funds spent on health care, and so on). However, inequality is one factor influencing life expectancy and makes a difference even in affluent countries.

From an individual standpoint, why should we be concerned with these larger patterns? It seems they are too large to do anything about. However, it *is* possible to implement policies that reduce inequality and improve nutrition, education, and primary health care, all of which are associated with better population health. In the United States, changes in policy could narrow the income and health gaps between the rich, middle class, and poor. For example, Chile is less wealthy than the United States but in the 1990s put in place policies that foster greater equality. The health benefits have appeared among Chile's children and in overall life expectancy.

As individuals and within our communities, we can support policies that foster greater equality and participate in organizations that work toward that goal. In addition, we can exercise participatory democracy by working at local and global levels to promote more equitable policies. Nongovernmental agencies and watch dog groups also provide avenues for individuals to have a collective impact on the policies of governments and corporations. As consumers we can apply pressure with our spending power, buying products from companies that are socially and environmentally responsible. With our children and in our communities we can model lifestyles that promote mental and physical well-being.

TABLE 1.1 *Relative Income Equality and Life Expectancy in Developed Countries*

Country	Gini Index/ Year Measured	Life Expectancy	
		Males	Females
Denmark	24.7 / 1992	73	78
Japan	24.9 / 1993	77	84
Sweden	25.0 / 1992	77	82
Norway	25.8 / 1995	76	81
Germany	30.0 / 1994	74	80
Spain	32.5 / 1990	75	82
Netherlands	32.6 / 1994	75	81
France	32.7 / 1995	75	82
Greece	32.7 / 1993	75	81
Switzerland	33.1 / 1992	76	82
Australia	35.2 / 1994	76	82
Israel	35.5 / 1992	76	80
United Kingdom	36.1 / 1991	75	80
United States	40.8 / 1997	74	80

Source: World Bank, *World Development Report 2000/2001: Attacking Poverty* (Washington, DC: World Bank, 2001), Tables 2 and 5.

How This Book Is Organized

The remaining chapters in the book expand the discussion and analysis introduced in this first chapter. Chapter 2 lays out theoretical perspectives and conceptual tools for analyzing health outcomes from a social perspective. Chapter 3 presents a political economy approach to health. Chapter 4 presents evidence of health inequalities that correspond to social inequalities and analyzes this "social stratification of health" from structural and psychosocial perspectives. Chapter 5 provides brief international health profiles, examining world regions' health progress and challenges. Chapter 6 provides an overview of evidence of the stratification of health outcomes by gender, race, and ethnicity, focusing mainly on the United States. Chapter 7 provides a global survey of the current epidemiology of mental health and its stratification by class, gender, and position in the world economy. Chapter 8 examines the causes and consequences of poor health profiles in underdeveloped countries. Chapter 9 examines the relationship between development and health, pointing out both the benefits of economic growth and its detrimental effects. Chapter 10 presents policy recommendations, some offered by experts in global health and some suggested by the evidence and analysis presented in the preceding chapters.

2

Theoretical Foundations for Studying Health Inequalities

> *I have found that, despite such changes as the rising general levels of education, increased participation of women in paid employment, and expansion of newer nonmanual forms of work at the expense of traditional proletarian occupations, class inequalities in the industrialized countries have remained more or less constant throughout most of the twentieth century. The central problem for class theory is not therefore, as generations of critics have supposed, to account for the demise of social class in advanced societies. The real challenge is to explain why class has persisted as such a potent social force.*
>
> —Gordon Marshall, *Repositioning Class: Social Inequality in Industrial Societies*

This chapter outlines theoretical foundations for studying social inequality and health. Instead of focusing on individuals and their health, we treat *social groups* as the units of analysis—social classes, ethnic or racial groups, male and female genders, age groups, generation cohorts, residents of regions or countries. What effects does social hierarchy (or social inequality) have on physical and mental health? Sociologists refer to systems of inequality as *stratification systems*. These are the official and unofficial, visible and invisible means by which individuals and social groups are located at various positions of wealth, power, and status in a society.

In addition, we consider the following questions:

- What effect does *social cohesion* have on individual and population health?
- How does worse health result from economic inequality?
- How does a deficit of trust or social capital cause poorer population health or prevent faster health improvements?

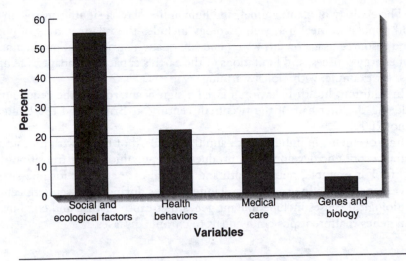

FIGURE 2.1 *Explaining Variations in Health*

Source: A. R. Tarlov & R. F. St. Peter, Introduction. In A. R. Tarlov & R. F. St. Peter (Eds.), *The Society and Population Health Reader: A State and Community Perspective* (New York: New Press, 2000), x–xvi.

Explaining Variations in Population Health

Just how much of a group's health is explained by social variables? This is a complex question; answering it involves varied evidence. At the risk of oversimplification, the following and Figure 2.1 present an overview based on current research.

By far the greatest amount of variation—approximately 56 percent—is explained by social and ecological factors (Tarlov & St. Peter 2000, x–xii). Next in significance is health behaviors, at 21 percent. Next is the quality of medical care and the public health system at about 19 percent. The smallest proportion of variation in disease burden is explained by genes and biology—only about 4 percent.

Social factors exert a major impact on individual and population health. overlapping with behavioral and ecological categories. Patterns include the following:

- Disease and death rates vary according to sociological categories within nations, states, cities, and neighborhoods.
- The health–social hierarchy gradient is continuous throughout the socioeconomic spectrum.
- Overall, individuals' socioeconomic position influences their health to a greater extent than the reverse.
- Within developed nations, the poorer health on the lower part of the gradient is influenced by social inequality, not just by material conditions.
- Within developed nations, the slope of the health gradient corresponds to the extent of income and social inequality (for example, Sweden and Japan, with flatter gradients, as compared to the United States, with a steeper gradient) (Wilkinson 1996).

The ecology of plant, animal, and human life plays a significant role in individual and population health as well. Ecology includes the relative stress of population size and resource usage on air, water, and soil quality; agricultural production; depletion of energy sources; and limitations of the earth's capacity to adapt to temperature swings, for example, with global warming.

In addition, health behaviors played a significant role in the reduction of disease during the first half of the twentieth century in Britain and the United States (Marmot 2000).

Improvements in public health and the standard of living with industrialization and other economic developments produce the epidemiological transition that prolongs life. For example, public health and medical care account for one-sixth of the forty-year increase in life span in the United States during the twentieth century.

Biological causes include mutant genes that cause disease and combinations of normal genes that predispose individuals to chronic diseases.

Foundations for a Social Science of Health and Inequality

Several existing theories provide conceptual building blocks for analyzing social inequalities in health. Promising leads come from three fathers of modern social science: Emile Durkheim, Karl Marx, and Max Weber. All three grappled with the transformation from traditional to modern societies, from agrarian to industrial capitalist economies, and from peasant/aristocratic to modern social classes. They could see that the individual's relationships with work, family, and community were fundamentally transformed during these historical shifts. What are the health effects of economic and social transformations? Are various social groups affected differently? Are there beneficial as well as harmful effects?

The Social Group and Health

Emile Durkheim was a leading French sociologist (1858–1917) interested in the emotional and moral bonds that hold societies together. From his study of European countries, he found that the act of suicide varied systematically by the sociological characteristics of suicidal individuals (1897/1966). In other words, this most personal act expressed *social* dynamics. Durkheim found that socially isolated individuals were more likely to commit suicide than those well integrated into a network of social relationships. He also discovered that suicide rates increased during times of economic recession as well as during times of dramatically increasing prosperity. Coping with positive as well as negative aspects of social change is stressful for individuals, and for some it brings on serious depression. Durkheim also was concerned with the increased *anomie* (normlessness) in rapidly changing societies, in which traditional codes of behavior and morality no longer guided behavior. He was concerned that a weak sense of belonging and higher rates of crime, deviant behavior, and suicide are the price that societies pay for their modernity. Durkheim believed the situation could be improved through participation in organizations, such as workers' collectives, through which emotional ties and moral norms could be maintained.

How does connection to others promote better health in an individual's body and mind? Certainly, not all contacts with others support health and well-being. Demeaning and abusive relationships surely are not conducive to good health. We do know that social isolation—not having individuals available for practical help and emotional support—is harmful. And we know that supportive ties promote health. There are several pathways through which social support improves health. Some have direct relationships to the body and mind, whereas others have an indirect effect (Stansfeld 1999, 159).

Social support encourages healthy behaviors (good nutrition, good sleep and exercise habits, talking with others) and discourages unhealthy or risk-taking behaviors (smoking, alcohol abuse, reckless driving, sedentary lifestyle). Positive contacts with others spur biochemical processes, including enhanced immune functioning and feelings of well-being, which in turn may reinforce positive social relations and health-promoting behaviors. These connections are investigated by the field of psychoneuroimmunology, the study of the interactions between consciousness, the brain and central nervous system, and the immune system. The positive effects of contact with others must be distinguished from the potentially harmful effects of population density, discussed below. Social support buffers the impact of stressful life events on the body and mind, such as during times of loss of a loved one, disappointment at work, troubled family relationships, illness of a child, or recovery from illness, surgery, or heart attack.

This pattern occurs across the life cycle. Adequate attachment in childhood increases the ability to develop personality characteristics that are conducive to maintaining social support during adolescence and adulthood; this, in turn, buffers life events from harmful effects on mind and body (Stansfeld 1999, 158). The absence of harmful personality characteristics (such as hostility and pessimism), which are more likely to develop from lack of healthy child and adult attachments, helps prevent unhealthy life trajectories. Hostility, for example, prevents supportive relationships from developing and can result in isolation and coronary heart disease (Barefoot et al. 1995; Williams 1989).

Social Stratification and Health

Social stratification refers to the system by which individuals, families, or classes are located at varying positions in a social hierarchy. Societies differ in what determines this hierarchy, for example, in agrarian societies, whoever owns and controls the land typically also has the most power and prestige. In a modern capitalist society, those owning and controlling major enterprises typically control economic and political institutions and have higher social status as well. In addition, some societies are much more unequal than others. For example, Brazil and Colombia are highly unequal societies, whereas Japan, Denmark, Norway, Sweden, and Finland are far more egalitarian.

Street children sleep on the pavement in an elite shopping district of Rio de Janeiro, Brazil. Poverty as well as social inequality worsen population health.

Types of Societies and Risks to Population Health

The degree of inequality in societies depends on the amount of surplus resources available above and beyond survival needs. Inequality is also determined by the organization and distribution of political power and social status. For example, contemporary developed societies are wealthier than the ancient Inca and Roman empires, but modern societies are more equal. Modern societies have "flatter" stratification systems than wealthy agrarian states because modern societies have cultures and political structures that have equalizing effects. Gerhard Lenski (1966) offers a typology of stratification systems based on material conditions, technology, and degree of surplus. Not all societies fit neatly into Lenski's "ideal types," and one type does not evolve into the next. But these are tools for comparative analysis, formulated to emphasize structural differences and degrees of social inequality.

For example, *hunting-and-gathering societies* have a relatively low surplus of food and other resources, small populations, and a low degree of inequality. Few hunting-and-gathering societies remain today, with the expansion of urban and agricultural development. Their health risks stem from loss of habitat, food shortages, and weak protection from the environment.

Horticultural societies rely on subsistence farming and ecologically favorable conditions to maintain a surplus that can be saved, bartered, or sold. Horticultural populations are vulnerable to changes in the weather that affect crops and bring flooding

*Copenhagen Square, Denmark. Developed countries with relatively
equally distributed incomes and low poverty rates (e.g., Denmark, Japan,
Sweden, and Norway) have generally healthier populations.*

and other disasters. Food shortages, malnutrition, and diseases spread by mosquitoes
and other vectors are health risks, especially in tropical regions. Many horticultural
societies persist today in rural parts of Asia, Africa, and Latin America, although they
are dwindling for the same reasons that hunting-and-gathering societies have mostly
vanished. Threats to subsistence farming come from the modernization of agriculture,
the expansion of capitalism, forest depletion, industrialization, and other developments that move indigenous people off the land and toward urban areas, to seek work
in formal or informal economies.

Societies that have *advanced horticultural* production use plows for tilling large
acreage, are more sedentary and large, and have greater inequality than hunting-and-
gathering and horticultural societies. The elite is composed of aristocrats, chiefs, and
priests, who extract labor and tribute from lower classes. Historical examples include
the Maya of Mexico, the Inca of Peru, the Azande of East Africa, and other large societies in Dahomey and Nigeria in West Africa (Collins 1975; Collins & Coltrane
1995). Greater population density increases risk of bacterial and viral infectious dis-

eases, and malnutrition and weakened immunity are risks for the less privileged. In ancient Mesopotamia, the combination of increased population density and lack of systems for disposal for human and animal wastes created the health risks of "pestilence, plagues and epidemics" that destroyed the society (Tarlov & St. Peter 2000, xiv).

Agrarian societies enjoyed ample food surpluses and had the greatest degree of social inequality. In many agrarian societies, a large-scale state exercised considerable control, and a military aristocracy, along with political and religious leaders, often made up the elite class. Society was organized around large aristocratic households that included relatives, servants, agricultural laborers, and military staff. Agrarian societies in Europe, ancient China, and ancient Egypt witnessed the growth of urban areas, which brought the health risks of population density.

For 4,500 years prior to the beginning of the twentieth century, bacterial and viral infections were the primary causes of death in human populations, primarily in the more crowded agrarian societies. Crowded areas today and historically, with people traveling from various destinations, risk the spread of infectious diseases. For example, bubonic plague during the fourteenth century reduced Europe's population by 45 percent. In addition, colonization efforts like that in the Americas resulted in death for a large proportion of the indigenous population, vulnerable as they were to foreign pathogens. The wealth of European, Inca, and Egyptian agrarian societies allowed travel to foreign lands for trade and discovery. In the lands of exploration, for indigenous populations without the antibodies to European pathogens, the results were devastating. An estimated 95 percent of Native American populations were killed by war, slavery, and diseases brought by Europeans, in what sociologist Eric Wolf has called "the great dying" (Robbins 2002, 72; Wolf 1982, 133). This disastrous effect of economic exploration foreshadows some of the harmful effects of development found in the world today. (Chapter 9 examines the relationship between development and health.)

Industrial societies have enormous surpluses beyond what is needed to sustain life, but they are not as unequal as the agrarian states. Typically, a large middle class enjoys a high standard of living with substantial disposable income. Industrial societies use modern machinery and inanimate energy sources, with an extensive division of human labor. Large bureaucratic organizations administer such major social institutions as government, education, major religions, financial institutions, and large businesses. There is a cash economy and modern social classes, the largest of which is workers dependent on wages.

As industrial economies and technologies evolve, income differences among workers increase, and clear lines between working, middle, and upper-middle classes become blurred. However, some industrialized countries, such as Sweden and Japan, have remained fairly egalitarian, with large middle classes and relatively small income disparities. In terms of population health, the degree of inequality corresponds to the extent of excess morbidity and mortality—beyond what would be expected from the population's age and other characteristics. Inequalities in industrialized countries also roughly correspond to inequalities in health care. For example, even with British universal health care, those who can afford private physicians get the quickest and best care. In the United States, health insurance through employers is the most secure way to maintain care; however, jobs carrying health benefits are becoming fewer, and costs are rising faster than inflation rates. Symptomatic of inadequate health care protection is the decreased proportion of the population covered during the economic boom of the 1990s. The proportion of the uninsured continued to climb, and preventive care and prescription costs continued to spiral upward, making them less available even to the middle class and especially to the elderly.

The Two Transitions of Developed Countries

Two major transitions that affected developing countries occurred with industrialization around the turn of the twentieth century. As the overall standard of living improved and with better nutrition and sanitation, infectious disease was replaced by chronic disease as the leading cause of death. This meant that diseases such as tuberculosis and pneumonia were replaced in prevalence by coronary heart disease, high blood pressure, stroke, diabetes, cancer, emphysema, cirrhosis, and other chronic conditions (Tarlov & St. Peter 2000, xiv).

The second transition has occurred since the middle of the twentieth century. During the first half of the twentieth century, behavioral factors explained more than half the prevalence of chronic disease. However, during the second half of the century in developed countries, behavioral factors accounted for less of chronic disease variation, and social inequalities explained more (Tarlov & St. Peter 2000, xiv–xv; Wilkinson 1996). This was the "postindustrial" transition.

Postindustrial societies are rapidly evolving into the twenty-first century. These are affluent developed countries, undergoing rapid social change as they respond to global markets and stock market fluctuations. They employ sophisticated technologies in highly diversified economies, including the manufacturing, financial, service, and telecommunications sectors. Labor markets respond quickly to fluctuations in global demand, technological innovation, and profit levels. To protect stock values, managers preemptively lay off workers when upcoming earnings are below projected gains. A survey of U.S. companies by the American Management Association found that 49 percent had eliminated jobs between June 1995 and June 1996, despite overall job growth of 68 percent during that period (American Management Association 1997; Amick & Lavis 2000). Today's productive worker becomes tomorrow's underemployed or unemployed, seeking a new niche in a rapidly changing economy. Those with less education and skill often get left on the sidelines or must compete with young adults at low-wage, entry-level jobs. Even the skilled and educated are susceptible to job loss and underemployment, and must be willing to seek employment in new locations. Expanding service sectors of economies absorb displaced workers, often at lower pay and minus the benefits of earlier industrial sector jobs. New industrial jobs are likely to be outsourced to countries with lower pay and weaker environmental protections; jobs remaining within developed countries are likely to pay lower wages, prevent unionization, and have minimal job security and benefits.

Health risks in postindustrial society are unequally distributed within the labor market and class system, and include those resulting from insecure employment, higher-risk jobs, parsimonious welfare states, inequality, and status systems emphasizing consumption. Dangerous jobs persist for workers lower in the social hierarchy, including those in mines and slaughterhouses, as well as jobs that require exposure to hazardous substances. Chronic diseases, emotional problems, and substance abuse are often related to efforts to cope with these labor force stresses and the contradictions of a consumer culture.

Lenski's types of societies, their corresponding levels of inequality, and related health risks provide a set of tools for comparing societies. Even today, the health of the least technologically sophisticated societies is highly dependent on the weather and other aspects of the environment. In societies with more sophisticated technologies, greater agricultural surpluses help populations survive unfavorable ecological conditions. The poor in the most unequal developed as well as developing countries continue to suffer from higher infant and child mortality than their affluent counterparts, as well as from asthma, other respiratory illnesses, and other maladies. Poor and low-income individuals and families also have inadequate access to preventive and early intervention medical treatments.

Social Inequality in the Modern World: Social Classes

Karl Marx (1818–1883) developed his theory of modern social classes and capitalism in response to the exploitation of workers by capitalists. He theorized that, over time, workers who spend long hours in dull, repetitive jobs develop a *class consciousness*—that is, a view of the world from the perspective of their position in the social structure—and take action collectively. *Alienation* describes the personal and psychological separation of workers from the work process and fruits of their labor under capitalism. No longer a meaningful source of personal identity and satisfaction as a craft, the worker's labor must be sold to an employer, forcing the worker to surrender control over the work process and its products. Workers produce more value in products than is paid to them; this "surplus value" is a source of profits, which capitalists pay to themselves and reinvest in additional profit-making enterprises.

Since Marx's day, differences in wealth and income between owners and laborers have widened, and poverty exists in even the wealthiest industrial countries. However, most workers are dramatically better off than they were during the early industrial period. Beginning in the late nineteenth century, workers made gains in collectively resisting oppressive working conditions, risking their jobs and sometimes their lives to organize unions. Modern welfare states have offered some protections to workers in organizing rights, length of the working day, and minimum wages. However, battles are ongoing between workers and employers over these and additional labor issues, and unions have been largely excluded from some regions, such as the southern United States. Oppressive and harsh labor conditions persist in many parts of the world, including developed countries, such as in some factory assembly work, meat packing, and mining.

Did Marx recognize health problems as an aspect of class inequalities? He believed that modern class relations caused workers to be alienated from their own bodies and "spiritual essence." "Estranged labor . . . estranges man's own body from him, as it does external nature and his spiritual essence, his *human* being" (from *Economic and Philosophic Manuscripts of 1844*, quoted in Tucker 1972, 63; emphasis in original). Marx also noted the destructive effect of a whole family's need to work for wages in order to survive.

> In so far as machinery dispenses with muscular power, it becomes a means of employing labourers of slight muscular strength . . . enrolling, under the direct sway of capital, every member of the workman's family, without distinction of age or sex. Compulsory work . . . usurped the place, not only of the children's play, but also of free labour at home . . . for the support of the family. (from *Capital*, quoted in Tucker 1972, 292)

Stratification, Life Chances, and Lifestyles

Max Weber (1864–1920) was also concerned with the dehumanizing effects of modern social institutions. In mass society, decision making is based on impersonal rules and laws, often within large bureaucratic organizations. Weber feared that the *rationalization* and routinization of labor create an "iron cage" that stifles human creativity and passion. Class divisions result from a combination of factors, including one's skills, credentials, and qualifications. Weber's notion of class position is not as fixed as Marx's; Weber said that there is some fluidity and mobility in modern class systems. Greater skills and credentials bring managerial and professional workers higher incomes, and skilled manufacturing workers are able to secure better pay and positions than unskilled workers. More satisfying jobs and a higher standard of living in turn produce better health in those privileged social groups. Statistics showing greater mental and physical health risks in routine, monotonous work coincide with Weber's concerns about the kinds of work available in modern societies, in both blue-collar and white-collar positions.

To Marx's theory of modern social class relations Weber added dimensions of social status and political power (Weber, 1946/1969, 180–195). *Status*, or prestige, is social honor bestowed differentially across social groups and occupations. Social status is a more subjective ranking of individuals than are income or wealth, and the jobs and styles with which it is associated may change over time. For example, in the United States, Supreme Court justices are often ranked in the highest status category but may have lower incomes than some Wall Street investors. Even more striking is the renowned status of Mother Teresa, who devoted her life to fighting poverty, in comparison to that of a Colombian drug lord—wealthy but without social honor. Occupation (or unemployment), income, race, and ethnicity all play a role in situating individuals in a status hierarchy. Residential segregation and job discrimination occur as a result of both income differences and social attitudes toward lower-status groups. Higher status has a positive effect on physical and mental health, produced through many pathways, including a higher standard of living, safer neighborhoods, better medical care, feelings of self-worth, greater investment in the future, and health-promoting behaviors.

Political parties are a third variable in Weber's model of stratification. Parties organize and struggle to control state power and resources. Weber defined the state as "a human community that (successfully) claims the *monopoly of the legitimate use of physical force* within a given territory" (quoted in Gerth & Mills 1969, 78). Political power groups can emerge out of social groups, classes, status groups, or even from within the state itself (Collins 1988, 152–153), for example, in corporate or religious lobbies, union coalitions, ethnic group coalitions, elderly lobbies, or "free-trade" lobbies. Political power helps privileged groups in society maintain their position and therefore also maintain greater chances of staying healthy and having long, satisfying lives.

The health gradient reflects Weber's model of stratification. It is not simply the material standard of living that determines whether individuals in modern societies will find themselves at the low or high end of the health gradient. For example, political power among the upper and upper-middle classes is exercised to ensure their continued influence over the distribution of resources by the state through laws and policies. And, although income is a major indicator of where an individual is located on the health gradient, social status also plays an important role. Our occupation, level of education, and other aspects of lifestyle influence how others treat us in everyday life.

Life Chances and Lifestyles: Structural Constraints and Personal Agency

Weber's concept of *life chances* describes the structural constraints on individuals' economic opportunities, choices, and life trajectories. His concept of *style of life* refers to the choices individuals make within those constraints and related to the expectations of others. The reference group for lifestyle choices may be, for example, a person's occupational peers or ethnic community. Weber contributed these insights:

> lifestyles (1) are associated with status groups, and therefore are principally a collective rather than an individual phenomenon; (2) represent patterns of consumption, not production; and (3) are shaped by the dialectical interplay between life choices and life chances, with choice playing the greater role. (Cockerham 1999, 59)

A lifestyle need not be simply an expression of conformity to a peer group. The works of Anthony Giddens (1991) and Michel Foucault (1973, 1978, 1979) suggest that individual expression may be a form of resistance to oppressive working or living conditions. Self-definition may resist authorities' characterizations or stereotypes, for example, as propagated in mainstream popular culture. Lifestyle is not just something that the affluent adopt; highly expressive styles may be even more important to those with limited resources. If lifestyle helps to transcend the rigid and demeaning aspects of modern social life, as well as a place lower on the hierarchy, then it has the potential to improve a person's health and life chances.

Personal and community agency may have positive health effects. This may entail the *active* creation and maintenance of an alternative subculture and supportive ties. Collective social action can transform a community as well as influence the dominant culture. Perhaps not surprisingly, the civil rights movement had positive effects on identity and health among African Americans, improving longevity for African Americans during the years between 1968 and 1978 (Cooper et al. 1981; Mullings 1989). For example, during the third administration of the National Study of Black Americans in 1988, the reported levels of physical and mental well-being were at their highest (Jackson et al. 1996). Not coincidentally, these positive reports came while Jesse Jackson was making his bid for the presidency (Williams & Collins 1995, 362). Latinos were slower to politically mobilize than African Americans, but by the turn of the new century there were numerous Latino leaders in local, state, and national politics. The positive health effects are not yet known, but it seems reasonable to guess that they will be significant. However, there is evidence of persistent income inequality and racism in the United States, and therefore we cannot stray too far from a structural analysis of ethnicity and health. If inequality between marginalized ethnic groups and other social groups continues to grow, we should expect further increases in the health and longevity gap between the more and the less privileged.

Labor Force–Health Relationships

What does the research evidence today say about workers' relationships to work and their effect on their health? Key findings are listed in Table 2.1. They suggest relationships between health and work that update Durkheim's, Marx's, and Weber's observations. The patterns reflect the concerns of these theorists for the physical, psychological, and social well-being of individuals in modern societies. Problems of harsh labor conditions, lack of control (including unemployment), and exploitation remain salient issues in the labor force today.

Theoretical Foundations for Understanding Gender Differences in Health

In most societies, women live longer than men. The reasons are not fully understood, but the difference is in part due to biological factors and in part due to behavioral and social factors. Estrogen seems to provide protective effects for premenopausal women, and men engage in more behaviors that cause them to die prematurely (smoking, drinking, violence, and other forms of risk taking). We also know that inequality between the sexes is nearly universal across societies, although it varies in its organization and degree—and inequality in social position produces inequality in health. Contemporary health evidence suggests that the female advantage in longevity would be even greater if women's and men's positions and resources in family, work, and community life were more equal. Women experience two independent sets of social forces in their positioning in the labor market: one based on their gender and the other based on their class. Both influence mental and physical health, but class and position in the global economy are stronger influences on health than is gender. (Chapter 6 addresses gender and health in greater detail.)

TABLE 2.1 *Labor Force and Health Outcomes: Key Observations*

Unemployment	Unemployed men have higher risk of death. This relationship is modified by labor market conditions, cultural views, and government policies. Social support, policies that minimize layoffs, and safety net programs cushion the effects of job loss on health.
Working in a job with little control	This heightens the risk of disease and death. For men, small changes that increase control can lower mortality risk. For women, only substantial increases in authority make a difference in health outcomes. (See also the table section "Work characteristics.")
Underemployment or underutilization of skills	This has a negative impact on health, in addition to the negative effect of lower-quality working conditions.
Work characteristics (e.g., repetitiveness, psychological demands, worker's decision latitude, job position within the hierarchy)	These affect worker control, level of interest and stimulation in the work process, status within the workplace, and strain on the mind and body. These, in turn, affect health. Less-routine, more stimulating, and higher-status positions with more control and decision-making power tend to produce better mental and physical health.
Job culture, structure of control, and rewards	The following affect employees' health risks and health buffers: work organization, compensation system (including benefits), flexibility in managing family-work demands, skills development programs, and workplace governance. These shape workplace conditions and affect level of control, job security, supervisor-employee relationships, and handling of layoffs.
Government laws and policies	Policies directly and indirectly affect labor market conditions and, therefore, workers' mental and physical health. U.S. examples include policies to prevent discrimination and unequal treatment of women, the disabled, and people of color. Governments supporting child care enable entry of women into the labor force. The Earned Income Credit helps keep workers' families from falling below the poverty line. European countries' policies provide more generous unemployment insurance programs and parental leave. European countries and Canada provide universal public health insurance.

Source: Data from B. C. Amick & J. N. Lavis, Labor markets and health: A framework and set of applications. In A. R. Tarlov & R. F. St. Peter (Eds.), *The Society and Population Health Reader: A State and Community Perspective* (New York: New Press, 2000), 178–210.

Friedrich Engels (1820–1895), who is famous for having been Karl Marx's close colleague, described the family in modern industrial societies as a microcosm of capitalist society in his *The Origin of the Family, Private Property and the State* (1884/1972). Engels displayed an early feminist perspective in his identification of women's household work as *labor*. He said that household labor is unpaid because of women's structural position in marriage and families. In effect, wives become their husbands' property in marriage, legally obligated to perform household labor and child care, and to submit sexually to their husbands. Like modern feminists (Hartmann 1981), Engels disagreed with conventional economic formulations by noting that work done in households is not "out of the labor force." In fact, unpaid household labor makes it possible for other adults (husbands and young adults) to go out into the paid labor force. Work done at home "reproduces" the labor power needed in the formal economy. How is this harmful to women's mental and physical health? As a job, housework's characteristics fit several of those that produce stress and poor health: It is routinized, monotonous, poorly remunerated, low status, and in the middle classes of developed societies, isolated from adult company.

Some societies, such as the Soviet Union and Israel, started out with intentions to rectify the patriarchal structure of family-work relationships by providing better opportunities and protections for women, but none were able to fully accomplish that goal. Nonetheless, loss of those protections with the dissolution of socialist governments brought a decline in women's social position. For example, the recent losses of job protections to East German women following the reunification of the country were accompanied by downturns in their health as well.

One way to examine the potential for women's greater equality with men is to look at their position in the economy. The relative strength of women in the labor force is related to

- The strategic indispensability of women's labor.
- The effects of the kinship system on female property ownership.
- The overall stratification of the society (Blumberg 1984).

Where women's labor is indispensable, women will have relatively greater economic power, as well as greater control over their sexuality and reproductive choices (Blumberg 1978, 1984; Collins 1975). Under these conditions, women's health is predicted to be better than in societies where their labor is not as crucial and where husbands' families have authority over wives and children. Not surprisingly, where women have little economic power, they are more likely to have little choice in marriage, reproduction, or divorce. Governmental and local policies can improve women's position by providing girls and women access to education, training, public offices, jobs, and technological resources. In horticultural societies, tools and fertilizers may be most in demand. In developed countries, access to computers and the Internet may expand skills and opportunities. The state can also legislate and enforce protections against domestic violence and restrict the availability of guns.

Gender "segregation in the occupational structure means that men and women are likely to end up in different destinations . . . that generate sex segregation in employment (hence women's restricted opportunities)" (Marshall 1997, 108). To the extent that women do not have access to equal income and status with men, their health will be disadvantaged. In addition, in Western societies, cultural values placed on female attractiveness add to competitive pressures. Achieving "the perfect body" has become part of the agenda for success, leading to unhealthy dieting and eating disorders, often starting in adolescence.

What are the health implications of women's working conditions? In the United States, where women raise small children in relative isolation and without pay or status, work at home is simply a harder job physically and emotionally. By contrast, in many Latin cultures, women seem less vulnerable to isolation, anxiety, and depression in their roles as wives and mothers. There, this position has higher status, and women often carry out their responsibilities within a network of kin and community relationships. However, if a woman's husband is abusive, she may suffer under his patriarchal authority and there are few avenues for changing the situation.

In societies and social classes where motherhood is isolating, affluent women can afford more choices. If they choose to work, they can purchase child care and enjoy more social stimulation and income. Because they do not necessarily need the income for basic subsistence, they can also quit jobs that do not sustain their interest. Mothers in part-time work report the highest satisfaction with their lives; they benefit from the rewarding aspects of raising their children while also gaining income and social stimulation. Low-income women do not have many choices; they must bring in money to purchase basic needs and are likely to be poorly paid, doing uninteresting work. This negatively affects health, especially if family members have negative attitudes about their working wife or mother. She then must endure a "double day" of home and labor force work plus the disapproval of her husband and children. This is a recipe for deteriorating mental and physical well-being.

Domestic violence against women is also a health issue. Engels's structural analysis locates women as the private property of their husbands, with the husband's right protected by both the state and norms of family privacy. The limit on how much coercion and overt force can legitimately be used against women in marriages and intimate relationships varies across cultures. In Western societies, there are long-standing legal and folk traditions respecting the rights of husbands to domestic labor, child-rearing, and sexual service from wives, and acceptance of a degree of coercion if a wife is noncompliant. The "rule of thumb," part of English common law that was imported to the United States, governed how thick a rod could be used for beating one's wife into submission (Dobash & Dobash 1979). This "discipline" reflects the structure of the patriarchal family, in which men and women do not simply fill functional social roles but occupy different structural positions of authority and control.

Social Hierarchy's Effects on Mind and Body

Analyzing human social inequality becomes more meaningful when examined in cultural context. Cultures create a social place and identity for individuals, sustain a sense of meaning and purpose, create rules, and distribute resources among members.

Other primates do not come close to matching the complexity of humans' capacity for creating culture, yet the baboons studied by Robert Sapolsky (1993) offer some clues about the stress caused by inequality. These primates spend just four hours a day foraging for food, leaving twelve hours out of each day for social interaction. "They have complicated social relations with patterns of dominance and subordination, alliances and friendships, and their competitiveness gives rise to a clearly defined social hierarchy" (Wilkinson 1996, 193). Sapolsky found that low-ranking males have higher levels of a group of stress chemicals called glucocorticoids than high-ranking males. These are steroid hormones released when danger is sensed in a "fight-or-flight" reaction. This chronic state of vigilance among lower-status males is physiologically costly. The energy taken up with this semi-alarm state takes away from rest and repair to the body. Over time, the neural feedback mechanism that regulates the release of glucocorticoids fails to work because of the death of neuron receptors in the hippocampus (Wilkinson 1996, 194). Similar patterns of chronic alarm and damage have been found in other primates.

Among humans, there are several ways in which poorer health results from the chronic release of stress chemicals into the system. It causes elevated blood pressure for longer periods, which in turn increases the risk of cardiovascular disease and stroke. In addition, higher levels of stress chemicals are associated with a lower ratio of high-density to low-density lipoproteins. The higher proportion of low-density lipoproteins leads to a more rapid accumulation of cholesterol deposits in the blood vessels, which can form plaque and narrow the coronary arteries. Narrowed arteries slow blood flow (and therefore oxygen) to the heart, increasing risk of blockage and heart attack.

The Whitehall study of British civil servants working in London is discussed in Chapter 4, but here we note the physiological effects of the hierarchy in this workplace. The study found dramatic results roughly parallel to the hierarchical health effects found in Sapolsky's primates. The death rates from heart disease were four times as high among the lowest levels of male civil servants as among the highest levels (Brunner 1996). The levels of low-density lipoproteins overall were gradated by place in the civil service hierarchy, accounting for about a third of the higher rates of heart disease among the lower ranks of civil servants.

Within groups of both baboons and British civil servants, it is theoretically possible that males at the bottom of the hierarchy *could be at the top*. Among baboons, the jockeying for position occurs until a clear hierarchy emerges. The hierarchy changes as older dominant baboons age, die, and are replaced by new dominant males. Among British civil servants, where social class is important, social position is in large part determined by the individual's family of origin and educational training, but it is possible for persons toward the lower level of the civil service to have reached the upper rungs. How does interaction within the status hierarchy affect health? Face-to-face interactions involve sizing up an individual's status vis-à-vis others, reflecting and reaffirming status differences that include family status, education, personal confidence, and appearance. For example, being tall is given social status, and, remarkably, the physical height of Whitehall civil servants was more closely related to their position in the occupational hierarchy as adults than to the social class of their families when they were children (Marmot 1986).

Those with lower status develop an alertness to being challenged or shamed. This protective alertness involves the limbic system's (the emotional brain's) being attuned and "switching on" the sympathetic nervous system's stress response as needed. The costs to the body may be considerable, including higher baseline and acute levels of stress. Chronic activation of the system takes energy away from immune functioning and may leave the body vulnerable to infectious diseases and even cancers. High blood pressure may result from a persistent stress response, and atherosclerosis may develop from increased lipids and proteins in the bloodstream. We will see in Chapter 6 that African Americans' higher rates of high blood pressure may in large part be caused by the protective alertness provoked by racism.

Lifestyles express our individuality, and yet also conform to peer cultures among co-workers, family, and friends.

"Coronary-prone" hostile behavior is associated with hostile individuals of any social class (Williams 1989), but those least able to meet perceived social demands are most vulnerable to its effects. During the 1970s, hostility was conceptualized as part of an overall "Type A" personality. This type is especially salient in U.S. culture, where individuals are held personally responsible for reaching success on an uneven playing field. The ideology of the American dream promises affluence and status to those who work hard. Success is demonstrated by home and car ownership, and by high levels of consumption. Advertisements propagate the myth that everyone can consume at affluent levels; Americans respond by accumulating credit card debt and neglecting to save for the future. This cultural context may partially explain Americans' higher rates of heart disease in comparison to Europeans. Researchers at Yale studying second heart attacks among men concluded that it may not be anger alone that increases the risk of death from heart disease, but any intense negative emotional state that regularly sends waves of stress hormones through the body (Powell 1990). Failure to achieve "success" through conspicuous consumption may provoke such negative emotions.

Human Bodies in Modern Vehicles: The Case of Hierarchy on the Road

Automobiles perhaps epitomize American individualistic culture. We select our cars as extensions of our identity; our vehicles boost our ego and provide us time alone. We expect to get to our destinations quickly, and when traffic and annoying drivers get in our way, watch out! In *How Emotions Work*, sociologist Jack Katz (1999) reports findings from his studies of drivers in Los Angeles traffic. He finds that acting out angry dramas allows drivers to physically and emotionally express their frustration and moral indignation at other drivers, helping them to regain a sense of control. Encapsulated within their cars (which function as extensions of their body), drivers suffer insults to these auto "bodies" and respond with their dramas of rage. Once finished with their dramas, most drivers return to equilibrium. However, drivers with chronically switched-on anger are at risk for serious health problems, such as elevated blood pressure and cardiovascular disease. In a chapter titled "Pissed off in L.A.," Katz writes,

> Becoming "pissed off" when driving may be an unfortunately inescapable fact of public life in many places, but in Los Angeles it is a naturally occurring cornucopia for social psychology. Because this form of anger is known in memorably dramatic instances by virtually everyone who drives in L.A., because it is a brief and infinitely recurring experience, and because angry responses to other motorists are typically felt to be so deeply justified that they can be recounted readily to strangers without concern for loss of face, the experience of becoming "pissed off" while driving provides extraordinarily useful data for exploring fundamental issues about the nature and contingencies of anger as it emerges and declines in social interaction. (Katz 1999, 18)

In modern societies, how we drive provides an opportunity to self-diagnose our degree of impatience and hostility. Whether the driving conditions are bad or we have impatient personalities, if we are chronically angry and hostile, our health will suffer. Some individuals develop a habitually aggravated response to their daily commute. Many have sought affordable housing a long and congested distance from work. Other drivers are short tempered even when driving short distances in less-busy areas. Impatience and intolerance with others' behavior contribute to hostile responses that signal danger to the brain and flood the body with glucocorticoids, lipoproteins, and other chemicals involved in the stress response, which were linked with cardiovascular disease in Sapolsky's baboons and Whitehall civil servants.

Beyond chronically getting "pissed off" in traffic-clogged cities, when human face-to-face relationships grow fewer and more attenuated, social life pays a price. People do not learn how to get along and accomplish tasks despite their differences. Interactions do not generate sufficient trust for individuals to think of themselves as part of a community. When this happens, cities get physically and socially uglier, and interactions do not sufficiently buffer individuals from the stresses and strains of daily living.

Social Cohesion and Income Inequality

In the Durkheimian tradition, Ichiro Kawachi and Bruce Kennedy (1997) use the concept of social cohesion to describe what a society loses when it becomes less equal. As the gap grows between rich and poor, divisiveness grows between social groups, reducing social solidarity and increasing anomie and alienation. Participation in local organizations declines, and local governance deteriorates. Sociologist Melvin Tumin (1953) describes the unfortunate consequences of social stratification when individuals are aware that they *could* be equal.

> [T]o the extent that inequalities in social rewards cannot be made fully acceptable to the less privileged in a society, social stratification systems function to encourage hostility, suspicion and distrust among the various segments of society and thus to limit the possibilities of extensive social integration. (Tumin 1953, 393)

Conversely, social *equality* creates positive social and health effects. Populations in more equal countries like Japan and Sweden have greater longevity than their more unequal counterparts in the United States and Great Britain. But this has not always been the case. During the two world wars, Britain achieved greater income equality and fuller employment. These conditions led to a healthier population and an increase in life expectancy. Of course, policies to achieve full employment and equality are preferable in peacetime rather than in war. In addition, as Durkheim recognized, an outside threat to a social group enhances social cohesion. During both world wars, solidarity surely increased British social cohesion and contributed to health, along with a more equal distribution of income.

Another case example is the mid-twentieth-century community of Roseto,

Pennsylvania. Researchers studied Roseto because its rates of heart disease were approximately half of those in communities around it and the nation as a whole. Roseto enjoyed high civic participation in a tightly knit community in which "everybody knew everybody." With the economic opportunities and rapid social changes of the 1960s, income differences in Roseto increased, civic participation decreased, and community cohesion dissipated. A sharp increase in deaths from cardiovascular disease followed, and researchers concluded that the town had lost the high level of social capital that had served as its collective health buffer (Bruhn & Wolf 1979).

Income inequality and mortality in the United States also provide convincing evidence of social cohesion as a buffer against disease and death (Kawachi et al. 1997). Ichiro Kawachi and his colleagues found results parallel to those suggested by Roseto's experience: Inequality was associated with detrimental patterns in community life and health. The "density of associational life" was measured by participation in organizations (sports or church groups, labor unions, local clubs), and social trust was measured by questions about whether most people could be trusted. In the thirty-nine states studied, both low associational life and social distrust were associated with income inequality and higher overall mortality. The authors conclude that income inequality results in lower social capital, which in turn results in higher mortality.

Summary

This chapter has offered theoretical foundations for studying health in social context. The following is a summary of key contributions:

1. From Durkheim:
   - The group is a unit of health analysis.
   - Social cohesion is a factor in the health of communities.
   - Social cohesion promotes mutual support within a population, which is associated with positive health outcomes.
   - Social inequality (an aspect of heterogeneity) in a population weakens social cohesion and increases anomie; both have negative effects on health.
2. From Marx:
   - Modern class relations produce alienation among a considerable proportion of the population, making these groups more vulnerable to the psychosocial causes of ill health: depression, anxiety, and risk-taking behaviors such as smoking, drinking, reckless driving, and poor eating and exercise habits.
   - Pressures to maximize profits contribute to harmful working conditions, for example, in mining, agriculture, factory, and assembly work. Jobs that have low pay, low job security, and few benefits are associated with poorer health and more accidents and disability. Producing surplus value often comes at the expense of workers' health and well-being.
   - The need for surplus labor to keep wages down requires that a part of the population be unemployed. There are known associations between unemploy-

ment and disease and premature death, experienced most strongly by working-age men.

3. From Weber:
   - Rationalization of social processes in large bureaucratic organizations and workplaces stifles human creativity and individuality. These affect psychological health and health-related behaviors.
   - Life chances (including occupational opportunities, wealth, and health) are constrained by a person's place in the social structure.
   - Social class, cultural status, and political power contribute to an individual's place in the social structure.
   - Lifestyles are choices a person makes within the constraints of his or her culture and social position; the more disadvantaged, in general, the more limited the choices for health.
   - The state plays a role in mediating class relations. Policies that reduce social inequality, ensure care of basic human needs, and enhance human capital through education and primary health care have the potential to improve population health.

4. From the sociology of gender:
   - Labor performed in households is an essential part of the economy; it is unpaid, repetitive, and low status. The gendered division of domestic labor in modern societies has harmful effects on women's mental and physical health. The harmful effects are felt much more strongly among women of the lower and working classes, who must contribute economically for their families to make ends meet. Financial and physical strain often are chronic conditions. Middle-class women strain under the double day of work and home responsibilities in order to maintain a middle-class lifestyle. Upper-middle-class women have more choices and protective benefits from their class position.
   - The household division of labor has a corresponding relationship to the division of labor in the paid labor force, with built-in disadvantages for women in narrower opportunities and in the timing of careers around motherhood. These market disadvantages have detrimental effects on women's health and longevity. Low-income women (and especially ethnically marginalized women) experience these harmful effects the most, whereas upper-middle-class women are protected by their class position.
   - When and where women's labor is valued and needed by a society, their social position will be elevated; women are not as likely to suffer economic and health disadvantages under these conditions.

The following chapter builds on this foundation, to describe a political economy approach to health and quality of life.

3

A Political Economy Approach to Health

Every morning . . . Pedro and his youngest son Jaime wake up coughing and wheezing. . . . Pedro never experienced health problems before coming to work in the copper smelters of Ilo, six years ago. He worries now because he has seen several fellow workers die from lung cancer and other respiratory complications.

But what troubles Pedro most is his ailing child. When his wife took eight-year-old Jaime to the local medical clinic, the doctor gave the boy cough medicine and vitamins. But the remedies did little, and Jaime's cough is often so bad he is forced to stay home from school. Many of Jaime's young friends complain of similar symptoms.

—J. V. Millen and T. H. Holtz, "Dying for Growth. Part I: Transnational Corporations and the Health of the Poor"

Southern Peru Copper is the largest mining company in Peru, yet it is a U.S.-owned company. Its careless industrial practices are costing many Peruvians their health. In the southern Peruvian town of Ilo, 2,000 tons of sulfur dioxide are spewed into the air every day from the company's smelters (Millen & Holtz 2000, 192).

Among the social factors that influence health and life chances is location in the global economy. Economic projects designed by capitalists in affluent parts of the world have ripple effects in the countries where the production occurs. "Global economy" means that there is a system of economic relationships, worldwide in scope and hierarchical in its distribution of resources. For example, 20 percent of the world's population receives 80 percent of the income (United Nations Development Programme 1997). Mexican workers may stitch together garments from cloth made in India that was cut into patterns in Indonesia. The final product may be sold in department stores in Los Angeles, Paris, and other cities. A person's location in this

*Workers in the global economy, these women package cosmetic cream in
an Avon subsidiary factory in Guatemala City.*

global economic web of production and consumption is likely to influence how well
he or she is fed, clothed, and housed, and what kinds of educational and occupational
opportunities he or she has.

Depending on where workers are located in the global economy, the risks and
rewards of their jobs, the security of their family life, and the quality of their living
conditions vary enormously. Even within wealthy countries, some workers have
unhealthy working conditions, low pay, and risk of unemployment, and low-income
families or the elderly may find rents or health care unaffordable. It is also the case
that in underdeveloped countries an elite often benefits from "extractive sectors" of
the economy, which export oil, precious metals, or timber to wealthier countries. This
chapter explores these issues of economics, power, and health, and presents a model
summarizing the social influences on health (Figure 3.1).

We consider the following questions:

- How do living conditions vary in different parts of the global economy?
- How do those differences correspond to health?
- Which factors protect or worsen health?

The World Economic System

Latin American scholars crafted *dependency theory* in response to an increasingly obvious question: Why is so much of the world so poor and dependent, despite centuries of trade and contact with more advanced nations? Dependency theory posits that imperialism and multinational expansion by powerful, developed countries maintains *underdevelopment* in less-powerful countries. Trade relations and political interventions ensure continued dependency on and exploitation by more powerful nations and transnational corporations.

Immanuel Wallerstein (1974/1980) built the dependency approach into a fully developed *world systems theory*. Although this theory has its weaknesses, it has proven a valuable tool in understanding the dynamics of development and underdevelopment in the modern world. It is an essential component of a political economy analysis of health. According to the theory, there are three types of countries that make up the world economic system: periphery, core, and semi-periphery.

Periphery countries have less-developed economies; that is, they produce relatively few products and are limited by less infrastructure and technology. Their economies are often based in subsistence agriculture and a few simple "extractive" commodities, such as fruits, coffee, tea, vegetables, grains, precious metals, or lumber. They have weak states and are exploited by affluent countries for their resources, inexpensive labor, and markets. Periphery countries are less able to take care of basic human needs (and therefore often have malnourished populations) because they have low incomes, inefficient production, and few social services.

Periphery countries also suffer economically, according to world systems theory, because they are kept in dependent economic relationships, for example, in needing foreign capital, jobs, and foreign investments in production. Periphery governments often make agreements with corporations, giving them special privileges regarding environmental impacts, labor conditions, or product marketing. Corporate investments from the core of the global economy most often do not help periphery countries to develop their own industries and infrastructure. Periphery countries have low incomes and standards of living, often with a majority of their populations living on the equivalent of $1 or $2 a day. A few examples are Cambodia, Bangladesh, Haiti, Kazakhstan, Peru, Ethiopia, and Zambia.

Core countries have diversified economies, strong and stable states, and large middle classes. Civil liberties are extensive, and overt class conflict is minimal. Corporations based in core nations exploit periphery and semi-periphery countries by extracting raw materials (oil, timber, and metals); employing inexpensive labor for assembly and other labor-intensive production; and using them as potential consumer markets. This occurs primarily through trade relations but is also supported by the governments of core countries and by international financial institutions. Examples of core countries include the United Kingdom, the United States, Japan, Germany, France, Spain, and Sweden.

Semi-periphery countries have more diversified economies than periphery countries but are far less diversified than core countries. They have substantially higher incomes than periphery countries, from an abundance of a valued natural resources, such as oil; from well-developed and somewhat diversified industries; or from prolific agricultural production. Semi-periphery countries are likely to include a middle class, although smaller than in core countries, and also may have a substantial proportion of the population living in poverty. The states of semi-periphery countries are not as stable as in the core; they are more likely to experience coups d'état and other governmental disruptions, and have a higher potential for class conflict. Transitions of power from one regime to the next are especially vulnerable to conflict, as various personalities and mobilized groups vie for control. Semi-periphery countries often have the greatest income inequality among their populations. Examples of semi-periphery countries include Saudi Arabia, Brazil, Chile, Mexico, Argentina, South Korea, and Libya.

Over time, the economies of periphery and semi-periphery countries may become increasingly less able to develop independently. Foreign firms and investors gain considerable control over periphery countries' economies, and core states intervene with financial or military punishments against trade barriers. If conditions are no longer favorable, corporations pull out, often leaving few infrastructure improvements, depleted natural resources, and a spoiled environment.

The overall increases in longevity worldwide during the twentieth century (including substantial reductions in infant and child mortality in poorer countries) seem to discount a world systems analysis of global health. The model has the weaknesses of not predicting health outcomes in particular countries and not explaining why some periphery countries have had gains in life expectancy and become more independent. Nonetheless, the theory does predict the increasing inequalities both within and between countries. These divides have the harshest effect on those on the bottom rungs of periphery and semi-periphery countries. The following global health conditions identified by the Institute for Health and Social Justice (based in Cambridge, Massachusetts) paint a grim picture of living conditions in the periphery:

- More than 50 percent of the people in the world's forty-six poorest countries are without access to modern health care.
- Approximately 3 billion people in less-developed countries do not have access to sanitation facilities.
- More than 1 billion individuals in less-developed countries do not have access to safe drinking water.
- At least 600 million urban dwellers in Africa, Asia, and Latin America live in what the World Health Organization calls life- and health-threatening homes and neighborhoods (Kim et al. 2000, 4).

In summary, the political economy perspective contributes the following to theoretical foundations for studying health:

1. Location in the global economy or world economic system generally determines the standard of living and life chances.
2. In periphery countries, absolute poverty threatens population health. Chronic

hunger, malnutrition, and lack of access to safe drinking water compromise infant and child health, and result in lowered immunity and vulnerability to disease among the poor generally.

3. Location in the periphery of the economic world system jeopardizes health in part because core and semi-periphery countries exploit the natural resources and labor of the periphery with the assistance of the indigenous elite, without protecting workers and the environment. Periphery countries often become stuck in debt and are forced by international financial institutions to cut back social spending that supports basic needs. Cuts in nutritional programs, literacy campaigns, education, and primary health care hamper improvements or worsen population health.

We now place the political economy approach within an overall model of social influences on health.

A Global Model of Social Influences on Health

Figure 3.1 presents a model that situates individuals in the political economy, along with the other social influences on health. This model offers analytical tools for examining case studies and for considering ways to ameliorate the health-damaging aspects of social inequalities. Its political economy approach emphasizes the structural aspects of varying living conditions, life chances, and health outcomes.

1. Location in the Political Economy

Location in the political economy describes an individual's position vis-à-vis market forces in terms of country, social class, ethnicity/race, gender, and age. The global trend of rural-urban migration, especially in periphery and semi-periphery countries, is an example of shifting location from the subsistence farming sector to the urban pool of wage laborers and "informal economy" workers. The latter includes those who do not work in established businesses or agencies; instead, they sell or exchange services or products informally, outside of transactions that are tracked and measured by business and state agencies. For example, without the ability to grow and barter food (whether because of environmental deterioration, civil war, or agribusiness dislocation), husbands, wives, or whole families migrate to the city to seek work.

In another migration pattern common in semi-peripheral countries, young women are recruited to do factory assembly work, taking them away from home and family. Hardships may include living in a shantytown, having insufficient food and poor sanitation, and being exposed to coercion or violence. The anonymity of urban areas or free-trade zones fosters little trust, and employers are often not held accountable for poor treatment of workers. With the push and pull of forces away from rural areas toward cities, family and community supports weaken and are less able to protect individuals from harm. Thus, in addition to the loss of social support,

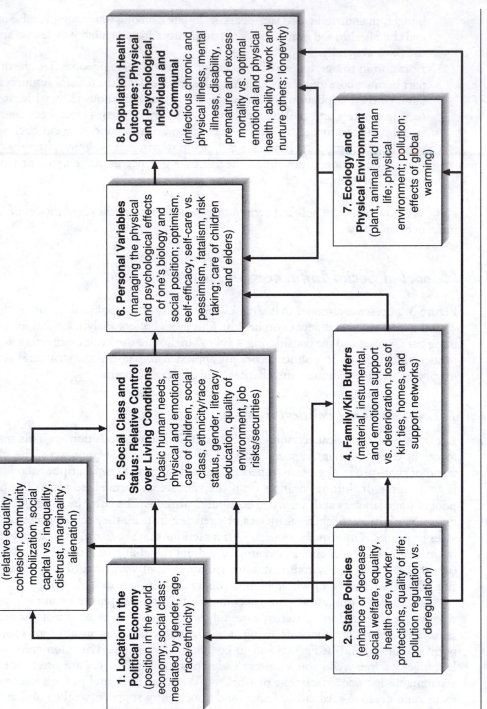

Boxes in figure:

8. Population Health Outcomes: Physical and Psychological, Individual and Communal (infectious chronic and physical illness, mental illness, disability, premature and excess mortality vs. optimal emotional and physical health, ability to work and nurture others; longevity)

7. Ecology and Physical Environment (plant, animal and human life; physical environment; pollution; effects of global warming)

6. Personal Variables (managing the physical and psychological effects of one's biology and social position; optimism; self-efficacy, self-care vs. pessimism, fatalism, risk taking; care of children and elders)

5. Social Class and Status: Relative Control over Living Conditions (basic human needs, physical and emotional care of children, social class, ethnicity/race status, gender, literacy/education, quality of environment, job risks/securities)

4. Family/Kin Buffers (material, instumental, and emotional support vs. deterioration, loss of kin ties, homes, and support networks)

3. Community Buffers (relative equality, cohesion, community mobilization, social capital vs. inequality, distrust, marginality, alienation)

2. State Policies (enhance or decrease social welfare, equality, health care, worker protections, quality of life; pollution regulation vs. deregulation)

1. Location in the Political Economy (position in the world economy; social class; mediated by gender, age, race/ethnicity)

FIGURE 3.1   *Political Economy, Basic Human Needs, and Health Outcomes*

Poverty and the drive to keep production costs down are the main causes of child labor and exploitation of children. This young girl and others like her sew together soccer balls in India.

harsh environmental and work conditions often result in poor care of basic human needs.

In affluent core countries, relation to the market is also a major factor in whether social relations will enhance or harm health. The upper and upper-middle classes control investment capital, the physical means of production (land, factories, and offices), and the hiring and firing of workers (Wright 1978). Professionals and highly trained technology workers enjoy higher incomes, more control over their work, and more prestige than other workers. Less highly educated workers can find opportunities in the building trades and service industries during boom times, but when there is recession and an oversupply of workers, jobs, wages, and benefits decrease. Creative entrepreneurs can make the ascent to financial success if they tap into market opportunities and work hard, but more frequently businesses fail. There is an overabundance of semi-skilled individuals in affluent countries competing for both white-collar and blue-collar jobs that pay middle-class to lower-middle-class wages. In the United States, working-class and middle-class incomes have stagnated or slid since around 1973. Income increases, concentrated in the upper echelons of the labor force, began in the 1980s, and the highest incomes continued to pull the average income upward until a recession emerged in 2001.

In rapidly fluctuating labor markets, laid-off workers accept lower-paying jobs in services or retail, often without health care and retirement benefits. Displaced workers know too well the punishments of fluctuating markets. Workers from the Enron bankruptcy of January 2002 lost not only their jobs but also their retirement savings, as these were heavily invested in Enron stock. The downward mobility from job loss takes its toll on mental and physical health and has ripple effects on families and communities. Sociologist and psychotherapist Lillian Rubin interviewed several laid-off working-class couples for her study *Families on the Fault Line* (1994). A twenty-nine-year-old father of two lost his factory job when his employer's company was restructured during the 1990s. As he described it, "I worked there for two years, but I didn't have seniority, so when they started to lay guys off, I was it. We never really had a chance to catch up on all the bills before it was all over" (Rubin 1994, 104). Rubin noted that depression was a common problem among the unemployed men she interviewed. One said to Rubin, with his head bowed, "It's a real shocker to realize that about yourself, to feel like you're all slowed down. . . . I don't know how to explain it exactly, maybe like your mind's pushing a load of mud around all the time" (Rubin 1994, 110).

Unfortunately, job insecurity is likely to plague growing numbers of workers in postindustrial core countries, as it does workers in periphery and semi-periphery countries.

2. State Policies

The state to some extent regulates business and may provide a safety net to protect individuals, social institutions (families, schools), and the environment from the damaging effects of the market. Where there is only a limited safety net and a paucity of regulatory efforts, communities and individuals are left to their own devices in coping with harsh working conditions and deteriorating environments. When jobs that pay a living wage are unavailable, psychological depression, deviant behavior, and participation in informal and underground economies are possible adjustments. In addition, taxation and welfare benefit policies can contribute to a safety net or further increase population inequalities. Policies that protect the environment and improve education, job conditions, housing, and nutrition benefit population health and well-being.

3 and 4. Community, Family, and Kin Buffers

The institution of the family continues to provide a front line of defense against harsh material and social conditions in all kinds of countries. Ideally, communities integrate individuals into social life, moderate their behavior, and protect them from hunger and other dangers. Families and communities do not always perform these functions well, of course; resource shortages and domestic abuses are all too familiar. None-theless, according to social psychologist Lisa Berkman, health outcomes are heavily influenced by "the degree to which people are embedded in a web of social relation-ships that provide intimacy, love and meaning as well as a larger sense of belonging and 'fit' with a larger community" (Berkman 2000, 260). For example, following a surgery, if one or more people are available to assist the recovering patient, that recov-ery is likely to go more smoothly. And, following an accident or natural disaster, if people rally around to help one another, recovery of the community enables the recovery of individuals.

Following Durkheim's early work, contemporary studies show that family and community relationships influence individual as well as social aspects of health and disease. For example, the quality of care during infancy and early childhood years influences cognitive abilities and therefore children's ability to focus and perform well in school. Healthy eating, sleeping, and exercise patterns during childhood and early adulthood influence health and illness throughout life. But there are more than indi-vidual effects, as Durkheim's study of suicide demonstrated. At the community level, the quality of relationships influences the prevalence and progression of disease, as well as overall mortality rates (Berkman 2000, 260).

Nurturing relationships may require special effort in modern societies, because social relations are often more fleeting and anonymous than in smaller, traditional societies. Family and friends may become more important for emotional support. For example, when individuals or newly married couples move away from home, staying in contact by phone or e-mail helps to keep emotional bonds intact. Also, friendships may become family-type relationships, providing closeness, practical help, and emo-tional support.

Community disruptions and dislocations due to war, agricultural moderniza-tion, environmental devastation, and famine are much more widespread in periphery countries. For example, there were around 20 million official refugees in the world as of the mid-1990s, and that number is higher at the turn of the new century. These are displaced persons who have crossed national boundaries, mostly in poor countries. An additional 20 million or so are displaced within their own countries (Desjarlais et al. 1995, 136). Refugees are vulnerable physically and psychologically, dislodged from relationships and homes that provide subsistence and social support. Their physical health risks are considerable, including chronic hunger or famine, illness, rape, and other violent assaults. Their emotional risks are perhaps less visible but take a serious toll as well, with depression, anxiety, and chronic traumatic stress symptoms. Psy-chosis also afflicts the most vulnerable and traumatized individuals.

5. Social Class and Status: Relative Control over Living Conditions

Uncertainty is a major source of stress, and position in the stratification system to a large extent determines the amount of control individuals have (Sutton & Kahn 1987; Williams & Collins 1995, 378). Control over daily living conditions links social structure to health, including the ability to satisfy basic needs for food, shelter, and drinkable water. Fulfillment of basic needs enables parents to nurture and educate children, to work, and to carry on social relationships beyond the family. Public health researcher Leonard Syme (1991) suggests that *control* may be the key determinant of where individuals are located on the health gradient. The "effects of social support, Type A behavior, and stressful life events can all be interpreted to reflect the presence or absence of different aspects of control" (Syme 1991, quoted in Williams & Collins 1995, 378).

Perhaps the variable of control can be extended to whole communities. Efforts to increase control and bring about improved social conditions can have positive effects on individuals' sense of self and can improve the care of children. For example, LaVeist (1992) found that, where communities were mobilized in the movement for black political power, postneonatal mortality rates were lowered. He suggests that active involvement and political empowerment enhance health in communities drawn together by a sense of common purpose.

6. Personal Variables

The model in Figure 3.1 emphasizes structural variables shaping individual lives but also recognizes personal influences on health. This is the individual–social system paradox that we described in Chapter 1: Individuals are dependent on healthy social conditions for their mental and physical health, yet individuals are also purposeful decision makers, influencing their own health destiny. In Chapter 2, Figure 2.1 showed that individuals' health behaviors explain nearly one-fifth of the variations in disease and mortality rates. Therefore, we know that individuals are not passively living out predestined life courses; they make creative choices, resist coercion, and sometimes transcend harsh living conditions. Some people are born sturdy, whereas others become resilient through life experience. Other individuals deteriorate when faced with difficulties. Tragically, some privileged and gifted individuals seemingly throw away opportunities for a long, satisfying life because they cannot find purpose or inspiration.

Personal variables include the relative amount of psychological distress that individuals experience and also how they cope with that distress (Anderson & Armstead 1995). Personality also influences health; for example, whether a person is generally optimistic or pessimistic influences his or her view of the world and shapes health-related behaviors (Seligman 1991). Optimism is not a panacea for life's problems, but rather a way to harness personal resources to make the best of good and bad situations. Behaviors that increase the risk of disease, disability, and premature death include smoking, excessive drug and alcohol use, driving while intoxicated, and engaging in injury-prone sports. Conversely, sound eating, sleeping, and exercise habits enhance health and help prevent disease and accidents. (And those behaviors are highly predicted by an individual's social class position.) Self-care also has positive ripple effects on family, friends, and coworkers. Perhaps most important, children's development benefits when parents are healthy, attentive, and patient.

7. Ecology and Physical Environment

This category includes plant, animal, and human life, and the remainder of the physical environment. For example, population size and density affect the sustainability of usage patterns on air, water, and soil systems (Tarlov & St. Peter 2000, xi). Some experts argue that population growth does not automatically bring food shortages; they stress that unequal distribution of food prevents eradication of famine and chronic hunger (Lappé et al. 1998; Seaman 1994). Other experts point to global population growth with concern over food shortages and the earth's limited carrying capacity (Brown 1997). As urbanization accompanies population growth, population density creates opportunities for infectious diseases to spread, and in less-developed countries, improved sanitation and water supplies often don't keep pace with urban growth. In addition, agricultural modernization, such as irrigation projects and dams, often causes pollution and land degradation, and may spur disease (Bowman 1994; Bradley 1994). Even in developed countries, the waste from the mass production of beef, poultry, and eggs has caused serious environmental problems (Lacey 1994).

During the twentieth century, modern water, agricultural, and sanitation systems have dramatically improved the standard of living and curbed disease; these changes in human ecology have dramatically lengthened lives (Wilkinson 1996). However, overly optimistic World War II assumptions about abundance took their toll as well. Among the costs of economic development and affluence have been wasted resources and a damaged environment. British researcher Bryan Cartledge (1994) spent many years in the former Soviet Union and observed some of the worst environmental neglect from careless and hurried development. He describes the deterioration of the Central Asian Aral Sea,

> The two rivers which feed this large inland sea, the Amu Darya and Syr Darya, had been partially diverted in the early 1960s in order to supply water to new irrigation schemes in Uzbekistan and thus boost cotton production. As a result, the Aral Sea began to shrink and by 1988 its level had dropped by 13 metres. The consequential change in the regional microclimate, heavy deposits of wind-blown salt over a vast area to the south and west of the sea, and concomitant deposits of chemical fertilizers, herbicides, and pesticides blown from the drying delta regions on to populated areas had a devastating impact on the health of the local population. A representative of Karakalpakia told the Soviet Congress . . . on 30 May 1989: "There has been a sharp rise in the percentage of deformities in new-born babies . . . two out of every three babies examined were ill—mainly with typhoid, cancer of the oesophagus, and hepatitis. There are cases of cholera. In some areas of Karakalpakia doctors do not recommend breast-feeding: the milk is toxic." (Cartledge 1994, 4)

Two years later, official reports confirmed that overall and infant mortality had risen sharply. The Soviet Union was especially guilty of careless industrial strategies but is by no means alone in this abuse.

The Institute for Health and Social Justice chronicles environmental abuses by transnational corporations (TNCs). In their chapter "Dying for Growth," authors Joyce Millen and Timothy Holtz summarize,

> Throughout the world, TNCs release solid, liquid, and gaseous waste into the environment. Transnational energy, mining, forestry, fishing, manufacturing, and agricultural corporations affect human life on every continent by flooding huge tracts of land, depleting natural resources, eliminating fish stocks, and destroying vegetation and wildlife. (2000, 178)

8. Population Health Outcomes: Physical and Psychological, Individual and Communal

The factors described in boxes 1 through 8 in Figure 3.1 influence the health and disease patterns of individuals, groups, and societies. Health outcomes include infectious and chronic illness, mental illness, disability, premature death, and excess population mortality. Health includes the ability to work, care for children and households, and be an active member of the community.

The theoretical perspectives and concepts presented in Chapters 2 and 3 provide tools for comparing and analyzing social groups, as well as for considering case examples. The following chapter presents principles describing ways that health and disease vary systematically according to social inequalities.

4

Health and Inequality: Principles and Examples

The harm to health comes not only from material deprivation but also from the social and psychological problems resulting from living in relative poverty.

—Mary Shaw, Danny Dorling, and George Davey Smith, "Poverty, Social Exclusion, and Minorities"

While it is tempting to focus on the biological pathways that "explain" how inequalities in health are manifested in individuals, it is likely that only an understanding of economic, behavioral, social, psychological and community dynamics and their causes will lead us to remedies.

—George Kaplan and John Lynch, "Whither Studies on Socioeconomic Foundations of Population Health?" *American Journal of Public Health*

This chapter summarizes sociological health patterns as a set of principles. Principles 1 through 6 are discussed in this chapter; 7 and 8 are discussed in Chapter 6; and 9 is discussed in Chapter 9. All eight principles are listed in the appendix. These principles are based on information about health patterns globally, as well as within countries. Standard of living and inequality are key variables, and examples clarify some of the pathways through which social structure influences quality of life and health. Following the principles is a case example of deteriorating health in Russia. A discussion of social policies concludes the chapter, illustrating their potentially beneficial or harmful effects on health. Policy will be discussed in greater detail in Chapter 10.

We consider the following questions:

- What are the social dynamics that produce health differences?
- Can these patterns be altered by community and governmental policies?

Principle 1

Globally, the major factor determining whether individuals will live longer lives and experience less life-threatening illness is the availability of living conditions that meet basic human needs (Wilkinson 1996).

Poverty has direct, harmful effects on mental and physical health. "Absolute poverty" means that basic human needs for nutrition, water, and housing are not being met.[1] There are various ways to measure poverty, but chronic hunger and insecure food supply, along with inadequate housing, are nearly universal aspects. The particulars vary geographically.

For example, a project investigating poverty sponsored by the World Bank found that, in Guatemala, poverty is defined as not having enough food or being without housing (Narayan 2000, 36). In Cameroon, the poor distinguish themselves from the nonpoor by their chronic hunger and monotonous diet. In Nigeria, poverty is equated with preharvest food shortages and starchy diets. In Swaziland and Zambia, when food runs out, the poor eat roots and leaves foraged from the bush. In slum areas of Phnom Penh, Cambodia, poor people report that they have cut meals down to one or two a day. In rural Ukraine, some respondents noted that they were not really poor because they were not starving. In Togo, in West Africa, the poor associated poverty with the inability to work due to malnutrition (Narayan 2000, 36).

Improvements in life expectancy worldwide during the latter half of the twentieth century resulted from reduction of such conditions among many of the world's poor. The largest gains in life expectancy came from reducing infant and child mortality through improved nutrition and living conditions, which resulted in less vulnerability to and easier recovery from infectious and diarrheal diseases (Wilkinson 1996, 29).

Overall, rising living standards have produced the dramatic improvements in longevity over the past century.

[B]ecause the historical pattern is not so much a matter of getting over a temporary upsurge in infectious mortality before returning to pre-existing death rates, but is instead a reduction of infectious mortality of all kinds to levels unknown in any earlier historical periods, the primary [explanatory] place must be given to the rising standard of living. (Wilkinson 1996, 33)

Infant mortality is a good indicator of a country's care of basic human needs, because it reveals whether there is adequate nutrition, safe drinking water, and protective care by adults. It also reveals how well the most vulnerable members of the population are treated. Table 4.1 shows the countries (and Hong Kong) with the lowest infant mortality rates measured in 1998, as reported in the *World Development Report* (World Bank 2001).

[1] Approximately 90 percent of the world's 1,300 million "absolutely" poor people live in Asia and Africa (World Bank 1993). Gender, ethnicity, and race have some effects on health independent of social class and are addressed in the next chapter.

TABLE 4.1 *Lowest Infant Mortality Rates, 1998*

Country	Infant Mortality Rate (deaths per 1,000 live births)
Hong Kong, China	3
Finland, Japan, Norway, Singapore, Sweden, Switzerland	4
Australia, Austria, Canada, Czech Republic, Denmark, France, Germany, Italy, Netherlands, New Zealand, Slovenia, Spain	5

Source: World Bank, *World Development Report 2000/2001* (Washington, DC: World Bank, 2001), Table 7.

At the other end of the spectrum are the countries listed in Table 4.2. These have the highest infant mortality rates, as of 1998 measurements.

Except for Cambodia, all the countries listed in Table 4.2 are located in Africa, where absolute poverty widely compromises health. Warfare and social disintegration play a significant additional role in high risk of death for infants in Sierra Leone and Rwanda. Several countries listed in Table 4.2 (and additional ones) are deeply affected by the HIV/AIDS epidemic.

The United States does not make the list of lowest infant mortality despite a high standard of living and the highest per capita health expenditures of any country in the world. The United States has 7 infant deaths per 1,000 live births, ranking

TABLE 4.2 *Highest Infant Mortality Rates, 1998*

Country	Infant Mortality Rate (deaths per 1,000 live births)
Sierra Leone[1]	169
Malawi, Mozambique[1]	134
Rwanda[1,2]	123
Niger	118
Mali	117
Zambia	114
Ethiopia[1]	107
Burkina Faso	104
Cambodia[1]	102
Uganda[2]	101

[1] Affected by war in the 1990s.

[2] Affected by HIV/AIDS epidemic.

Source: World Bank, *World Development Report 2000/2001* (Washington, DC: World Bank, 2001), Table 7.

below, for example, Greece (at 6 per 1,000) and Spain, Italy, and Canada (at 5 per 1,000).

Principle 2

> Overall, people in affluent countries have greater life expectancy than those in poor countries.

Figures 4.1 and 4.2 illustrate the relationship between countries' per capita income and life expectancy. Populations in higher-income countries benefit with longer lives. At the left side of the scatterplot in Figure 4.1, countries with the lowest yearly incomes (of $1,000 or less per year in standardized international dollars) show dramatically shorter life expectancies than countries with just $2,000 to $4,000 more per year. Above $5,000, increases in life expectancy continue but are more gradual. Absolute poverty is the root cause of more disease and shorter lives in countries at or below per capita incomes of approximately $5,000 to $6,000. Poverty results in poor nutrition, transportation, sanitation, housing, and caloric intake for a large proportion of the population. These conditions hamper immune functioning and increase susceptibility to infectious diseases.

However, the overall association between average per capita income and life expectancy is not linear. Improvements are dramatic in poor countries up to a per capita income of between $5,000 and $6,000. Among richer countries, the relation-

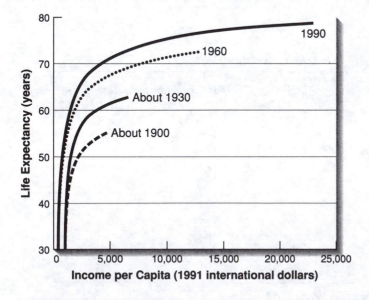

FIGURE 4.1 *Life Expectancy and Income per Capita for Selected Countries and Periods*

Sources: Reprinted from R. G. Wilkinson, *Unhealthy Societies: The Afflictions of Inequality* (London: Rouledge, 1996), 34; World Bank, *World Development Report 1993: Investing in Health* (New York: Oxford University Press, 1993).

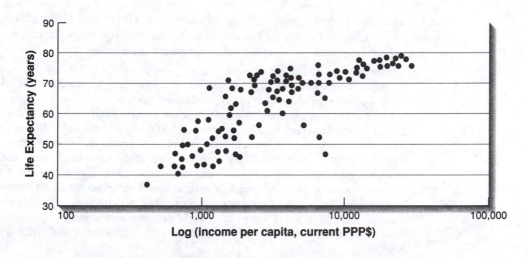

FIGURE 4.2   *Life Expectancy and Income in Purchasing Power Parity (PPP) Dollars 1997*

Source: World Bank, World Development Indicators, 1999. Reprinted with permission from Bloom and Canning (2000, February 18). The health and wealth of nations. *Science* 278, 1207. Copyright 2000 American Association for the Advancement of Science.

ship levels off, and further GNP increases bring small improvements in life expectancy (Wilkinson 1996, 43). Preston (1975) concluded that no more than 12 percent of the improvement in life expectancy was associated with the rising standard of living among affluent countries (Wilkinson 1996). The same number of additional years of life expectancy that costs $10,000 in richer countries costs $1,000 per capita in poorer countries, a pattern of sharply diminishing health returns with increases in income (Wilkinson 1996, 35). Using World Bank data, Wilkinson shows this dynamic graphically in Figure 4.1; the sharply rising lines signify dramatically increasing life expectancy among countries with per capita incomes up to approximately $5,000. Life expectancy inches slowly upward with increases in income in the wealthiest countries, whereas dramatic upward trends are achieved with slight increases in subsistence-level countries.

The political economy of food distribution, debt, and food exports also helps explain why populations in food-producing countries are sometimes malnourished. Thus, although Lester Brown (1997) of the World Watch Institute warns that food shortages are a looming global problem, other experts emphasize that distribution of food is the major problem. Lappé and colleagues (1998) argue that most countries produce enough food to feed their own population. However, in many cases food gets exported in exchange for foreign currencies that are used to purchase needed commodities (such as medicine, machinery, spare parts, computers, and the products of other modern technologies). Countries rely on their commodity exports (coffee, cocoa, or precious minerals) to purchase what they do not produce within their borders.

This analysis of food distribution fits the world systems model in which periphery countries' economies develop in distorted ways. Their trade relations with core and semi-periphery countries make them dependent on the export sectors of their economies, where production is externally oriented. Millen and Holtz (2000), of the Institute for Health and Social Justice, describe the consequences for export markets of the trend away from subsistence farming toward production.

> In India, Bangladesh, Thailand, Malaysia, Ecuador, and Mexico, for example, commercial projects produce tiger prawns and other "exotics" such as eels for export to rich countries. These commercial aquaculture schemes have been ecologically disastrous to coastal zones, damaging fragile mangrove and wetland systems and polluting sea water. They also tend to deplete groundwater and poison farmlands of surrounding villages, ruining previously rich agricultural land for generations to come. Because farmers are rarely compensated sufficiently for their losses and have no other sources of support, one net result of agro-industrial growth in developing countries has been greatly increased landlessness and rural impoverishment. The disruption of traditional subsistence agriculture in many parts of the world has been accompanied by massive migrations of displaced farmers into urban squatter settlements and slums. (Millen & Holtz 2000, 196)

The epidemiological transition occurs when living standards reach a threshold adequate to ensure basic material standards for most of the population (Omran 1971; Wilkinson 1996). During the 1990s, the average per capita annual income needed to make the epidemiological transition was estimated at $6,400 in U.S. dollars (Wilkinson 1996). This means that, at this level of per capita income, a society could afford to industrialize, improve its infrastructure (including water and sewer systems, and roads), and raise living standards and health across the society.

In the United States, the epidemiological transition occurred toward the end of the nineteenth century and in to the twentieth, as living conditions improved and deaths from infectious diseases, including tuberculosis, influenza, and typhus, decreased (Weitz 2000, 22). Improvements in health occurred *before* the medical treatments for these illnesses were applied (McKinlay & McKinlay 1977). A shift in the social distribution of chronic and infectious disease accompanies the epidemiological transition.

> During the epidemiological transition the so-called "diseases of affluence" became the diseases of the poor in affluent societies. The most well-known example is coronary heart disease which, in the first half of the twentieth century, was regarded as a businessman's disease but changed its social distribution to become more common in lower social classes. Several other causes of death, including stroke, hypertension, duodenal ulcers, nephritis and nephrosis, and suicide also reversed their social distribution to become more common among the least well off. . . . [O]besity also changed its social distribution to become more common among the least well-off. (Wilkinson 1996, 44)

This reversal of disease patterns, however, is not absolute. Despite modernization in much of the developing world, infectious diseases continue to plague the poor in these countries. However, analyses vary, and Murray and Lopez (1996) found chronic diseases to be the most frequent cause of death in more-developed as well as less-developed countries. Contributing to chronic disease is a high-fat, low-fiber diet, which is being adopted in urban, industrializing China and other urban areas in the developing world. Health problems among the elite in poor countries also often resemble Western patterns, with higher cardiovascular disease and cancer rates.

Principle 3

> Improvements in material living conditions among populations below the epidemiological threshold result in significant improvements in health and longevity. Smaller improvements occur in developed countries, where living conditions improve as a function of affluence or reduction of social inequality (Wilkinson 1996).

A country's economic growth typically improves the overall quality of living conditions, with improvements in water supply, nutrition, and housing. Health improvements will be greatest among infants and children, and adults will also have a better chance of surviving to old age (Wilkinson 1996). However, in the absence of redistributive policies, the inequalities that typically accompany economic development often have damaging effects on civic life and health. If development depletes a country's resources and brings about improved living conditions mostly for the elite, population health improvements are slower. In addition, harsh working conditions, environmental degradation, and increases in smoking, drinking, and automobile accidents are all aspects of development that negatively effect health (Millen & Holtz 2000, 178).

Poor countries are often politely referred to as "developing" in reports by international agencies such as the World Health Organization or the World Bank. However, lumping the categories of "developing," "less developed," and "underdeveloped" together conceals considerable social, economic, and health differences. The categories of developing and underdeveloped (or less developed) correspond roughly to periphery versus semi-periphery countries in Wallerstein's world systems model. In periphery countries, a substantial proportion of the population lives in absolute poverty, whereas in semi-periphery countries an elite and a middle class enjoy a fairly comfortable standard of living alongside sizeable working and poor classes.

The semi-periphery economies of China and Brazil are developing and have both substantial middle classes and high inequality. In China, this is especially evident in contrasting urban and rural populations. In Brazil, inequality within urban areas is glaring, with many homeless children among the poor. In developing countries, increasing cultural and income differences separate those who have experienced the rewards of economic development from other groups left behind. By contrast, in periphery countries such as those listed in Table 4.1, with high infant mortality rates (Sierra Leone, Malawi, and Mozambique), more illness and shorter lives reflect their relative disconnection from the global economy.

A limitation of technological innovations in the developed world is that they are typically aimed at growing food and fighting disease in temperate zones, although most poor and indebted countries are located in tropical zones (Sachs 1999). Only during crises of war and famine, which bring vivid images of suffering and death to

These children sleeping on the sidewalk in Bombay, India, suffer the effects of absolute poverty, which entails inadequate food, shelter, clothing, and care.

television viewers, do citizens of affluent countries turn their attention and open their wallets to poor countries (Waters 2001).

Developed countries enjoy an affluent standard of living, which guarantees an overall high level of population health. Modern nutritional and prenatal care of mothers and infants reduces maternal and infant mortality. Higher levels of education and access to preventive and curative health care enhance the understanding of a wide range of preventive activities that help to reduce disease and accidents. Social welfare programs, including medical care, also improve population health.

Affluence also helps prevent harsh working conditions. Workers with choices and unemployment insurance are less pressured into taking jobs with awful working conditions. Safer working conditions better protect workers from accidents, disease, and premature death. Greater affluence also makes a public education system possible, and a healthy, literate, educated public can aid the development of democratic

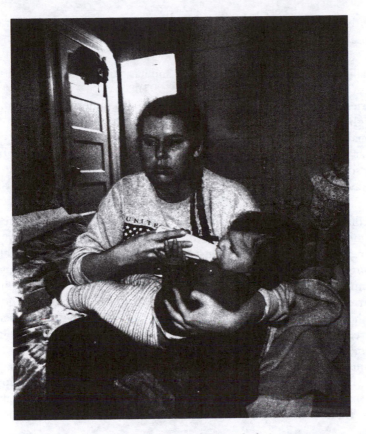

This mother and her children suffer the effects of relative poverty, temporarily housed in a run-down hotel and marginalized from the mainstream of social life.

institutions. Where jobs with a living wage are available, trained and educated workers contribute to their own mobility and to their country's economic development.

Principle 4

Across societies, there is an association between the degree of social inequality and the rate of disease and death: Higher inequality results in higher disease and premature death (Rodgers 1979; Wilkinson 1996, 2000).

When countries are compared, increased rates of disease and death are found where there are higher levels of social inequality (Kawachi et al. 1997; Pappas et al. 1993; Wilkinson 1996; Williams & Collins 1995; Kawachi et al. 1997). Inequality is implicated in the deterioration of social life and the physical environment.

Three explanations are offered for the role of inequality in health outcomes (Kawachi et al. 1997).

- Inequality increases levels of frustration and has damaging behavioral and health effects (Kawachi et al. 1994; Wilkinson 1997).
- Societies that permit more severe inequalities also underinvest in human capital through education, health care, and other institutions that promote social and personal well-being (Kaplan et al. 1996; Kawachi et al. 1994).
- Higher inequality leads to loss of trust and social cohesion (conceptualized as lower social capital), which damages population health in many direct and indirect ways (Kaplan et al. 1996; Kennedy et al. 1996).

According to Wilkinson (1997), the clear association between income and morbidity and mortality within countries contrasts sharply with the much weaker relationships found *between* them. In other words, it is not the amount of wealth per se, but the *quality of social life* (influenced by inequality) that predicts variations in health outcomes among developed countries. Wilkinson's analysis of twenty-three developed countries found that economic growth during recent decades did not produce substantial health improvements (Wilkinson 1997). His analysis suggests that less than 10 percent of the increases in life expectancy during the period from 1970 to 1993 were related to economic performance.

In summary, within and among developed countries, (1) higher living standards improve the quality of life, and therefore health and life expectancy inch upward over time; and (2) the best health is found where there is the greatest social equality among populations, whether in counties, regions, states, or countries.

Principle 5

Social inequality affects health in direct and indirect ways. High inequality entails a larger proportion of the population living in relative poverty and governmental policies that neglect human investments (such as in education, health, and an array of services). Inequality also affects health indirectly through psychosocial factors related to our place in the social hierarchy. Social capital (trust and civic participation) declines with greater inequality.

The healthiest developed countries, such as Japan and Greece, have a relatively equal distribution of resources. This enhances social interaction and the viability of social institutions. Such social "wealth" results in better mental and physical health for the whole society. This pattern is more common in relatively homogeneous populations, which are minimally affected by immigration.

Increases in inequality in Britain and the United States during the last two decades of the twentieth century are reason for concern (Danziger & Gottschalk 1993; Karoly 1993). During the 1980s, life expectancy for some groups in Britain decreased for the first time in fifty years. For example, in the poorest areas, mortality rates rose among men under forty-five and among women aged sixty-five to seventy-five, reversing previous improvements. A widening pattern of social class differences in mortality is also evident in France, Finland, Norway, and the Netherlands (Department of Health and Social Security 1980; Knust & Mackenbach 1994; quoted in Williams & Collins 1995).

Within the United States, race and ethnicity have a major impact on social class and health. African Americans have an infant mortality rate of over 15 per 1,000 births, almost double the national average. Explanations include the following:

1. Pockets of poverty exist where basic human needs are poorly met.
2. High social inequality worsens health, with African Americans disproportionately at the lower end of the income and status hierarchy.
3. Close proximity between residentially segregated rich and poor populations enhances the harmful effects of inequality (Massey 1996). Residential segregation generally is associated with higher mortality for both adults and infants (LaVeist 1989; Polednak 1991, 1993).

Principle 6

Higher social class or socioeconomic status gives individuals greater health and longevity chances. Some of the causes are direct, such as through nutrition, but many are indirect, through psychosocial influences. Relatively poor people experience more illness and live shorter lives than affluent people.

In the United States and all other countries that researchers have studied over four decades, there is a relationship between social class position and physical health, morbidity, disability, and mortality (Krieger et al. 1993; Rogers et al. 2000; Williams & Collins 1995). The lower the socioeconomic status, the poorer are the chances in terms of health and longevity. The higher the socioeconomic status, the greater are the chances to live a long life untroubled by disability and disease. Mental health is also associated with social class. Self-reported distress, depression, hostility, and locus of control (internal personal control versus external causes of events) all have been found to be inversely associated with socioeconomic status. In the United States, mortality differences between the upper and lower ends of the socioeconomic scale have been widening since 1960.

Occupational status as a predictor of health was confirmed by the remarkable Whitehall study of 17,530 male British social servants working in London. The study found that a man's grade of employment was a stronger predictor of his subsequent risk of death from coronary heart disease (CHD) than any of the other major coronary risk factors, including smoking and family history. Messengers, the lowest grade of worker, had over three and a half times the CHD mortality of administrators, the highest employment grade. Junior staff members were absent six times as much as senior staff working in the same offices. Remarkably, health status correlated with job status at all occupational levels. The study controlled for other factors that might have caused the greater disease rate among lower-level employees (Marmot et al. 1978).

> Men in the lower employment grades were shorter, heavier for their height, had higher blood pressure, higher plasma glucose, smoked more, and reported less leisure-time physical activity than men in the higher grades. Yet when allowance was made for the influence on mortality of all of these factors plus plasma cholesterol, the inverse association between grade of employment and CHD mortality was still strong. (Marmot et al. 1978, 244)

A U.S. study based on occupation found similar results. Gregorio and colleagues (1997) used the National Longitudinal Mortality Study for information on principal occupation and nine-year follow-up data for 229,851 people aged twenty-five through sixty-four years. A "Slope Index of Inequality" was used to quantify differences in death rates across occupational categories. The authors used four different measures of occupational hierarchy, and despite some variations, each measure revealed a consistent pattern of increased risk of death for persons at lower positions in the occupational hierarchy (Gregorio et al. 1997, 1473).

Income also has a strong relationship with life expectancy, especially for individuals under sixty-five years of age. McDonough and colleagues (1997) studied data from the U.S. Panel Study of Income Dynamics for 1968 through 1989. Whether income was measured one year at a time or grouped for multiple years, higher and lower incomes were associated with death rates. From 1972 through 1989, people forty-five and older, with household incomes averaging less than $20,000 over a five-year period, were two to three times as likely to die in the next five years as those with average incomes over $70,000. Families with incomes in the middle range, from $20,000 to $70,000, had a 50 percent higher chance of dying than the high-income group (McDonough et al. 1997). Having a low income had especially harsh effects. A household income of less than $20,000 for four to five years raised the risk of death above those only temporarily at this low income. All low-income individuals had higher mortality rates than those financially better off.

For middle-class individuals, income instability increased mortality risk. An income loss of 50 percent or more from one year to the next had the biggest impact on those earning $20,000 through $70,000. No apparent effect on mortality from such a loss was found for those persistently or temporarily in high-income groups (McDonough et al. 1997, 1479). The harmful effects of income fluctuations on health are especially noteworthy for middle-income groups increasingly faced with layoffs in a volatile labor market.

For men, being employed is associated with better health. For women, the association is positive, although less strong. A longitudinal study of 6,191 British men found an increased risk of mortality among middle-aged men who lost their jobs after stable employment (Morris & Cook 1994). Those who became unemployed or took early retirement were twice as likely to die during the following five and a half years as those who continued to work. Even healthy and wealthier men who retired early had a significantly higher risk of dying than those who remained employed.

The Russian Case Example

Russia in the 1990s illustrates some of the dynamics of population health, as well as unique aspects of the Russian experience. A failing economy, chaotic social conditions, and pessimistic feelings about the future had harmful effects on Russians' health. Poverty and inequality increased, and state services (including the public health system) collapsed.

Russia is in the midst of a major health crisis. At the turn of the twenty-first century, deaths exceeded births by about 700,000 persons. Vodka production is one of Russia's few booming businesses. Drinking is expected behavior among adults, and among men the pressure to drink heavily is strong. The health consequences are serious. Headlines in the winter newspapers include body counts of the intoxicated found dead of exposure. In 1996 alone, 35,000 people died from accidental alcohol poisoning (Francis 2000), and in 1997 the Interior Ministry announced that around 43,000 people had died in Russia that year from drinking vodka (Garrett 2000, 131). Indeed, Russians have the highest per capita consumption of alcohol in the world. Smoking is also part of Russians' unhealthy lifestyles. Two-thirds of men and one-third of women smoke, which accounts for 20 to 30 percent of deaths from heart disease and cancer. Russian heart disease and cancer death rates are double those in the United States. Are there underlying causes of this health crisis? Is it the collapse of the Soviet Union, in which Russia fell from superpower to political and economic weakling? The effects of the collapse during the 1990s were devastating and have accelerated the decline in health. Russian authors offer an explanation.

> The recent upsurge in criminality, in synergy with alcoholism, is above all the aftermath of the sweeping economic reforms and accompanying lower standards of living and of the dismantling of the former political and administrative system. (Shkolnikov et al. 1996, quoted in Garrett 2000, 131)

However, the decline in Russian men's life expectancy began much earlier, in 1965, long before the dissolution of the Soviet Union (Cockerham 1999). The economy had begun to stagnate and, along with the increasingly unhealthy lifestyles of men since World War II, resulted in increased cardiovascular disease and cancer. But health worsened with the fall of the Soviet Union. By the mid-1990s, public drunkenness was rampant. As journalist Laurie Garrett chronicles, "In devastated old industrial cities, from Bohemia to Vladivostock, unemployed men [were] no longer able to imagine their futures" (2000, 136). She notes that, by 1999, Russian men were consuming an average of three liters of vodka every week, resulting in an alcohol poisoning rate about 2,000 times greater than in the United States.

During the 1950s and 1960s, the Soviet Union made major technological and economic advances, and the Cold War was in full swing. Life expectancy in Eastern European communist countries during mid-century up to the mid-1960s equaled or exceeded those in the West (Cockerham 1999, 9). But there were disturbing trends developing. The Brezhnev regime (1964–1982) hid worsening Soviet health with deceptive statistics. By the early 1970s, both infant and adult mortality were increasing. Infant mortality then improved beginning in 1975, but the increase in overall adult male death rates continued. Two American demographers, Christopher Davis and Murray Feshbach, analyzed several data sources and made a shocking discovery in 1980: The Soviet Union was the first industrialized country to experience an increase in infant mortality and an overall decline in life expectancy (Cockerham 1999, 9).

Death rates for Russians rose between 1975 and 1994, with the sharpest increases among men with the least education: Middle-aged men with manual jobs had the highest death rates. Women's death rates did not increase, but their increased longevity was much lower than in other European countries during that time. However, middle-aged women's health *was* negatively affected.

The most developed regions of Russia had the greatest declines in life expectancy, revealing social and economic dynamics different from those in periphery countries. In part, increased disease resulted from the many industrial and mining areas that were severely polluted. Therefore, both unsafe, polluted working environments and unhealthy lifestyles were contributing factors in worsening health.

> Data from Russia . . . show that circulatory disease caused 48.3% of the increase in deaths in 1991–92, followed by accidents (13.5%), respiratory diseases (8.9%), murder/suicide (7.5%), alcohol (6.1%), digestive/infectious diseases (4.6%), and cancer (1.7%). (Cockerham 1999, 23, citing Haub 1994)

The Soviet health care system was a massive infrastructure, with more nurses, doctors, and hospital beds per capita than anywhere else in the world (Garrett 2000, 123). And yet it was ill suited to respond effectively to this emerging health crisis because the system was oriented toward treating infectious disease, and it failed to gear up for the more individualized and technologically sophisticated treatment of cancers and cardiovascular disease (Cockerham 1999). It also failed against alcoholism, drug addiction, and tuberculosis. The lack of preventive public health campaigns and poor response to unhealthy behaviors and increased illness left rising death rates unabated through the end of the twentieth century and into the twenty-first. The health care system did not *cause* the health crisis, but it was not able to mitigate the problem, let alone generate solutions.

The fall of the Soviet Union and the political and economic chaos that ensued only intensified the trend, which included the revival of infectious disease. With the "radical privatization" of the economy, the elite rushed to buy up Russian assets, and the ensuing scramble left average citizens much worse off. Thus the economic and cultural malaise that eroded Russian health before the end of the Soviet Union worsened with post-Soviet financial deterioration and policy failure. The failure of leadership and shortage of funds resulted in shredded safety nets and a deteriorated public health infrastructure. Not only did policy makers neglect to provide leadership, the corruption of political officials also eroded their legitimacy and devastated citizens' hopes for the future.

Many more Russians fell into poverty and illness. In less than a year after the fall of the Soviet government in 1991, a series of epidemics broke out across Russia's enormous geographic expanse (Garrett 2000, 123).

Diphtheria infected 200,000 people regionally over this time period, killing 5,000; polio rolled into Azerbaijan in 1991, Uzbekistan in 1993, and Chechnya in 1995; and hepatitis was suddenly so commonplace as to be considered endemic, rather than epidemic. Flu hit so hard in 1995 that the Ukrainian government closed for more than a week; typhoid infected more than 20,000 in Tajikistan in 1996 and then stayed endemic; St. Petersburg coped with dual epidemics of cholera and dysentery four times from 1993 to 1998. AIDS grew exponentially, with 20,000 full-blown cases projected in Ukraine alone by the year 2001; TB, syphilis, and gonorrhea followed suit. And alcoholism, drug abuse, and suicide were by 1995 considered epidemic, according to international health standards. (Garrett 2000, 123)

For children, the collapse of the Soviet economy, public health system, and social services has meant greater malnutrition; more drunk, neglectful, and abusive parents; polluted environments; lack of medicine; and increased vulnerability to epidemics and drug-resistant pathogens.

Interpreting the Russian Case

Features of the Russian health crisis include

1. A stagnating and declining economy with increased poverty and inequality from the post–World War II period to end of the century.
2. Unhealthy lifestyles, especially among men, with heavy drinking, smoking, poor eating habits, and little exercise.
3. Implosion of the Russian economy in 1989, including declining oil revenues, a stock market crash, bank failures, skyrocketing inflation, government bankrupcy, and failure to collect taxes.
4. "Radical restructuring" under IMF direction, in which loans stipulated cutbacks in social spending and state-owned companies were sold to the elite.
5. Destabilization of the state, political system, and economy, weakening the rule of law.
6. Loss of funds to maintain social services and the public health infrastructure.
7. Social malaise and downward mobility, felt both personally and nationally.

Although the Russian case is somewhat unique, the principles described in this chapter, which relate social conditions to health, help us to understand some of its causes and dynamics. Especially following radical restructuring, an increased number of Russians did not have the resources to meet their needs, and mental and physical health deteriorated as a result (as suggested by Principle 1).

Principle 2 indicates that affluent countries have greater life expectancy than poor ones. The standard of living stagnated or deteriorated for Russians during the second half of the twentieth century, most drastically during the 1990s. The stagnation hurt working-age men's health the most, helped along by their excessive drinking and smoking. The small gains in longevity that come with a gradually rising standard of living in affluent developed countries (Principle 3) have not occurred in Russia. And an increasingly unequal distribution of wealth, jobs, and other resources contributes to Russia's declining social capital in the form of distrust, crime, and corruption (Principles 4 and 5). In Russia, the majority of the population experienced economic downward mobility and a worsened standard of living. State policies did not cushion citizens from the worst effects of economic restructuring and inequality. Instead, state officials played key roles in dismantling the state's resources and buying up its valuable industries and properties for their personal gain.

Exploring the case of deteriorating Russian health, Kennedy and colleagues (1999a) attempted to measure the decline of civil society. Variables included relative trust or mistrust of government, level of crime, quality of work relations, and degree of civic engagement in politics. The study examined whether these measures were associated with life expectancy and mortality rates in post-Soviet Russia. The following are the authors' main findings:

- Regions with high levels of distrust in local government had higher male age-adjusted mortality. The relationship was strongest for circulatory diseases for both men and women. Distrust of national government did not show this effect.
- Lack of civic engagement (disinterest in politics, lack of voting) was strongly associated with male mortality, life expectancy, and deaths from circulatory diseases.
- Conflict at work and crime rates were both associated with overall male mortality. Crime was a particularly strong predictor of both male and female life expectancy and was associated with all major causes of death.
- Perceived economic hardship ("the economic situation in your city or region" is poor or very poor) was negatively associated with several social capital variables, such as trust and civic participation, as well as with life expectancy (Kennedy et al. 1999a, 271).

One aspect of the Russian post-Soviet situation that does not fit the principles outlined in this chapter is that the higher-income areas had *higher* crime and divorce rates, and there was a positive association between higher per capita income and higher mortality. Therefore, analyses of inequality and health must take into account short-term effects of social disruption during transition periods, as compared to longer-term, more stable conditions.

Policies Matter!

Throughout this chapter, we have examined principles and patterns for understanding how health varies in somewhat systematic ways across societies and social groups. Here we pause to remember that these are not immutable facts of life. For example, even though the gradient of unequal health is found across societies, some societies are more steeply unequal (and less healthy) than others. Why? The answer includes several components: the country's location in the world economic system and its class structure, the heterogeneous or homogeneous makeup of the population, and the effects of governmental policies.

Social policy plays a major role in alleviating (or worsening) the effects of poverty and inequality on health. The final chapter of this book will address policy issues in greater detail, but here Table 4.3 provides examples of policies that improved or worsened health.

The political climate influences policy decisions regarding health and social services. For example, California's policies toward immigrants during the 1990s illustrate this point. Passage by popular vote in 1994 of California's Proposition 187 allowed the state to deprive illegal immigrants of a wide range of services. Perhaps as damaging to the social climate was the message from leadership that immigrants were the cause of California's problems. California's Port of Entry Detection program, begun in 1990 and later discontinued due to a lawsuit, detained 10,000 migrants at the Mexican-

TABLE 4.3 *Selected Examples of Health Related Policies*

Policy/Policy Maker	Place	Health Consequences
Cuts in health and social service spending, implemented early in the Reagan administration (Williams & Collins 1995)	U.S. federal and state programs affected	• Reduced access to prenatal care, more anemia • Increased infant mortality in 20 states among the poor (Mandinger 1985) • In California, lower access to Medicaid; study found, 6 months following termination, 10-point increase in mean diastolic blood pressure (mm Hg) (Lurie et al. 1984)
Federally subsidized Child Health Insurance Program (CHIP), healthy families program	California; less than half of eligible poor signed up. Pete Wilson's administration instituted a 30-page application for families to apply	Lost opportunity to improve child health and reduce health inequalities; uninsured children and adults increased
State spending puts highest priority on human services, education, and civic needs, despite a meager budget.	State of Kerala, India	Health statistics and literacy rates far above those of societies with more wealth, but without the civic-minded policies of Kerala
State spending puts high priority on primary and preventive health care and education.	Chilean administrations during the 1990s	Increases in infant and child survival rates, overall longevity, and literacy; slightly decreased income inequality

American border. They were told they would have to repay the costs of any benefits they had received illegally in California. Catching the California anti-immigrant spirit, in 1996 the U.S. Congress stripped *legal* immigrants of benefits they had long enjoyed.

Also symptomatic of callousness toward low-income people, Governor Pete Wilson's administration developed a thirty-page application that discouraged many families (immigrant and local) from applying for the new "Healthy Families" health insurance program (Freedberg 2000). Only after several more years and a different state administration did the program more successfully enroll low-income children for health care.

Policies that allow growing disparities in income and wealth are detrimental to health. Wages have stagnated for the majority of the U.S. population since around 1973 (with some increases during the 1990s), causing increasing income inequality. Sociologist Douglas Massey (1996) contrasts recent decades with the affluent postwar period of more widespread upward mobility.

> For a short time after World War II, mass social mobility temporarily halted the relentless geographic concentration of affluence and poverty in developed countries. The postwar economic boom that swept Europe, Japan, and the United States created a numerically dominant middle class that mixed residentially with both the upper and the lower classes. After 1970, however, the promise of mass social mobility evaporated and inequality returned with a vengeance, ushering in a new era in which the privileges of the rich and the disadvantages of the poor were compounded increasingly through geographic means. (Massey 1996, 395)

During the 1980s and 1990s in Britain and the United States, the gap between rich and poor widened. President Reagan declared that government was the problem and vowed to pare down programs and spending. He proceeded to defund social and regulatory programs and to finance with debt the largest peacetime military buildup in history. An aggressive policy of criminalization was applied to the drug trade, which had attracted many unemployed persons to the informal economy in the mid-1980s. The "war on drugs" has been a war on (especially minority) unemployed men, dramatically swelling the prison population. Increased numbers of women also find themselves incarcerated on charges related to the drug trade. The United States now has the highest rate of incarceration in the world. In early 1999, one in every 163 Americans was in jail or prison, a rate six times the average for European countries. Prisons and jails are crowded with Latinos and African Americans, enhancing patterns of inequality that were already damaging to American society. Scott Christianson (1998) describes a growing "prison-industrial complex," bringing an economic boost to smaller towns and cities willing to be sites for new prisons. He describes this recent trend as consistent with a long history of American popular support for incarceration. This policy succeeded in locking up many individuals (some for life) who might have committed crimes through their late twenties, even though most men stop breaking the law after that age. Without a meaningful effort to reduce the widespread availability of guns, the policy may have contributed to a more dangerous and unhealthy society in the long run. Criminalization and incarceration for nonviolent crimes fail to remedy problems of unemployment and alienation. These conditions are bad for law breakers' health, but statistics reveal they are bad for the society as a whole as well.

Policies generally don't restructure economies (as they did in Russia) or revolutionize social relations (as they did in Castro's Cuba). However, policies hold the potential to establish baseline protections for population health. Policy makers can lead societies toward a more equitable distribution of resources and lessen the distance between social groups. This can be accomplished without stripping the wealthy of their comforts. Research by the "social capital" school demonstrates that the benefits of greater equality are felt throughout society. Lower death rates are the clearest evidence of this, but there are countless subtler benefits of living in a more egalitarian society. Not the least of these are less hostility and greater personal safety. In the two next chapters, we look at health variations globally, among men and women, and among ethnic groups.

5

Thinking Globally About Health

> The miracles of science could and should be shared equally in the world. There is a growing chasm between those of us who are rich, powerful, and healthy and those who are poor, weak, and suffering from preventable diseases. If we are to improve health, we must concentrate on existing disparities in opportunities, resources, education, and access to health programs. Only to the extent that we can eliminate these inequities will our dreams for global health in the twenty-first century be realized.
>
> —Jimmy Carter, "Foreword," in *Critical Issues in Global Health*

We consider the following:

- What are global health trends today?
- How do they vary by region?

Global Trends

During the second half of the twentieth century, the less-developed world experienced dramatic improvements in standard of living and life expectancy. Average life expectancy in relatively low-income countries, such as the Democratic Republic of the Congo, Egypt, and India, rose from forty to sixty-six years. Infectious diseases were tamed, although not eradicated, by vaccinations and medications. Average infant mortality rates fell from 28 percent to 10 percent of live births, and nearly half of adults are now literate (Desjarlais et al. 1995). Access to clean drinking water and provision of sewage systems are by no means universal early in the twenty-first century but are far more available than at mid-century. These improvements, combined with greater availability of primary health care and vaccinations, have lifted many populations from being chronically vulnerable to life-threatening disease through an epidemiological transition, which allows a majority to live through middle age. Ironically, this shift in population health involves more chronic disease among adults.

Governments' and international agencies' commitment to public health improvements greatly contributed to global health. The year 2000 *World Health Report* summarizes,

> A second generation of reforms . . . saw the promotion of primary health care as a route to achieving affordable universal coverage. This approach reflected experience with disease control projects in the 1940s in countries such as South Africa, the Islamic Republic of Iran, and former Yugoslavia. It also built on the successes and experiments of China, Cuba, Guatemala, Indonesia, Niger, the United Republic of Tanzania, and Maharashtra State in India. Some of these countries, and others such as Costa Rica and Sri Lanka, achieved very good health outcomes at relatively little cost, adding 15 to 20 years to life expectancy at birth in a span of just two decades. In each case, there was a very strong commitment to assuring a minimum level for all of health services, food and education, along with an adequate supply of safe water and basic sanitation. (World Health Organization 2000, 14)

Technologies and medications now exist that have the potential to improve health both within and outside the developed world. There is wider distribution at the turn of the century of life-saving vaccinations and treatments for infectious diseases. Influenza, smallpox, measles, whooping cough, rubella, diphtheria, tetanus, and tuberculosis have been curbed or eradicated. Oral rehydration therapy, developed in Bangladesh, has saved millions of babies from dying of diarrhea. This therapy is a simple mixture of sugar and salt dissolved in water, administered to babies and small children to prevent the dehydration that results from diarrhea. Because millions of children in poor areas have only impure drinking water, access to this treatment is crucial for continued improvements in infant and child health. In Ethiopia and Burkina Faso, for example, only 20 percent of those who need oral rehydration therapy receive it, as compared to two-thirds worldwide ("Brains v. bugs" 2001, 7).

There are also technologies and medicines that can help control fertility, manage mental disorders, and lessen the burden of disabilities (Desjarlais et al. 1995). However, yet wider and more equitable access to these resources is needed. Despite reductions in infant and child mortality, 30,000 children under five die each day from preventable causes ("Brains v. bugs" 2001, 6). Access to preventive and life-saving treatments for children has greatly improved but is not close to the goal of universal access to primary care set by the World Health Organization.

There is an ironic downside to the breakthroughs in health and longevity made during the twentieth century. As more people survive infancy and childhood, adult populations grow, and chronic disease and mental illness increase. For example, there is a global increase in the number of people experiencing clinical depression, schizophrenia, dementia, and other forms of chronic mental illness, as well as cardiovascular disease and cancers. In addition, modern technologies and more impersonal social relations increase problems such as substance abuse, traffic accidents, and in some cases, violence.

To better understand population health, researchers and policy makers have sought to measure not only deaths but also injuries and disabilities from accidents and disease. In 1994 a new measure was introduced for a study of "The Global Burden of Disease," called "disability-adjusted life years," or DALYs (Murray 1994). This is a measure of years lost to disability due to injury or illness; those years spent in disability are subtracted from an individual's life expectancy. Table 5.1 provides examples of DALYs alongside the average life expectancy for a range of countries. By developing measures of life years lost to disabilities, epidemiologists, policy makers, and economists can more accurately assess and debate the costs of certain risks, be they from land mines, bad roads, diseases, or impure drinking water.

Beneficial aspects of policies can also be measured with DALYs; for example, inoculations against polio prevent its life-long crippling effects. Prostheses allow people who have lost limbs to be ambulatory and perhaps to care for their children or work in the labor force. Disabilities have a variety of causes. An estimated 34 percent of years lost to disability are due to individual behaviors and behavior-related illnesses. These include sexually transmitted diseases such as HIV/AIDS and gonorrhea, as well as drunk driving accidents (Desjarlais et al. 1995).

Poverty remains a barrier to health worldwide. Despite life-saving improve-

TABLE 5.1 *Life Expectancies and Disability-adjusted Life Expectancies (DALYs)* for Selected Countries, Estimates for 1997 and 1999*

Country	Life Expectancy at Birth (years)	Male DALY	Female DALY
Japan	74.5	71.9	77.2
Finland	70.5	67.2	73.7
Argentina	66.7	63.8	69.6
Saudi Arabia	64.5	65.1	64
Suriname	62.7	60.2	65.2
Iran	60.5	61.3	59.8
Egypt	58.5	56.7	59.6
India	53.2	52.8	53.5
Haiti	43.8	42.4	45.2
Madagascar	36.6	36.5	36.8
Sierra Leone	25.9	25.8	26

*Disability-adjusted life expectancy is calculated by subtracting the number of estimated years that individuals will spend disabled from total average life expectancy.

Source: World Health Organization, *The World Health Report 2000 and Statistical Annex* (Geneva, Switzerland: World Health Organization, 2000), Annex Table 5. These countries are selected from 191 countries in the report; each nineteenth entry in the table is included here, from highest life expectancy (Japan) to lowest life expectancy (Sierra Leone).

ments, the substandard living conditions, environmental degradation, and human exploitation that accompany absolute poverty remain serious health problems in underdeveloped countries. In developing countries, where living conditions continue to improve, pockets of extreme poverty persist as well, amid increasing social inequality. Even within affluent populations of the United States and Britain (the most unequal among wealthy developed nations), high levels of inequality and harsh working and living conditions persist for less-privileged groups. Chronicles of worker injuries in U.S. meat-packing, agricultural, and mining industries are but three examples. For example, an investigation of Nebraska's meat-packing industry by the lieutenant governor found that there were unsafe and unsanitary working conditions, abusive and discriminatory language and behavior used by supervisors toward workers, and inadequate communication of company policies to workers (Maurstad 2000). The meat-packing industry employs one-fifth of Nebraska's manufacturing sector workers, now mostly immigrant workers. Over the past twenty years, wages for meat-packing jobs have dropped from today's equivalent of $16.00 an hour to between $6.50 and $8.00 an hour, with benefits cut back ("Community organizing . . ." 1998).

Does economic development automatically improve the plight of the poor? We address this question in Chapter 9 but here point out that distribution of resources hinges on institutional arrangements. Vested interests often block food, housing, education, or loans from getting to the most needy—even when these resources were specifically intended for them. An analysis of food supply in less-developed countries from 1970 to 1990 by sociologists J. Craig Jenkins and Stephen Scanlan (2001) found that the increased amount of food that accompanies economic growth does not greatly reduce child hunger. Domestic investments in economic growth improve the food supply to underfed children somewhat more than do foreign investments. However, social and political institutions prevent dramatic reductions in child hunger overall. The authors' analysis revealed that the *political* conditions that protect the status quo best explained persistent child hunger in economically developing countries. Therefore, we should not assume that nutritional and health improvements automatically result from economic growth.

> The child hunger problem is not simply a question of growing more food, but of distributing it so that disadvantaged children, minorities, women, and rural households have secure access to this supply. Our evidence suggests that entrenched inequality, especially that associated with ethnic political discrimination and internal violence against minority and other groups, is key to the persistence and increase in child hunger rates. Hunger . . . must be addressed through political change—especially political democratization, restrictions on arms trade, and the reduction of generalized violence. (Jenkins & Scanlan 2001, 738)

Regional Trends in World Health

For the purposes of this chapter, we use the World Health Organization's regions of the world to discuss global health trends. These regions are displayed and their countries listed below.

World Health Organization Regions

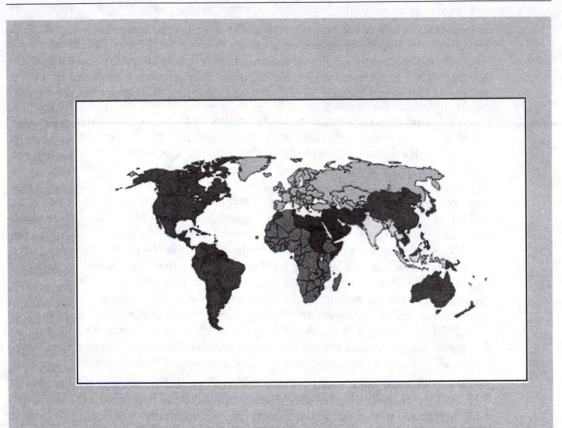

African Region
Algeria, Angola, Benin, Botswana, Burkina Faso, Burundi, Cameroon, Cape Verde, Central African Republic, Chad, Comoros, Côte d'Ivoire, Democratic Republic of the Congo, Equatorial Guinea, Eritrea, Ethiopia, Gabon, Gambia, Ghana, Guinea, Guinea-Bissau, Kenya, Lesotho, Liberia, Madagascar, Malawi, Mali, Mauritania, Mauritius, Mozambique, Namibia, Niger, Nigeria, Republic of Congo, Rwanda, Sao Tome and Principe, Senegal, Seychelles, Sierra Leone, South Africa, Swaziland, Togo, Uganda, United Republic of Tanzania, Zambia, Zimbabwe

Region of the Americas
Antigua and Barbuda, Argentina, Bahamas, Barbados, Belize, Bolivia, Brazil, Canada, Chile, Colombia, Costa Rica, Cuba, Dominica, Dominican Republic, Ecuador, El Salvador, Grenada, Guatemala, Guyana, Haiti, Honduras, Jamaica, Mexico, Nicaragua, Panama, Paraguay, Peru, Puerto Rico (associate Member State), Saint Kitts and Nevis, Saint Lucia, Saint Vincent and the Grenadines, Suriname, Trinidad and Tobago, United States of America, Uruguay, Venezuela

Eastern Mediterranean Region
Afghanistan, Bahrain, Cyprus, Djibouti, Egypt, Iraq, Islamic Republic of Iran, Jordan, Kuwait, Lebanon, Libyan Arab Jamahiriya, Morocco, Oman, Pakistan, Qatar, Saudi Arabia, Somalia, Sudan, Syrian Arab Republic, Tunisia, United Arab Emirates, Yemen

European Region
Albania, Andorra, Armenia, Austria, Azerbaijan, Belarus, Belgium, Bosnia and Herzegovina, Bulgaria, Croatia, Czech Republic, Denmark, Estonia, Finland, France, Georgia, Germany, Greece, Hungary, Iceland, Ireland, Israel, Italy, Kazakhstan, Kyrgyzstan, Latvia, Lithuania, Luxembourg, Malta, Monaco, Netherlands, Norway, Poland, Portugal, Republic of Moldova, Romania, Russian Federation, San Marino, Slovakia, Slovenia, Spain, Sweden, Switzerland, Tajikistan, Turkey, Turkmenistan, Ukraine, United Kingdom of Great Britain and Northern Ireland, Uzbekistan, Yugoslavia, the former Yugoslavia Republic of Macedonia

Western Pacific Region
Australia, Brunei Darussalam, Cambodia, China, Cook Islands, Federated States of Micronesia, Fiji, Hong Kong (special administrative region of China), Japan, Kiribati, Lao People's Democratic Republic, Macau (special administrative region of China), Malaysia, Marshall Islands, Mongolia, Nauru, New Zealand, Niue, Palau, Papua New Guinea, Philippines, Republic of Korea, Singapore, Solomon Islands, Tokelau (associate Member State), Taiwan (province of China), Tonga, Tuvalu, Vanuatu, Vietnam, Western Samoa

South East Asia Region
Bangladesh, Bhutan, Democratic People's Republic of Korea, India, Indonesia, Maldives, Myanmar, Nepal, Sri Lanka, Thailand

Africa

During the twentieth century, the mortality rates of African infants and children declined, and several infectious diseases, such as smallpox, cholera, and measles, were brought under control (Lucas 2001). Tuberculosis was nearly brought under control, except for an upturn toward the end of the century, associated with increased poverty in the 1980s (Wilkinson 1996, 31). Nonetheless, Africa still has the highest child death rates in the world, and HIV/AIDS is having devastating effects in several African countries. According to UNICEF (1998), for children under age five, the mortality rate in sub-Saharan Africa was 183 deaths per 1,000 live births, compared to the Middle East and North Africa, where it was 86 per 1,000 live births (Lucas 2001, 14). After a century of improvements, increases in African life expectancy stopped after 1990.

Adetokunbo O. Lucas is chair of the Global Forum for Health Research (2001), which studies problems affecting the poor. He identifies several factors that play a role in the relatively poor health status of Africans.

- *Poverty* causes malnutrition and suppresses immune functioning. Low revenues limit governments' abilities to prevent and respond effectively to health problems, including sufficient and new medicines, and additional technologies to fight disease.
- *Geographical and ecological factors* favor parasitic and other infectious agents and their vectors (that is, carriers of disease, such as mosquitoes).
- *Poor infrastructure* causes neglect of essential services, adequate housing, safe drinking water, and food.
- *High fertility* strains resources and is associated with high-risk pregnancies, low–birth weight babies, and unsafe abortions.
- *Low literacy rates*, especially among women, make it difficult to expand the knowledge "people need to promote, protect, and restore their health" (Lucas 2001, 13). Approximately 45 percent of Africans receive a primary education. Illiteracy also limits employment options and the potential for financial independence.
- *Civil wars and unrest* disrupt social life, economies, and infrastructure; they cause civilian deaths and disabilities, refugee flight, widespread homelessness, and trauma (including to thousands of children). Widespread violence is harmful to individual and social health in countless ways.
- *Inefficient and corrupt leaders, and unstable governments* siphon off precious resources to themselves and their supporters, and fail to invest in infrastructure and population needs.

Health challenges for Africa include continued management of infectious diseases; effective response to newer diseases, especially HIV/AIDS; and response to the steady increases in chronic ailments, especially cardiovascular disease and cancer (Lucas 2001, 13). These challenges need to be met in the context of poor infrastructure, food shortages, drought, and high population growth rates; therefore, outside help is essential.

Reform of public health systems in African countries is a priority for the World Health Organization. Programs begun by WHO and UNICEF (the United Nations child relief agency) need to be integrated into national health systems. These include programs focused on infant, child, and maternal welfare, including growth monitoring, oral hydration, breast feeding, immunization, family planning, female education, and supplementary nutrition for pregnant women. Another need is for training of more doctors, nurses, and health management staff to deliver services and coordinate African health systems (Lucas 2001). Chapter 8 examines in greater detail the health problems of African countries in terms of coping with underdevelopment.

Latin America and the Caribbean

Substantial progress was made in Latin America in the last quarter of the twentieth century toward improving access to safe drinking water, immunizations, and life expectancy. Child mortality declined, especially due to control of infectious diseases.

According to UNICEF, in 1998 child mortality in Latin America stood at 48 per 1,000 live births. This was better than in East Asian and Pacific countries (at 57 deaths per 1,000 live births) and also in the Middle East and North Africa (at 86 per 1,000). However, Latin America's rate is still far behind that of industrialized countries' 11 deaths per 1,000 live births (Lucas 2001, 14).

Infancy has also become more secure. The infant mortality rate for Latin America and the Caribbean for the period from 1995 to 2000, according to the Pan American Health Organization (PAHO), is 25 deaths per 1,000 live births. Between the periods of 1980 to 1985 and 1995 to 2000, infant mortality fell approximately 30 percent (Pan American Health Organization 2000a, 5).

Latin American and Caribbean health indicators are likely to continue to improve (Alleyne 2001). However, as people live longer, disease patterns will continue to shift away from infectious disease and toward chronic disease and behaviorally related causes of death.

Latin America has the highest social inequality in the world, which has a negative impact on population health. A poll taken in Latin American countries in the year 2000 found some of the social symptoms of income inequality. For example, Latin Americans reported distrusting one another. Only 16 percent reported that they trust "most people," and roughly two-thirds have little or no trust in their politicians, political parties, congress, police, or judiciary ("Angola: A Third Force" 2000, 34). Respondents in relatively more equal countries, such as Costa Rica and Uruguay, were more satisfied with their institutions. Among Latin American respondents generally, only 37 percent were content with the way democracy works in practice, whereas in Uruguay, 69 percent were satisfied with their public institutions, and in Costa Rica, 61 percent were satisfied. The most dissatisfied citizens were found in Paraguay and Brazil—two of the most unequal countries in the world—with only 12 and 18 percent, respectively, reporting satisfaction with their democracy.

Social inequality hampers improvements in health that otherwise result from improvements in the standard of living that development brings. For this reason, the Pan American Health Organization's year 2000 report identifies a goal to help reduce inequalities among Latin Americans through better public health systems (Pan American Health Organization 2000a, 3). The organization urges member countries to target health interventions at the greatest needs and inequalities. For example, increased access to local health clinics, especially in rural areas, would decrease infant and child deaths. Among Costa Rica's relatively more equal population, the poorest fifth of the population experiences almost one-quarter of the country's infant deaths, whereas the richest fifth accounts for 15 percent. In relatively less equal Guatemala, 35 percent of infant deaths occur in the poorest fifth of the population.

If inequalities within and between countries are to decrease, they need to be targeted by social and economic policies as well as by health programs. Chile's health- and equity-enhancing reforms of the 1990s are an example of how social and health inequalities can be targeted, with promising results in health, literacy, and improved income equality. (These reforms are described more fully in Chapter 9.) In Brazil, one of the most unequal countries in the world, the benefits of development have reduced child malnutrition[1]; however, urban homelessness and mistreatment of children are still rampant.

The greatest recent reductions in infectious disease in Latin America occurred where disease rates were highest: the Central American and Andean regions (Alleyne 2001). Nonetheless, communicable diseases remain a problem, including tuberculosis, malaria, dengue, and HIV/AIDS; these require prevention, screening, and treatment.[2] One million cases of malaria were reported in the region in 1997 (Alleyne 2001). A quarter of a million AIDS diagnoses have been made since the start of the epidemic, and about half of those individuals have died. However, the annual incidence of AIDS cases in Latin America seems to be falling early in the new century, so there is room for cautious optimism (Alleyne 2001).

Cardiovascular disease already accounts for about one-third of Latin American and Caribbean deaths at the turn of the twenty-first century. Estimates are that rates will increase to 38 percent by 2020 (Alleyne 2001). However, cancer deaths have not increased, and there is hope that prevention efforts may reduce cancers caused by tobacco use. Additionally, early detection and treatment may lower rates of breast and cervical cancer.

As life expectancies in Latin America improve and disease profiles continue to shift from communicable to chronic diseases, emphasis will need to be on preventive campaigns that promote healthy behaviors and diets. Prevention efforts also have the potential to slow the transmission of HIV/AIDS.

Mexico's effort to expand the provision of health care to all citizens is one example of Latin American civil reforms that have an effect on overall health. The Program for Health Sector Reform (1995–2000) sought to guarantee access to a basic bundle of health care services for all Mexican citizens (de la Fuente et al. 2001). The program was made available to 10 million people who had previously had little or no health care. Additional reforms moved some of the employee health care burden from private employers to the state, enabling wider coverage for workers.

In addition to expanding health care, targeted programs have achieved health goals. For example, nearly all Mexican children between ages one and four received vaccinations, preventive health programs for women were expanded, and treatments for AIDS patients were provided free of charge. Salaries for health professionals were also substantially increased in 2000, adding stability to the public health system. Mexico's health system will continue to be a publicly funded one, with private fee-for-service providers playing a complimentary role (de la Fuente et al. 2001). Ability to

---

[1] Malnutrition is a state of deficiency in energy, protein, or other micronutrients such as vitamin A, iodine, and iron. The World Health Organization measures malnutrition by the weight of the infant or child. The child is defined as malnourished if his or her weight (for age) is two standard deviations or more below the expected means.

[2] Over the latter two decades of the twentieth century, dengue fever and dengue haemorrhagic fever have become major public health threats throughout the tropical and subtropical world. Prevention is almost totally dependent on controlling the *Aedes aegypti* mosquito, the main vector of the disease. These efforts as of the turn of the century were not very effective, and the disease has continued to spread globally.

provide consistent services and to support a strong public health infrastructure will depend in part on political policies that favor civil protections and equality, and in part on the strength of the economy.

Canada

Canadian citizens are among the healthiest in the world, and their life expectancy continues to inch upward. Infant mortality is below 5 per 1,000 live births, and life expectancy as of 1998 was seventy-six for males and eighty-two for females (World Bank 2001, Tables 2 and 7). Levels of schooling increased for all population groups over the last fifteen years of the twentieth century, and fatal traffic accidents declined substantially, due to increased use of seatbelts and safer driving. Canadian civic life also undoubtedly contributes to population health, with high levels of volunteerism, civic participation, and social support (Rootman & Hancock 2001, 102). In addition, environmental quality is generally good, as is the quality of the food and water supply.

Good health is not experienced equally, however. Canada's aboriginal peoples experience poorer living conditions and poorer health than the general population. In addition, growing inequality has increased the percentage of Canadians with low incomes from 16 to 20 percent between 1990 and 1995. "Low income" in developed countries such as Canada and the United States refers to a poverty line calculated on the basis of minimum levels of household spending required to meet essential expenditures on food, clothing, shelter, health, and education. In 1996 the U.S. poverty threshold for a family of two adults and two children was set at $16,036. For poor and low-income Canadians, inadequate and unaffordable housing is a problem; 200,000 are estimated to be homeless or in substandard housing (Rootman & Hancock 2001).

Tobacco smoking continues to be a Canadian health hazard, with increasing use among adolescents. Among high school–age youth, multiple drug use has increased as well. Also having a negative impact on health is the growing proportion of overweight Canadians, a trend since 1985. Finally, there is concern about the potential future hazards of accumulating toxins in the land, air, and water.

Similarly to those in Western European developed nations, Canadians benefit from universal access to publicly insured health care. This system is undoubtedly partially responsible for the continued improvement of most health indicators. Pressures for greater efficiency have brought recent cost-trimming efforts in health care services in the Canadian provinces. Nonetheless, federal financial support for the public health system and universal care remains strong.

The United States

Life expectancy in the United States increased from around fifty in 1900 to nearly eighty in 2000 (Anderson et al. 1997; McGinnis 2001, 81). During the early decades of the century, industrialization improved living conditions and lengthened life. As a consequence, cardiovascular disease surpassed infectious diseases as the leading cause of death by the 1920s. By the turn of the twenty-first century, the leading cause of death was still heart disease (32 percent), followed by cancers (23 percent), and stroke (7 percent). As in other developed countries, modern living conditions in the United States also brought risks from human behaviors that enhance disease and disability. Medical researchers J. Michael McGinnis and W. H. Foege (1993) examined the underlying causes of death in the United States, with the following assessment: Tobacco use is the single most serious health threat, causing 19 percent of deaths, whether from oral use or from first-hand or second-hand smoke. Next are poor diet and sedentary lifestyle (causing 14 percent of deaths), then alcohol (5 percent), micro bial agents (4 percent), firearms (3 percent), sexual behavior (2 percent), motor vehicle accidents (1 percent), and illicit drug use (less than 1 percent).

Many behavioral factors that affect health are associated with socioeconomic status. Risk behaviors such as higher smoking and obesity are found across all social classes but are more prevalent among lower-income groups (Rogers et al. 2000, 318). For continued health improvements to occur, prevention and education campaigns must persist alongside policies to reduce economic inequality, and with campaigns against smoking, drug use, high-fat diets, sedentary lifestyles, riding bicycles and motorcycles without a helmet, and driving without seatbelts. In addition, education is needed to decrease the number of overweight Americans—a problem that often starts in childhood and causes an array of health problems.

The United States is the most unequal among developed societies, and the distribution of incomes and jobs is reflected in disparities in health and longevity. Chapter 3 offers explanations for the association between individuals' position in the social hierarchy and their relatively good or bad health. Despite the complexities of this relationship, there is a clear correlation between wealth and health. Consequently, socioeconomic differences in disease and death rates are a major public health problem in the United States (Rogers et al. 2000, 115).

African-American health patterns are of special concern. Not only are the effects of unemployment (and underemployment), lower pay, and lower occupational status reflected in poorer health outcomes, but racism, too, plays a role (Williams & Collins 1995). When considering whether population health in the United States will continue to improve, it is especially important to examine social class, racial, and ethnic group dynamics. In the conclusion of their book *Living and Dying in the USA: Behavioral, Health, and Social Differentials of Adult Mortality*, sociologists Richard Rogers, Robert Hummer, and Charles Nam recommend that "economic policies . . . provide an adequate level of living for everyone to permit better health standards and more widespread access to health care" (Rogers et al. 2000, 317). They also warn of the health risks to Americans without adequate social support, noting that those elderly adults living alone and parents raising children without the help of a partner need assistance. "Policies facilitating health-related assistance of single, divorced, and separated parents and those living alone would go a long way toward insuring longer life" (Rogers et al. 2000, 317). It is especially important that the elderly maintain friendships; old friendships are most meaningful, but new ones help prevent isolation and depression as well. Face-to-face contact is best, but letters, phone calls, or e-mails can also maintain feelings of closeness. One woman reported, "My best friend calls me

An Indian extended family. The close-knit ties of traditional extended families demand conformity but also often protect individuals against poverty, isolation, and poor health.

every morning at eight o'clock. Neither of us can get out any more, so we haven't seen each other for six months" ("ElderCare Skill Builders" 2000).

Rogers and his colleagues (2000) also suggest that the health consequences of immigration policies be examined. The health and survival advantages of more recently arrived immigrants over their counterparts living here for a couple of decades are significant. These differences are poorly understood, and immigration and health policies may well affect the greater vulnerability of longer-term immigrants in the United States.

The Eastern Mediterranean

As designated by the World Health Organization, this region extends from Morocco to Pakistan, including a population of nearly 457 million near the turn of the twenty-first century. The region's World Health Organization director, Hussein Gezairy, states that growing inequalities in the region, in part resulting from a global economy, are a challenge to health improvements (Gezairy 2001). For example, when countries borrow money from the International Monetary Fund (IMF), the loan conditions restrict spending on education, health, and other population needs. Therefore, for several economies in the region, financing debt has prevented improvements in the standard of living. Violence within a few countries has increased the rates of injury and death, and has restricted access to basic health care. This is the case in Afghanistan, Somalia, and southern Sudan. In Afghanistan, even before the U.S.

bombing following the September 11 attacks, 250 per 1,000 infants were estimated to die before their fifth birthday. This is close to Somalia's extremely high level of 265 infant deaths (Gezairy 2001, 31). Maternal life expectancy (a different measure than female live expectancy) in Afghanistan in 1996 was measured as forty-three and one-half years by the World Health Organization. Taliban warlord domination deteriorated a country already in disarray from years of Soviet invasion and civil war. In the wake of September 11 and retaliatory bombing in Afghanistan, there is further displacement of the population, worsened malnutrition, and increased injuries and loss of life.

Oil-rich countries with higher incomes have far more favorable health profiles. In descending order of per capita gross domestic product (GDP), the United Arab Emirates ($17,554 GDP per capita [GDPpc], 1996) has a rate of child mortality comparable to that in the developed world, of 11 deaths per 1,000 children, and a maternal life expectancy of seventy-three years. Kuwait ($17,482 GDPpc, 1997) has a rate of 16 child deaths per 1,000 and maternal life expectancy of seventy-five years. Qatar ($15,570 GDPpc, 1996) has a child death rate of 15 per 1,000 and a maternal life expectancy of seventy-four years (Gezairy 2001, 31).

Hussein Gezairy emphasizes the need to develop sustainable health care systems and to maintain existing health improvements, especially among the poor. He advises states to work on improving the quality of health services and equal access to them (Gezairy 2001, 34).

Europe

The World Health Organization's European region includes fifty-one countries, starting from Greenland and extending all the way to the Pacific coast of the Russian Federation. During the 1950s and 1960s, European countries' health status was fairly similar, in that health and life expectancies were improving in fairly parallel fashion. However, since the 1970s, health differences have grown, with Western European health improving and Eastern European health stagnating. Countries of the European Union experienced gradual progress upward in longevity, from approximately seventy-two years in 1970 to approximately seventy-six years in 1996 (Asvall & Alderslade 2001). Eastern European life expectancy remained fairly stable, except for the former Soviet republics, which experienced declining life expectancy (Cockerham 1999). Health in the countries of the former Soviet Union and its satellite states deteriorated after 1970 and declined even more steeply following the dissolution of the Soviet Union in 1989 (Asvall & Alderslade 2001). The exception to this trend was a temporary improvement in Soviet health during an intensive anti-alcohol campaign conducted during the mid-1980s. However, when the campaign stopped in 1987, heavy drinking resumed, and health continued to decline.

Two WHO experts with experience in the European region summarize the deterioration of health in Eastern Europe (Asvall & Alderslade 2001).

In the newly independent states of the former Soviet Union, the rapid rise in poverty, unemployment, criminality, and social alienation, together with sharp reductions in health care budgets, brought in their wake a new diphtheria epidemic, a sudden rise in tuberculosis prevalence, a sharp rise in sexually transmitted diseases . . . [including] HIV infection, and rises in infant and maternal mortality, accidents, suicides, homicides, drug abuse, and smoking. Even cholera epidemics reappeared and malaria returned to the southeast parts of the region, where they had been eradicated. (Alsvall & Alderslade 2001, 38)

Russian working-age men's health continues to deteriorate early in the twenty-first century, with heavy drinking and smoking, poor diet, and sedentary leisure habits (Cockerham 1999). This unhealthy lifestyle isn't just a tradition; it is an aspect of deteriorating social relations, including a stagnating economy and an increasingly inequitable distribution of resources. Feelings of alienation intensified with the social and economic chaos brought on by the "radical restructuring" of the post-Soviet Russian economy. Vladimir Bragin worked at a welding factory until, at age forty, he had his second heart attack, and chest pains indicated that a third was on the way. Bragin wanted to get out of the hospital and back to work because, without his job, he feared, "my family will not be able to survive." His doctors had no hope of an able-bodied recovery, however. His cardiologist reported that Bragin was reaping the harvest of an unhealthy lifestyle: two packs of cigarettes daily since age fifteen, no exercise, a diet of sausage and sour cream, and binge drinking up to eight pints of vodka a day (LaFraniere 2001).

In Western European countries, continued progress in health and longevity is uncertain due to demographic and policy trends. There is increasing urbanization and a growing elderly population. National economies are wealthy and highly competitive regionally and globally, but pressures are felt in the public sector to keep down costs, including in public health services. There is also political pressure from the right to privatize services and reduce government spending on public health. These trends, plus increases in social inequality, could slow or threaten overall health improvements.

The behaviors of European citizens will also affect their health. The incidence of disease, accidents, and injuries, as well as overall longevity over the next decades, will be influenced by population mental health and health-related behaviors. Public health campaigns are needed to promote health consciousness, including smoking cessation, education about the benefits of physical exercise, and use of bicycle helmets. Populations also need encouragement to adopt diets high in vegetables and whole grains, and low in fats and sugars. In addition, greater availability of condoms in public locations such as bars, hotels, and kiosks, along with public health messages, will help slow the spread of HIV infection as well as other sexually transmitted diseases. Finally, health experts in the region advocate increasing the price of alcohol to reduce consumption by youth and to help curb excessive consumption among adults (Asvall & Alderslade 2001, 41).

The Western Pacific

This Asian region includes a diverse array of countries, from the most populous in the world (China) to some of the smallest in the world. A few countries are affluent, for some time have been developed and characterized more by chronic than by communicable diseases, and have low birth rates (Australia, Japan, New Zealand, and Singapore). Several other countries are on their way to completing the "epidemiological transition," such as the Philippines, Malaysia, Vietnam, and China. Considerable progress has been made against several infectious diseases, including poliomyelitis (with no cases in the Western Pacific since March 1997), leprosy (with a 90 percent decline in cases over ten years), and a 60 percent decrease in cases of malaria (Omi 2001). However, malaria continues to be a significant public health risk in nine countries of the region, and tuberculosis and sexually transmitted diseases also continue to pose serious health risks (Omi 2001). New diseases, too, threaten populations, such as the H5N1 virus, avian flu in Hong Kong, and a new encephalitis virus in Malaysia.

Noncommunicable diseases like cancer, cardiovascular disease, and diabetes will continue to increase in the coming years in the Western Pacific region (Omi 2001). Disease from high rates of smoking will continue, including lung cancer and cardiovascular disease. Urbanization and cross-country migrations are trends that intensify the need for sound public health planning and delivery of preventive campaigns and basic health care services. If poorly managed by governments and without widespread access to primary health care, migrations will intensify existing health problems. In addition, urbanization tends to increase many behaviors that cause disease and injury, including smoking, drinking, drug use, driving, and sexual encounters. Public health campaigns are needed to educate city dwellers about the potential harm of these practices and to promote healthy behaviors.

China.   A snapshot of China's dramatic improvements in health over the past half-century is seen in its increased life expectancy. Average life expectancy before the founding of the People's Republic in 1949 was thirty-five years, whereas at the turn of the twenty-first century, it was seventy years (Wenkang & Schwarz 2001, 58). The infant mortality rate decreased from 42 deaths per 1,000 live births in 1980 to 31 in 1998, and the under-five mortality rate went from 65 per 1,000 to 39 (World Bank 2001, Tables 2, 7). Maternal mortality for the 1990s was 65 deaths per 100,000 live births, considerably lower than India's (over 400) but higher than Chile's (23). China has achieved success in population control, nutrition, and overall improvement of population health (World Bank, China Country Office, 2000).

There are conflicting reports about the quality of China's water supply and environment. The World Bank reports that, during the 1990s, 90 percent of China's population had access to safe drinking water (2001, Table 7), whereas the World Resources Institute in Washington, D.C., reports that over half the population lacks access to clean drinking water. Both sources agree that less than one-fifth of the population had access to adequate sanitation during the 1990s, with over half the urban population having access (World Bank 2001, Table 7). Related to China's water difficulties are pollution problems. The World Resources Institute has documented serious pollution in all of China's seven major watersheds (Huai, Hai, Liao, Songhua, Chang [Yangtze], Zhu [Pearl], and Huang [Yellow]). China is tremendously efficient in its use of energy compared to its developed Western counterparts. Its population is three and a half times larger than the United States but puts into the atmosphere four and a half times less carbon dioxide. It is open to question whether, as China gets richer, the government will control the use of vehicles and carefully monitor air pollution.

There is widespread agreement that China's state-directed birth control policy has dramatically curtailed fertility. The one-child policy has incentives for compliance and punishments for failure to meet this tough standard. The policy is reportedly more carefully enforced in urban areas than in rural areas, where children may continue to be an asset in agricultural production. The prevalence of contraceptive use (including sterilization) was reported at 85 percent during the 1990s (World Bank 2001, Table 7). The methods and consequences of the policy are strongly debated, however. The pressures of the one-child policy have led to serious concerns regarding female infanticide and the treatment of girl babies. In fact, the number of men is already thought to outnumber the number of women by more than 60 million. The policy, introduced in 1980, has been successful in reducing perhaps as many as 250 million births. It stipulates that each couple living in the cities should have only one child, unless one or both of the couple are from an ethnic minority or both are only children. In most rural areas, a couple may have a second child after a break of several years. The policy was introduced to ensure that the country, which historically has been prone to floods and famine, could feed its people ("China Steps up 'One Child' Policy" 2000). In the fall of 2000, the Chinese government again stepped up enforcement of the policy, due to the population increases expected during the first half of the new century. But, despite forced abortions and severe financial penalties, some couples still get around the policy by sending the pregnant woman away to stay with relatives until the baby is born. Couples may claim the newborn was adopted or belongs to a friend or relative. Local officials are called upon to enforce the policy, and abuses do occur. For example, in September of 2000, three officials were questioned about their killing a baby in central China in the course of enforcing the one-child policy ("China Steps up 'One Child' Policy" 2000).

Chinese economic development has brought longer lives but also increases in health problems that affect adults. These include cardiovascular disease, cancer, accidents, substance abuse, and sexually transmitted diseases. Prevention efforts related to these problems are of growing importance in both rural and developing regions of China. With development and increased wealth among some sectors of the population, unequal access to health care has become a major social and political issue in China (World Health Organization, Western Pacific Regional Office 2001). External financial and technical assistance in addressing health problems has come from other countries and international agencies. The World Health Organization in particular has assisted with the eradication of polio, surveillance of influenza, and control of sexually transmitted diseases. WHO's collaboration with China, especially in poor areas, continues. However, the agency states that, as China continues to become wealthier, this collaboration will focus largely on technical expertise to strengthen locally funded activities (World Health Organization, Western Pacific Regional Office 2001).

South East Asia

The World Health Organization's South East Asia region includes ten countries: Bangladesh, Bhutan, Democratic People's Republic of Korea (South Korea), India, Indonesia, Maldives, Myanmar, Nepal, Sri Lanka, and Thailand. In recent decades, most countries of the region have experienced economic development, which has at times been erratic. Between 1980 and 1995, the average annual growth rate in GNP per capita ranged from 2.2 percent in Bangladesh and Nepal to 6.3 in Thailand (World Health Organization, South East Asia Regional Office 2001b). Nonetheless, inequality has increased within and among South East Asian countries. For example, in the early 1990s, 78 percent of Bangladesh's population lived on less than $2 a day, and in 1995 82 percent of Nepal's population lived at that level. By contrast, less than 2 percent of South Koreans lived at such a poor level. Thailand's population has experienced reduced poverty with economic development. By 1998, 28 percent lived on less than $2 a day, while by contrast, 66 percent of Indonesians lived at that level in 1999 (World Bank 2001, Table 4). However, economic disaster hit the region during the mid- and latter 1990s, putting Asian countries into recession.

Moderate inequality characterizes both relatively affluent South Korea and poverty-stricken Bangladesh. Their great economic differences are reflected in their life expectancies; Bangladesh's is just under fifty years, and South Korea's is sixty-five (World Health Organization 2000, Table 5). In South Korea, the wealthiest 20 percent of the population reaps nearly 40 percent of the country's income. This is almost as unequal as Bangladesh, where the top 20 percent makes 43 percent of the income. Indonesia is slightly more unequal, with 45 percent of the income going to the wealthiest 20 percent. India has approximately the same inequality as Indonesia, with 46 percent of income going to the top 20 percent. Among countries in the region where data are available, World Bank figures indicate that Thailand is the most unequal, with over 48 percent of the income received by the wealthiest fifth of the population. Thailand's inequality is roughly the same as in the United States, where in 1997 over 46 percent of income went to the top fifth (World Bank 2001, Table 5). Asia's economic recession aggravated the problems of poverty and inequality in the region.

In Southeast Asia, infectious diseases are still the leading causes of disease and death (World Health Organization, South East Asia Regional Office 2001b). However, significant progress has been made in the eradication of polio, guinea worm disease (which has appeared in India), and yaws. (Yaws is found in tropical and subtropical regions, often infecting poor children. It is spread by a spiral-shaped bacterium from direct contact with a lesion. It destroys skin, bone, and other tissues.) Progress has also been made toward eliminating leprosy and neonatal tetanus. Tuberculosis and malaria continue to take a heavy toll in lives and disability, economically crippling many families and weakening overall economic prospects. These diseases are most problematic in poor countries and regions. In addition, new diseases threaten health in the region, including HIV/AIDS, dengue fever, Japanese encephalitis, and viral hepatitis (World Health Organization, South East Asia Regional Office 2001b). Although many infectious diseases are coming under better management and prevention in Southeast Asia, chronic diseases are increasing due to the increased longevity of populations and more affluent lifestyles among the privileged. Cardiovascular diseases, cancers, neurological and metabolic disorders, and other chronic conditions that trouble the young and the poor less often are becoming more common in Southeast Asian countries.

WHO and UNICEF have provided assistance and coordination in the region in public health planning. These agencies help move countries toward universal immunization and also toward self-sufficiency in vaccination programs. All countries in the South East Asia region meet at least 80 percent of their vaccination costs, as compared to African countries, which are far more dependent on outside assistance. Indonesia, for example, is able to produce all the vaccines needed for its program (World Health Organization, South East Asia Regional Office 2001b).

India.   India is the second most populous country in the world. It has seen health improvements in recent years, as reflected in reductions of its infant, maternal, and overall death rates (World Health Organization, South East Asia Regional Office 2001b). The mortality rate for infants and children under five years of age decreased from 177 deaths per 1,000 in 1980 to 83 in 1998 (World Bank 2001, Table 2). Life expectancy in 1998 was sixty-two years for males and sixty-four years for females, and infant mortality was 70 deaths per 1,000 live births (World Bank 2001, Tables 2 and 7). As of 1998, illiteracy, which inhibits healthy practices, remained relatively high, at 33 percent for men and 57 percent for women over fifteen years of age (World Bank 2000, Table 2).

Health problems that persist include communicable diseases, notably tuberculosis and HIV/AIDS. Noncommunicable diseases like cardiovascular disease and cancer are increasing. Birth control efforts have been less successful than in China, and population growth continues to be high, with significant variations among Indian states. Nevertheless, there has been a decline from an average 5 births per woman in 1980 to 3.2 in 1998 (World Bank 2000, Table 7).

As of 1997, the World Bank estimated that 86 percent of India's population lived on less than the equivalent of $2 per day (2001, Table 4). Consequently, malnutrition continues to be an important source of ill health in India, resulting in low–birth weight babies and underweight children. Anemia in pregnant and nursing women is related to numerous micronutrient deficiencies in infants and children. Immune functioning is also hampered by malnutrition, experienced by over half of children under five years old (World Health Organization, South East Asia Regional Office 2001a). An estimated 200 million Indians have an iodine deficiency, making them vulnerable to related disorders, including goiter, an enlargement of the thyroid gland on the neck.

Eighty-eight percent of pregnant women were found to be anemic in 1991. This alarmingly high rate is related to numerous health problems among mothers and infants. Anemia during pregnancy is associated with low birth weight and an array of developmental risks for the child. In at least some regions, half or more of the children under five had iron deficiency anemia at the turn of the twenty-first century (World Health Organization, South East Asia Regional Office 2001a). Public health responses are insufficient and often must be funded by international agencies.

Nonetheless, preventive campaigns have the potential to make an enormous difference. For example, in response to the vitamin A deficiencies that put preschool-age children at risk for blindness, India's National Institute of Nutrition administers a program giving vitamin A to a majority of young children.

Additional health risk comes from behavior and lifestyle. Smoking among youth has been increasing for the last couple of decades. Also damaging to health is a sedentary lifestyle among the affluent, along with consumption of fast food, substance abuse, and violence against women and children. The Indian government gains revenue from tobacco sales and therefore has been reluctant to be highly restrictive, although the government did ban smoking in public places. Nevertheless, the tobacco industry continues to sponsor sports events and engage in high-profile advertising.

Poverty and malnutrition are not the only problems of India's poor. Nearly one-fifth of the population did not have access to safe drinking water as of the 1990–1996 period (World Bank 2001, Table 7). Access to sanitation (which means hygienic excreta disposal facilities, not necessarily flushing toilets) was at 16 percent for the 1990–1996 period (World Bank 2001, Table 7). However, half of the *urban* population had access to adequate excreta disposal facilities, whereas less than 4 percent had these facilities available in rural areas as of 1995 (World Health Organization, South East Asia Regional Office 2001a). Most municipalities do not have systems for monitoring the quality of the water supply and are vulnerable to water-borne diseases. Rural water supply systems are even more neglected. Increased population awareness of the importance of a sanitary water supply is needed, in addition to technical equipment and skilled personnel to monitor the water supply and sewage disposal.

India has taken steps to provide medications to its citizens despite a lack of money. A list of 300 essential drugs was developed and price controls exercised on 78 of those (World Health Organization, South East Asia Regional Office 2001a). Several international organizations provide medical assistance to India, including the World Health Organization, the World Bank, USAID, and United Nations agencies such as UNICEF. The Indian government provides the majority of health care to the population, and its services are meager by the standards of developed countries. But the quality of health care available in India depends largely on one's social class. Private doctors and hospitals provide primary and specialized care to the affluent, whereas the majority of the population gets by with what is available in public clinics and hospitals, which are less available in rural areas. India actually has a relatively high number of doctors, but many leave the country for higher salaries in the United States.

Proposed strategies for improving Indian health include

- Reducing poverty and inequality.
- Making health services universally accessible through a regional organization of health services.
- Strengthening health promotion and protection, and coordination of these efforts.
- Strengthening specific health programs (for example, against malnutrition, malaria, polio, tuberculosis, and HIV/AIDS).
- Improving the use of health technologies.

- Strengthening international partnerships for health (World Health Organization, South East Asia Regional Office 2001a, 112).

Conclusion

Remarkable improvements in health have occurred over the past century. Infectious disease has declined, and life expectancies have increased. However, there are significant increases in chronic illness and inequality within and between nations. Poverty, malnutrition, and HIV/AIDS persist as serious global health threats. Drug-resistant strains of viruses and bacteria threaten to frustrate treatment and eradication efforts; tuberculosis is but one example. Among the relatively affluent countries of the world, lifestyles that include high-fat foods, sedentary routines, and substance abuse are major threats to health. Feelings of alienation, depression, and anxiety are serious concerns, related to insecurities of economic and social status and deteriorating community ties.

Although overall health gains have been impressive over the century, the gains of the past decade have benefited mainly the affluent; the "health gradient" associating wealth with health shows no signs of disappearing. All major causes of death are strongly and increasingly inversely associated with social class, regardless of the country's level of wealth.

The vast majority (90 percent) of poor people in the world live in Asia, the Pacific, and Africa; the remaining 10 percent live in the rest of the world (Sen & Bonita 2000). A high proportion of the poor are women, and when women are poor, their children are poor. Of the approximately 56 million deaths globally each year, 80 percent occur in the poorest regions of the world. Many poor countries and even some disadvantaged groups in wealthy countries have life expectancies and disease profiles typical of European countries of a century ago (Sen & Bonita 2000). For example, African-American men have a life expectancy at birth of nearly twenty years less than white men (Murray et al. 1994), and most developed countries have life expectancies (around eighty years) double the life expectancies in the most disadvantaged countries. And, even when economic development brings increased affluence to poor regions, political barriers prevent the elimination of child malnutrition and sometimes block improvements to overall health. Today, seven out of ten deaths in children under the age of five occur in low-income countries, from five preventable conditions: pneumonia, diarrheal diseases, malaria, measles, and malnutrition (Sen & Bonita 2000).

Brutal dictatorships, civil unrest, and social chaos prevent populations from receiving adequate food, shelter, and medical care; under these conditions, injury, disability, and death increase. This is true in developed as well as underdeveloped countries. For example, several countries of the former Soviet Union have experienced health and longevity downturns for men, as political and economic conditions worsened with the fall of the Soviet Union. Civil war in the territories of former Yugoslavia worsened mortality there, especially among young adult men. Fortunately, the World Health Organization and many nongovernmental agencies, such as the Red

Cross and Doctors Without Borders, play a major role in responding to health crises, whether caused by war, civil disorder, or natural disaster. Amnesty International, along with several global Human Rights Watch organizations and helped by volunteer support from many citizens, keeps watch over human rights abuses and turns the spotlight on governments or paramilitary organizations that carry out brutal practices. Such organizations play an important role in monitoring the well-being of global citizens.

6

Gender, Race, and Ethnic Influences on Health

In developing countries each year an estimated 585,000 women die from complications of pregnancy, childbirth, and unsafe abortion—about one every minute. Nearly all of these deaths could be prevented.

—"Women's Lives at Risk," *Population Reports*

While violence against women has become widely recognized as a major issue of women's human rights, more recently there has also been growing awareness of the impact of violence on women's mental and physical health. Violence against women in families dramatically increases their risk of poor health, with studies consistently reporting negative and far-reaching effects.

—"Violence Against Women: An International Health Issue,"
Women's International Network News

The research literature on ethnic inequality . . . shows that progress in narrowing the gap between minorities and whites and among white ethnics was made when the economy was expanding through the mid-1970s. After that, for many groups, the progress slowed, stopped, or reversed. . . . In addition, the evidence indicates that direct discrimination is still an important factor for all minority subgroups except very highly educated Asians.

—Mary Waters and Karl Eschbach, "Immigration and Ethnic and Racial
` Inequality in the United States." In John Hagan and Karen S. Cook (Eds.),
Annual Review of Sociology

This chapter describes patterns and offers examples of how improvements in health and patterns of illness vary for men and women, and among different racial and ethnic groups. The first part looks at continued barriers to health improvements among women in less-developed countries, then focuses on gender differences in the United States. The second part of the chapter examines some ways that ethnicity and race influence health patterns, with particular emphasis on the United States.

We consider the following questions:

- Do social class inequalities generally predict how healthy or ill social groups will be?
- To what extent do gender, race, and ethnicity have added causal impacts on health and illness?
- Is an expansion of equity-enhancing policies, such as the Earned Income Credit, which gives refunds to low-income families, needed to reduce inequality between social groups in the United States?

Gender and Health

Men are most vulnerable to violence from other men through war, civil unrest, and conflicts with male friends and family members. Where guns are readily available, violence is far more often deadly. We have also seen that work holds an essential key to men's mental and physical health. Unemployment, job insecurity, and even early retirement can bring disease and premature death, much more so than for women. Marriage and parenthood provide anchors for men emotionally, to some extent preventing smoking, excessive drinking and drug use, and other behaviors that put single men at greater risk for accident and disease. It is quite possible that the health benefits for men of work and marriage are found in all modern developed societies.

Men have health advantages from having access to more resources than women have—land, jobs, income, improved technologies, food and housing, retirement, health benefits, and so on. However, despite their higher status, men face considerable health problems. In less-developed countries, poor men, women and children face chronic uncertainty regarding income and adequate food supply. In more-developed countries, the working class and increasingly the middle class face uncertain working conditions. Corporate downsizing and mergers threaten loss of jobs, and fewer sectors of the labor force are protected from layoffs. In developed countries, even with high proportions of wives in the labor force, men continue to feel the weight of responsibility for supporting their families and continue to identify strongly with that provider role. In all societies, when earning a livelihood is unavailable to working-age men, stress on family relationships increases, often causing separation or divorce. We now turn to examples of some continued barriers to improved health among women.

Women may be protected from a number of diseases by their reproductive physiology and certain X-linked genes (Gage 1994; Rogers et al. 2000; Waldron 1983). Especially before menopause, estrogen protects women from heart disease and early death, as compared to men. Even among babies, boys have a greater prevalence of disease and other physiological problems (Cockerham 1998). The apparent female biological advantage partially explains women's greater longevity, but not its changes over time or its variations within and among societies. For example, there are considerable social class differences in sex-mortality differentials. Male-female health differences also vary by marital status, as mentioned above; studies in developed countries find better health among married than among unmarried men. For women historically, the picture is more mixed, but currently women benefit in terms of improved life expectancy from marriage as compared to their unmarried counterparts. Health differences between the sexes also change over time. From these variations, we surmise that biological differences play a modest role in explaining health differences between men and women, whereas social factors play a major role (Rogers et al. 2000, 32). Chapter 2, Figure 2.1, provided a graphic representation of the relative influences of social, behavioral, medical, and biological causes of health differences, showing the large explanatory role of social variables.

Women's Health and Poverty

Poverty has especially harsh consequences for girls and women, because they have fewer resources than their male counterparts. This is the case at all ages. Within households, sisters and wives have less access to resources such as food and education than do their brothers and husbands. Although poverty unfailingly causes chronic hunger, malnutrition, and lower resistance to infectious and chronic diseases, studies reveal different male and female patterns of psychological distress and disorder in response to it (Desjarlais et al. 1995, 179, 185). Women's chronic hunger, overwork, and economic dependence in less-developed countries often lead to hopelessness, exhaustion, anger, and fear. In conditions of scarcity, women's responsibility to feed and care for their children is a constant source of anxiety, and crop failures, weather problems, civil unrest, and other dilemmas may compromise food supplies and safety. "Understanding the sources of ill health for women means understanding how cultural and economic forces interact to undermine their social status" (Desjarlais et al. 1995, 179).

A case example from Peru, gathered by the Institute for Health and Social Justice, illustrates the damaging effects of poverty, periphery status in the world economy, and ineffective state policies.

> Benedicta Sanchez started coughing during the winter of 1994, but at first she paid it little attention. Born in a rural province north of Lima, the 38-year-old woman had moved to the shantytown district of Carabayllo . . . when her husband found agricultural work nearby. From the time of their arrival, amid the economic austerity imposed by President Alberto Fujimori in 1990, the couple and their two adult daughters had teetered on the brink of starvation. . . .
> But Benedicta had more than a cold. For months she'd been losing weight and waking up at night with drenching sweats. One Monday evening, Benedicta's oldest daughter Maria returned from night school to find her mother coughing up blood-streaked sputum. Maria had just heard a radio announcement that described the symptoms of tuberculosis and that urged people experiencing them to seek help. Maria

decided to stay home from work the next day in order to take her mother to the nearest public health center. . . . [T]uberculosis checkups are free. This, as Benedicta and
Maria were told, is because the Peruvian Ministry of Health sees tuberculosis as a very
serious problem.

[Because Maria feared she would lose her job, she returned to work, and]
Benedicta went alone to the nearest public hospital, a half-hour bus ride and 20-minute
walk from her home. There, health workers informed her that she needed to purchase
saline solution, surgical tubing, gloves, and a syringe before a definite diagnosis could
be made. Benedicta was also told that the national tuberculosis program would not
cover the cost. . . .

Benedicta panicked. She had been told at the clinic that her treatment would be
free.

"Señora, how can you leave your house and come all the way here with just one
sol?" the nurse asked her.

"Señorita," replied Benedict, "if I had known I was going to have to pay, I would
not have come at all."

Benedicta returned home without even being diagnosed. . . . Benedicta told
[Maria] that she . . . didn't have TB after all. . . . And she knew that to purchase the
supplies for her treatment, she would have to deplete the family's meager savings, and
perhaps threaten its survival. So Benedicta made a calculated choice: she said nothing,
and went on coughing. (Kim et al. 2000, 127–128)

Working in Brazil, anthropologist Nancy Scheper-Hughes (1992) interpreted
women's complaints of "nervousness" as a result of chronic hunger and hunger anxiety. The World Health Organization (1993) estimated that more than 60 percent of
women in less-developed countries are malnourished. Nearly two-thirds of pregnant
women in Africa and southern and western Asia, and half of those who are not pregnant, are believed to be clinically anemic (Merchant & Kurz 1993; United Nations
1991). Maternal ill health in poor countries is so common that people often view it as
normal and unavoidable (Defo 1997). Maternal mortality ranges from approximately
100 to 1,000 maternal deaths per million live births in poor countries, with the highest levels in sub-Saharan Africa and South Asia (Defo 1997; Kwast 1989). For every
woman who dies in pregnancy and childbirth, about sixteen more experience ill
health, which may last the rest of their lives (Walsh et al. 1993). The vast majority of
these pregnancy- and birth-related deaths and disabilities are preventable with proper
nutrition and basic health care. Before the AIDS epidemic reached its height in sub-
Saharan Africa, 10 to 20 percent of women's deaths in childbirth were attributed to
anemia (Desjarlais et al. 1995, 185). Now the AIDS epidemic adds another threat to
women's already-precarious life chances.

A longitudinal study of nearly 10,000 women in Yaoundé, Cameroon, measured
the impact of socioeconomic disadvantage on women's health (Defo 1997). The
research design examined risk factors during the time period from childbirth to the
onset of episodes of illness. The author found that women's health was worsened
when they lived in poor-quality neighborhoods, lacked modern amenities in their
households, and did not participate in the paid labor force (1024). These relationships were significant even when controlling for lack of prenatal care, poor obstetric

history, nutritional status, and partner's characteristics. These findings support Wilkinson's observation that higher income and standard of living are significant predictors of better health.

Chapter 2 offered conceptual tools for understanding gender stratification and pointed out that the overall class system and the strategic significance of women's labor are important in determining the relative power of women. Women's labor in less-developed countries is essential to their own and their children's survival. However, especially in less-developed countries, women's labor is culturally undervalued, and there is little chance for upward mobility or economic independence. Micro lending—small loan programs for individuals to start their own small businesses—has worked in Bangladesh and other locations to provide women some economic independence and improved social status (Yunus 1999). However, thus far, micro lending has not become a widespread solution to women's economic difficulties in periphery countries.

Men and boys continue to have more social status and greater access to whatever resources are at hand. For example, research in Bangladesh found that malnutrition was significantly higher among girls than boys (Chen et al. 1981), and another study in West Bengal found the same result for girls under five in two villages (Sen & Sengupta 1983). A male-female comparative study of daily caloric intake and energy expended in the rural Indian state of Karnataka found a calorie deficit for women alongside a calorie surplus for men (Batliwala 1983, cited in Desjarlais et al. 1995, 185). Greater access to food in poor countries is a male privilege; girls and women more often pay the price of malnutrition.

Steep inequalities between men and women are perpetuated by patrilineal kinship patterns, with inheritance and kin identity traced through male lines. Combined with poverty, these conditions encourage positive attitudes toward boy babies and disappointment with girl babies. Where the pressures are intense to have boys and few births, and where affluence and technology allow, couples often screen fetuses and abort females. Infanticide against girl babies serves the same purpose for couples who cannot afford a medical route to preventing the birth of female children. In a survey of 1,250 women in Madras, India, over half reported having killed an infant daughter (Anderson & Moore 1993).

In cultures where parents must pay the groom's family a dowry, the bride's family may become a target of abuse. Reports of dowry abuse in India have become increasingly widespread, with the groom's parents demanding more and more from the bride's family for extended periods after the wedding has taken place. The young wife often is harshly treated; sometimes it is only her death that brings an end to the exploitation (Desjarlais et al. 1995, 194). Indian Hindu brides are sometimes burned to death for not bringing sufficient dowry to the marriage, and in Pakistan, Muslim and Christian women are burned as a form of abuse. The crimes are claimed to be accidents, or "stove burnings," though few believe this to be the case. Activist Shahnaz Bukhari investigated two hospitals and found that 500 women had been burned to death during the years from 1994 to 1997, blamed on cooking fires ("Ghastly Domestic Abuse" 1997).

Women's health chances tend to reflect the standard of living of their social class. Women's conditions compared to those of their male counterparts will influence the extent to which they retain their female health advantage. For example, where men have harsh and dangerous working conditions, their health will reflect that hardship and further widen the gap. Where women are malnourished, they are likely to lose their advantage and be more susceptible to chronic and infectious diseases.

Earning income is generally good for women's physical and mental health. It enhances personal control over daily life, increases independence and safety, and helps prevent isolation. Income gives women some independence that may improve their leverage with husbands and extended family members. With income, women have more control over feeding and caring for their children as well. In fact, the United States Agency for International Development (1997) concludes from existing research that children's nutritional and health status is improved more by increases in household earnings from *women* because they spend more than men on food for the family.

Coercion and violence are additional factors that affect women's health. Sexual and reproductive violence includes rape, involuntary prostitution (sexual slavery), unprotected exposure to sexually transmitted diseases, involuntary sterilization and abortion, domestic violence, and female abortion and infanticide (Desjarlais et al. 1995). Women's economic and social status is far more vulnerable to these problems.

Rape can occur to privileged women, but it is far more likely to occur to disadvantaged women. In conditions of civil war or societal breakdown, rape can become a frequent occurrence. Refugee women are at great risk for rape. Nearly 40 percent of women Vietnamese boat people were abducted or raped by pirates while escaping their country by sea (Mullica & Son 1989). Three Bosnian Serbs began jail terms of up to twenty-eight years after being found guilty by the United Nations war crimes tribunal in The Hague, Netherlands. The defendants were found guilty of a range of crimes, including rape and sexual enslavement, after the court heard testimony from sixteen of their Muslim victims ("Rape War Crime Verdict Welcomed" 2001). In recent years, reports of rape also surfaced in Bangladesh, India, Malaysia, and South Africa (Desjarlais et al. 1995, 188). An episode in Kenya reveals the casualness with which rape is regarded in some male-dominated societies. At a boarding school near Nairobi, male students struck in protest over fees. When the girls did not take part, the boys attacked them. Seventy-one girls were raped, and nineteen were crushed to death. *Time* magazine reported that the school's deputy principal explained that "the boys never meant any harm against the girls; they just wanted to rape them" ("A Night of Madness" 1991). One aspect of male privilege is that rape is viewed neither as a serious offense nor even as criminal.

There are recent reports in some traditional societies of young women being doubly traumatized when rape occurs. Because a woman's worth on the marriage market is dependent on her virginity, a symbol of the bride's purity and a real part of the marriage bargain, rape renders a woman worthless as a prospective bride. As a result, at times in Fiji, the Philippines, Thailand, Mexico, and Peru, women who have been raped have been forced to marry their rapist in order to solve the family's predicament (Desjarlais et al. 1995, 189; Heise 1993).

Like rape, female sexual slavery has a long history. When societies fall into chaos and turmoil from war or rapid social change, women are less protected by their kin and are more vulnerable to abduction and coercion. Families may even sell daughters to try to survive financially. Often, sexual slavery begins with promises of a job or marriage; then women are transported to cities where they are sold to brothels or bars and forced to provide sexual services. They face violence and brutality if they resist or try to escape. Under the strain of this coercion and harsh working conditions, their mental and physical health deteriorates. Katje, a nineteen-year-old Moldovian woman, was rescued early in 2002 from a seedy brothel in Pristina, the capital of Kosovo, where Albanian gangsters dominate a lucrative slave trade. When Katje did not meet her quota of servicing ten men per night, she and others like her were locked up in a dark cellar for a month (Lee 2002). Moldova is located between Romania and Ukraine; its severe poverty during the post-Soviet period makes it easy for sex slave traffickers to bribe police and customs officers. Worldwide, the U.S. State Department estimates that 700,000 to 2 million women and girls (some as young as five) are smuggled across borders each year, bought and sold for sexual purposes (Lee 2002).

Violence against women may also originate in state or local policies regarding women's health and reproduction. For example, enforcement of China's one-child policy included coerced abortions. The increase in sterilization started in 1991 with stepped-up enforcement of the one-child policy. Another example is the Indian government's advocacy of abortions in its "family-planning" efforts, employing ultrasound and amniocentesis to detect female fetuses, which are aborted (Anderson & Moore 1993).

Female genital mutilation is another example of violence against women. Rooted in cultural traditions and gender inequalities, it is often carried out by elderly women of the community. Procedures range from removal of the tip of the clitoris to removal of the entire clitoris and labia minora; parts of the labia majora are removed, and remaining tissues are sewn together, with a small opening left for urination and menstruation. These rituals mark the shift to womanhood as well as social control over women's sexuality. The procedures reduce or eliminate female sexual pleasure and introduce considerable pain. The resulting health problems include infections, sterility, and damage to the vagina and urinary tract during childbirth and sexual intercourse. The practice is found in societies in sub-Saharan Africa, as well as in Egypt, the United Arab Emirates, Bahrain, Oman, Indonesia, South Yemen, Pakistan, Malaysia, and some parts of Russia (Desjarlais et al. 1995, 192).

Gender and Health in the United States

During the twentieth century in the United States, a dramatic gap between male and female longevity developed (Rogers et al. 2000).[1] In 1920 women lived an average of less than two years longer than men did; the gap increased until it peaked in the mid-1970s at eight years (Knudsen & McNown 1993; Rogers et al. 2000). During the

---

[1] Rogers, Hummer, and Nam (2000) analyze the most comprehensive mortality data source available for the United States: the National Health Interview Survey matched to the Multiple Cause of Death file through the National Death Index (NHIS-MCD).

last two decades of the twentieth century, the longevity gap has narrowed to a six-year advantage for women (Peters et al. 1998). Most of the advantage occurs before old age, with less heart disease, respiratory disease, accidents, violence, and cancers (Nathanson 1984). What caused these changes? Rogers and colleagues' (2000) analysis of a recent data set for the United States yields some answers.

Contributing to men's higher mortality risk are their physically riskier jobs at lower occupational levels and their higher rates of cigarette smoking, alcohol and drug use, and other risky behaviors. Increased smoking among men contributed to their mortality over the first half of the century. A decline in male smoking toward the end of the century reduced male mortality. Between 1910 and 1962, greater male smoking accounted for three-quarters of the increased gender difference in longevity (Retherford 1975). Smoking among both men and women declined after 1964, helped along by the surgeon general's warning (in 1965) on cigarette packages that "smoking may be hazardous to your health" (Rogers et al. 2000, 243). By 1990 smoking had stabilized, with one quarter of both men and women smoking. However, new concerns are arising over signs that smoking is increasing again among some young groups (Nam et al. 1996).

Nathanson and Lopez (1987) have pointed out that class differences in smoking and other behaviors affect the gender-health gap. For example, in the United States, health risk behaviors have become more concentrated among the lower and working classes. In addition, among upper- and middle-class men, there are more supports for health-promoting behaviors. The result is narrower mortality differences between the sexes within more affluent classes. Another way in which social stratification interacts with gender is in women's positions in the labor force. Women are concentrated in lower-paying and lower-status occupations compared to men. This labor force disadvantage weakens women's longevity gains (Rogers et al. 2000). With greater gender equity in the labor force, women's longevity would most likely increase and widen the gender gap.

Despite reductions in smoking among men, male-female differences in smoking before 1990 are estimated to cause at least one quarter of the gender difference in longevity. The percentage is larger when smoking-related cancer and respiratory disease are added into the equation. Consequently, further reductions in smoking among men (and continued low levels among women) have the potential to further reduce the gender mortality gap and improve overall population health in the United States (Rogers et al. 2000, 49).

Men who are unemployed, separated, or divorced are at a distinct health disadvantage in developed countries. They weather these life situations more poorly than women, who actually experience these conditions more frequently than men. In the United States, for instance, women are more likely to be separated and divorced than men, remarry less frequently, and are much more likely to be widowed. Women also live in households with lower mean incomes than men and are less likely to have a college degree (Rogers et al. 2000, 35). These disadvantages lower women's life expectancies.

For men in developed countries, being employed is associated with better health—far more so than for women. Women are unemployed more often than men are, but that seems to affect women's health less. For example, Morris and Cook's

(1994) longitudinal British study found that even healthy and socially advantaged men who retired early had a significantly higher risk of dying than those who remained employed. Most women take positive mental and physical health benefits from their identity as mothers and in their relationships generally. For men, the positive effects of identities as husband and father seem to be weaker, as compared to their benefits from being formally employed. Nonetheless, combining marriage, parenthood, *and* work is healthiest for working-age men.

The "healthy worker effect" may emerge because work provides intrinsic life-promoting benefits, including a sense of worth, accomplishment, and community (Rogers et al. 2000, 155). Like men, women benefit from paid work but may not be as reliant on it for their good health. Women may experience some of the positive effects of work from being mothers and homemakers. Also contributing to the healthy worker effect are the benefits that come with better jobs, including health insurance, health screenings, and alcohol and drug treatment programs.

Along with the advantages of paid work for women comes the strain of the double day of wage labor and household responsibilities. This is a demanding daily routine, causing considerable stress and fatigue. Affluent women can purchase services (quality child care, prepared food, cleaning help) to lighten the load, but low-income and poor women cannot afford such luxuries. There are considerable differences in the quality of working-class versus professional women's jobs and pay. These influ-

Work offers a health benefit for both men and women, despite women's "double day" of home and work responsibilities, child care expenses, and lower pay than men.

TABLE 6.1 *Possible Social Trends in the United States and Their Potential Impact on Health*

Possible Social Trend	Impact on Gender Differences in Health
Greater job insecurity, underemployment, unemployment	Worsens population health, especially men's; widens the health gender gap
Increased inequality in distribution of income and wealth among social classes	Widens the health gap between rich and poor, men and women
Greater use of social support, friend and kin networks, and medical care by men	Improves male health and narrows the gender health gap
Increased equality in jobs and pay for men and women	Improves female health and widens the gender health gap

ence their health (and their children's health) as well as their position vis-à-vis men in their families.

Although social factors favor mostly men, their behaviors put them at a health disadvantage. Accident rates show that men take more risks in driving, sports, and other leisure activities, and the availability of guns affects their safety as well. Rogers and colleagues caution that "powerful efforts to curb dangerous and violent behavior disproportionally exhibited by (and harmful to) young males must be made if the substantial gap in mortality due to social pathologies is to be closed" (2000, 50).

Rogers and colleagues' analysis of historical trends in health and current class differences demonstrates that higher mortality figures for men are not fixed by biological differences (2000, 51). For example, the gap between men and women is much smaller among the most economically privileged social groups. Table 6.1 lists possible future trends and their effects on the health gender gap in the United States. Notice that, although class and gender dynamics operate simultaneously, social class is the more powerful determinant of health.

Women's Status and Health: A Study of the United States

Kawachi and colleagues (1999) compared the social status of women in the fifty states and examined how those results correspond to gender differences in health. The authors cite Connell's (1987) theoretical framework for gender and power, identifying two processes to explain the relationships between women and men: the division of labor and power structures. Connell's analysis is closely aligned with gender stratification theory as described in Chapter 2; Blumberg and Collins focus on the overall class structure and the strategic importance of women's labor, in addition to other factors. The study of women's status examined a combination of measures, developed by the Institute for Women's Policy Research (1996), shown in Table 6.2. Health outcome measures in the study were female and male mortality rates, female death rates by specific causes, and mean days of activity limitations reported by women during the previous month.

TABLE 6.2   *Indices of Women's Status Used to Compare the Fifty United States*

Women's political participation	Women's voter registration and turnout; representation in elected office; women's institutional resources
Economic autonomy	Women's access to health insurance; educational attainment; business ownership; percentage of women above the poverty level
Employment and earnings	Women's earnings; male-female wage gap; women's representation in managerial and professional jobs; women's participation in the labor force
Reproductive rights	State scores on 8 legislative and political indicators: (1) access to abortion services without mandatory parental consent laws for minors; (2) access to abortion services without a waiting period; (3) public funding for abortions under any circumstances if eligible; (4) percentage of counties that have at least one abortion provider; (5) whether the governor or state legislature is pro-choice; (6) public funding of infertility treatments; (7) existence of a maternity stay law; (8) whether gay/lesbian couples can adopt

Sources: I. Kawachi, B. P. Kennedy, V. Gupta, & D. Prothrow Stith, "Women's Status and the Health of Women and Men: A View from the States." In I. Kawachi, B. P. Kennedy, & R. G. Wilkinson (Eds.), *The Society and Population Health Reader: Volume I, Income Inequality and Health* (New York: New Press, 1999), 476–477; Institute for Women's Policy Research, *The Status of Women in the States* (Washington, DC: Institute for Women's Policy Research, 1996).

The authors found that higher status among women was correlated with lower female mortality rates and lower activity limitations. For example, women's political participation was highest in Kansas and lowest in Tennessee, and their employment earnings were highest in Alaska and lowest in West Virginia (Kawachi et al. 1999). In states where women control more resources, have more autonomy, and are more involved politically, they live longer and have less activity limitations. Greater wage equality between men within states also was associated with lower female mortality rates and lower activity limitations. These findings suggest that Principle 6 (in Chapter 4) applies to gender stratification as well as to overall social stratification. Applying this principle to gender, we add Principle 7.

Principle 7

Within societies or communities where women have more equitable political and economic status with men, and ample reproductive rights, women will be healthier, less often disabled, and longer lived compared with women who live in places with less gender equality.

Kawachi and colleagues (1999) found that women's status was strongly correlated with male mortality rates as well. For example, where women's health was poor, it reflected "more general underlying structural processes associated with material deprivation and income inequality" (474). A wife's access to resources and better health is also connected to her husband's class position. For example, nonemployed women married to high-earning husbands benefit from their husbands' resources and social status. Their health relative to women lower down the social hierarchy reflects that advantage. However, if an upper-middle-class woman lives in Mississippi, which has the lowest score for women's economic autonomy (as defined in Table 6.2), then she will benefit less than a woman from Maryland, the state with the highest score for women's status (Kawachi et al. 1999).

Kawachi and colleagues found regional patterns in women's status. States in the Southeast (Kentucky, Virginia, West Virginia, Tennessee, Georgia, Mississippi, and Louisiana) had the lowest scores in at least two out of four of the composite indices of women's status (described in Table 6.2). Midwestern states generally had the highest scores, including Minnesota, Wisconsin, Iowa, Kansas, and Missouri. These states were more likely to be among the highest-scoring third on two or more of the indices.

Although the measures of women's status are complex, we can be fairly confident that they were measuring similar patterns and processes related to women's status, because the correlations among the four indices were high.[2] An exception was the low correlation between women's political participation and reproductive rights. This suggests, for example, that women may participate in voting and other aspects of political life at high levels within a state that does not support women's reproductive rights. Using the four indices together helps to minimize the lack of uniform association between all the measures of women's status.

In the analysis of the fifty states, women's economic autonomy was negatively associated with female death rates from cerebrovascular disease (which causes stroke), cervical cancer, and murder. (Women are most often murdered by their husbands, boyfriends, former husbands, or former boyfriends.) Infant mortality was also lower in states with greater female economic autonomy. This resembles the trend in World Health Organization data that shows that, where women's standard of living and health improve, infant and child health improves as well.

A parallel study examined how violence against wives varies with the relative status of women in the fifty states. Kersti Yllo (1999) hypothesized that wives would experience less wife beating in states with greater gender equity, due to three factors.

1. Husbands' historically protected rights to use physical force against their wives would be weaker.
2. Women's greater economic independence would help them to leave abusive relationships.
3. More services and protections would be available to women in more equitable states.

---

[2] Correlations between the four indices were from 0.5 to 0.89. There was a low correlation between political participation and reproductive rights, which had an r of 0.24, for reasons discussed in the text.

Yllo measured women's status using clusters of variables organized into categories of economic, educational, political, and legal conditions. Violence was defined as an act carried out with the knowledge that the likely consequences would be physical injury or pain to another person (Yllo 1999, 452). The data were gathered in a national sample of 2,143 adults who were living with a person of the opposite sex (Straus et al. 1980). Over 98 percent were legally married. Hour-long interviews were done in subjects' homes. In the analysis, states were divided into five groups according to their overall ranking regarding the status of women.

Yllo's study found that the level of violence is highest in those states where the overall status of women is lowest, and the level of violence drops as women's status improves in more equitable states. However, the statistical relationship for all five groups of states and violence against women was not linear. A different pattern emerges in the one-fifth of states with the highest female status. In those states, the violence is almost as high as in the states with the lowest female status. What should we make of this pattern? One interpretation is that, during the period studied, the late 1970s and early 1980s, a transition in women's status was under way. The states with highest female status may be seen as the vanguard of the trend toward improved structural positions and social status for women. Steinmetz and Straus's (1974) notion of short-term and long-term trends in wife beating helps to explain why, during transition periods in which patriarchal and egalitarian norms clash, there may be increased marital conflict and violence.

Yllo's findings do *not* suggest that sexual equity increases domestic violence. Rather, she concludes that, under conditions of greater gender equity, there is less violence against wives. This coincides with theories of gender inequality: When women have greater access to resources and social institutions support greater equity, women and their children benefit in a variety of ways. Under more equitable conditions, women are more able to take care of their household, secure education for themselves and their children, care for their health, find employment that pays a living wage, and gain protection when they encounter violence.

A Global Approach to Racial and Ethnic Differences in Health

At a Harvard Medical School commencement address in 1999, the surgeon general of the United States, David Satcher, drew attention to American health inequalities.

> An African-American baby born in this country today is almost two and a half times as likely to die in the first year of life as his or her white counterpart; an American Indian baby, one and a half times more likely. . . . A Vietnamese woman in this country today is five times as likely to suffer cervical cancer; Asian Americans, three to five times as likely to experience liver cancer. . . . And some of our American Indian tribes are three times as likely to be diabetic. . . . African-American men are twice as likely to suffer prostate cancer before age 65. ("Satcher Calls for Nation to Close Disparities in Health and Care" 1999, 1)

Ethnic and race relations are fairly specific to societies, although they spill over national borders as well. Here we present perspectives for thinking about racial and ethnic health disparities. The first is an extension of Principle 6, which recognizes inequalities in health according to one's position in the social hierarchy. By recognizing that race and ethnicity concentrate groups at various locations in that social hierarchy, we see that health advantages or disadvantages correspond to that position. In large part, health differences among ethnic and racial groups are statistically explained by social class position. However, ethnicity or race explains an additional amount of the statistical variance. Consequently, we may add Principle 8 to our list.

Principle 8

Ethnicity and race have effects on health that are independent of social class.

Marginalized ethnic and racial groups have less access to resources such as well-funded schools and safe neighborhoods. In extreme circumstances, ethnic minorities can even become the target of state-sponsored genocide. This occurred in Iraq when Saddam Hussein waged a campaign against the Kurdish minority in the northern part of the country. In the United States, police have been accused of using deadly force more often in low-income African-American and Latino communities. And police in several communities and on several highways have been found to pull over cars driven by persons of color more frequently. This is but one way that stress from racist treatment causes higher baseline and acute physiological stress responses, which cause higher rates of disease and death.

It can be argued that racist ideologies have played a role in maintaining global as well as national inequalities. Racist justifications are sometimes offered to rationalize poor living conditions or violent conflicts in peripheral countries. For example, "ancient hatreds between tribes" were offered to explain the genocide against the Tutsis by the Hutus in Rwanda and surrounding countries. This view obscured the roles played by African leaders seeking to expand their control over territory, the historical influences of Belgian colonial powers, corporations wishing to extract the region's natural resources, and the effects of IMF and World Bank structural adjustment programs in the 1980s.

Many peripheral nations have histories of colonial domination in which social Darwinist ideologies of cultural superiority were used to justify their rule. Influence today by more powerful countries is exercised primarily through trade relations, with political and military interventions used as needed to maintain conditions conducive to "free trade." These neocolonial relationships have a major impact on people of color throughout the world, even though their working and living conditions are still invisible to many Western consumers.

That race and ethnicity continue to play a role in disadvantaging the health of people in less-developed countries has become painfully clear in the AIDS pandemic. "Global apartheid" is the concept that two authors from the organization Africa Action (Booker & Minter 2001) apply to the global dynamics of AIDS. The term *apartheid* suggests an "international system of minority rule," in which disparities and separation become entrenched and institutionalized (15). The authors point out that, of the 3 million AIDS deaths during the year 2000, 2.4 million occurred in sub-Saharan Africa. They argue that inequalities of race, class, gender, and geography have determined access to life-saving medicines and care for people with HIV disease (Booker & Minter 2001, 11).

Health Differences Among Racial and Ethnic Groups in the United States

Health differences among various racial and ethnic groups in the United States are due mostly to social class differences. For example, we know that poverty causes poor health and that there are three times as many African Americans and Latinos as whites living in poverty in the United States. However, ethnicity and race account for a substantial proportion of the variation in health as well (Williams & Collins 1995).

Racial and ethnic lines often become drawn between social groups in the process of competition over such resources as territory, wealth, or prestige. Cultural differences exist between groups but often are exaggerated to rationalize competition and conflict. As health and race expert David R. Williams (2000) describes it,

> Although widely shared in our society, the belief that races are human populations that differ from each other primarily in terms of genetics is not supported by the existing scientific data. There is more genetic variation within races than between them, and racial categories do not capture biological distinctiveness. Regardless of geographical origin or race, all human beings are identical for about 75 percent of known genetic factors. (240)

Created by cultures, the effects of race become institutionalized and woven into behavioral norms. Erroneous beliefs about gene pools and other biological differences are sometimes used to rationalize racist beliefs. Cultural differences in areas such as language or dress also become symbolic cues for drawing distinctions between "us" and "them." Even indigenous peoples such as Native Americans have been made to feel foreign and "other" by their repeated displacement. In the contemporary United States, we think of ethnic groups as Asians, Latinos, African Americans, and other peoples "of color," but the United States is a country of immigrants, all of whom have been seen as ethnic groups at various times. "Whites" are really a variety of ethnic groups, at earlier periods distinguished from one another by language, dress, and customs. In waves of immigration, Italians, Germans, Irish, Jews, and many other groups experienced prejudice and competition over jobs, neighborhoods, and social status.

"Internal colonialism" is a concept meaning that, within national boundaries, particular groups are treated as inferior. The effects of internal colonialism (Blauner 1969) are evident in the strikingly higher disease and death rates of Native Americans and African Americans. Neighborhoods that are dirty and crime ridden, along with residential segregation, have bad effects on health. Violence and illegal drug use, sometimes stereotypically associated with particular ethnic groups, are in fact more closely related to social class. For example, rates of violent deaths in New Jersey were found to be associated, not with race, but with living in a poor environment. Violent deaths were associated with residence in those urban areas having a concentration of environmental risks, such as waste incinerators, landfills, and deserted factories (Greenberg & Schneider 1994). Poison exposure and violence are the prices paid for being among the urban poor, and sometimes among the rural poor as well. The greater concentration of toxic dumps in low-income African-American and Latino neighborhoods is called "environmental racism." In the New Jersey study, violent deaths, poisonings, overdoses, fires, and suicides in poor areas were ten times higher for men and six times higher for women than among other New Jersey residents. Deaths were higher across all ethnic groups and ages living in these dangerous, polluted areas (Greenberg & Schneider 1994; Williams & Collins 1995).

Carl Bell's study (1997) of stress-related disorders among African-American children in Chicago found that many children were suffering from posttraumatic stress disorder (PTSD). PTSD takes its toll on health by overactivating the body's alarm system; stress chemicals flood the bloodstream, triggering changes in tissues and organs. Over time, too much of this stress reaction causes increased wear and tear on the body and in particular contributes to plaque buildup on the walls of the arteries. In Bell's study of children, symptoms of PTSD showed up as problems in school, as illness, or as acting-out behavior, but Bell discovered that the underlying causes were related to poverty and violence. Among these children, 26 percent reported that they had seen a person shot, and 29 percent reported having seen a stabbing. The children showed a variety of adverse effects. A ten-year-old's grades dropped, and he reported feeling sick to his stomach. In counseling, it came out that the boy had been with his father during the father's shooting death in an elevator. Only following grief therapy was the boy able to return to focusing on his studies. Another victim of violence, a thirteen-year-old girl, saw her school grades drop from A's to D's and stay there for two years. The school counselor advised two additional hours of study a night, but therapy revealed that she was having flashbacks to a sexual assault by her father when she was six years old. She had received therapy following the incident, but at age thirteen, flashbacks took over whenever she sat down to study. With another round of therapy sessions, she was able to function normally again. Bell encourages teachers, counselors, and other professionals to explore whether children with a variety of symptoms are experiencing posttraumatic stress disorder and to offer PTSD therapy (Bell 1997).

African Americans.   At each level of socioeconomic status, African Americans generally have worse health status than whites (Williams & Collins 1995). African Americans have shorter lives and more years with chronic health problems. The racial gap in health is spread across all domains of health (fatal and nonfatal chronic diseases, impairments, and functional difficulties). By controlling for variables, analysis of the evidence has revealed that socioeconomic conditions, not health risk behaviors, are the primary causes of African Americans' health disparities (Hayward et al. 2000).

In their extensive review of the literature on race and health, Williams and Collins (1995) note that income measures of socioeconomic status underplay the actual economic differences in wealth and standard of living between African-

American and white households at the same income levels. Inheritance, assets, and accumulation of wealth are much lower among African-American and Latino households than for whites with the same incomes (Eller 1994).

From review of the evidence, Williams and Collins conclude, "A growing body of theoretical and empirical work suggests that racism is a central determinant of the health status of oppressed racial and ethnic populations" (1995, 366). Lower incomes and less access to jobs may be viewed as an aspect of racism; by every measurement of socioeconomic status, African Americans are lower than whites (Farley & Allen 1987; Jaynes & Williams 1989). In addition to economic disadvantage, racism involves negative attitudes, behaviors, and differential treatment by agencies and businesses. Now reported in the media, "racial profiling" involves systematically different treatment of persons of color while they are engaged in public activities such as driving or shopping. For example, a recent study by the Immigration and Naturalization Service found that African-American women reentering the country were systematically strip-searched in airports more frequently than other citizens ("State Woman Testifies About Strip Search Humiliation" 2001).

Residential segregation greatly intensifies the harmful effects of inequality. In African-American neighborhoods, food, housing, goods, and services are often of poorer quality and are more expensive (Cooper 1984; King & Williams 1995). African Americans' lower-quality public schools are also a result of residential segregation and partial reliance on local funding for elementary and high schools. Poorer education, in turn, reduces access to jobs and further training. Even with higher education, the economic returns are lower for African Americans, and lower for African-American men than African-American women (Williams & Collins 1995). This structural disadvantage has major impacts on quality of life, family stability, emotional and physical health, and longevity.

The following examples illustrate the pervasive effects of racism on health:

- Employed African Americans are more likely than whites to be exposed to hazards and carcinogens, even when the data are adjusted for relative amounts of job experience and education (Robinson 1984).
- Racial discrimination has adverse effects on psychological well-being and can increase risk of cardiovascular disease. Racist disrespect can increase the likelihood of depression, anxiety, and substance abuse.
- A study of racial disrespect in the fifty states found that the degree of collective prejudice varied geographically and that a high rate of African-American mortality is associated with locations where racist views are pervasive (Kennedy et al. 1999b).
- African Americans who internalize racist ideologies have increased risk of disease and premature death (Williams et al. 1994).
- Persons with darker skin combined with a higher-status lifestyle were found to have the highest levels of blood pressure (Dressler 1993).
- Skin color was a stronger predictor of income and occupational status than parental socioeconomic status in the National Study of Black Americans (Keith & Herring 1991.)

Perhaps symptomatic of racism are African Americans' higher rates of hypertension. When class is controlled for, the difference from whites weakens but does not disappear. Middle-class African Americans have lower rates of hypertension than low-income African Americans, but higher rates than white middle-class people. Thus upward mobility into the middle class improves but does not eliminate the higher African-American risk for hypertension. Racism influences African Americans' greater vulnerability to health problems at all socioeconomic levels (Anderson & Armstead 1995). There is also evidence that disadvantages from childhood have cumulative effects. Consequently, a life course perspective, which examines experiences and changes over a lifetime, is needed to appreciate health patterns. It provides depth of understanding beyond examining income differences and health at fixed points in time. For example, some studies find that mortality rates are high even for African Americans at higher economic levels; this suggests cumulative harmful effects of racism even when a middle-class lifestyle is maintained during adulthood.

It is a reasonable hypothesis that spending childhood in a racially segregated, low-income neighborhood predisposes individuals to greater physical and mental health problems throughout life. For example, obesity and high blood pressure are similar among ethnic groups in childhood, but differences become evident in early adulthood (Kumanyika 1987; Williams 1992). For some reason, infant mortality rates decrease with the age of white and Latino mothers, but *increase* for African-American and Puerto Rican mothers (Geronimus 1992). The effects of poor living conditions perhaps accumulate over time for low-income mothers.

For psychological distress, there are mixed findings regarding race and ethnicity. One study found that controlling for socioeconomic status reduced but did not eliminate the higher psychological distress among African Americans as compared with whites (Kessler & Neighbors 1986). Another study found that low-socioeconomic-status white males had higher rates of psychiatric disorders than did their African-American peers (Williams et al. 1992). Overall, African Americans have lower rates of drug and alcohol abuse than whites. The exception is low-income African-American females' higher levels of substance abuse than their white peers (Williams et al. 1992). Williams and Collins urge caution about making generalizations from the available evidence. Psychological distress, which is not mental illness, must be distinguished from mental disorders, and the interplay of race, gender, and class needs to be recognized in mental health.

There is some good news on the apparent resiliency of African Americans. Long periods of low income are associated with poorer health for adult men generally, and we can surmise that there are stressful effects on their family members as well. However, a national study found that, for African-American children in the category of lowest long-term income, ongoing poverty was unrelated to either stunting of growth or a wasting condition. By contrast, there are strong indications of these problems among Latino and white children in the same economic category (Miller & Korenman 1994). Another study found that, among neonates (infants up to twenty-seven days old), low birth weight was more strongly associated with mortality for African Americans than for whites (Hogue et al. 1987). What this means is that high

The combined effects of poverty and racism are harmful to health and have lifelong effects.

infant mortality among African Americans is more clearly linked to the problem of low birth weight than for whites, where there is more diversity of causes for infant mortality. The reason for this difference is unknown, but perhaps social networks of extended family, church groups, and friends partially buffer the effects of low income and low birth weight on African-American babies' health.

There are differences in health care as well. A review of medical care services found that African Americans are less likely to receive a wide range of services than are whites (Council on Ethical and Judicial Affairs 1990). The relationship held up even when the researchers controlled for the severity of the illness, socioeconomic status, and insurance status. An example is provided by a study of cardiologists; they were found to refer African-American women for a cardiac catheterization 60 percent less than white women (Schulman et al. 1999). This procedure is commonly used to test blood flow, and the study authors surmise that African-American women are denied access only due to doctors' prejudice.

A surgeon general's study of mental health services found that minorities receive inferior and fewer services. The study examined the mental health care received by African Americans, Latinos, Asian Americans and Pacific Islanders, and Native Americans and Alaska Natives. These groups are overrepresented among the most vulnerable, including the poor, homeless, institutionalized, incarcerated, and survivors of traumatic events (Goode 2001).

Unfortunately, class disparities in African-American health are increasing (Williams & Collins 1995). To reduce inequalities in chronic diseases such as hypertension, heart disease, and prostate cancer requires preventive and primary care, as well as structural changes to reduce inequalities.

Latinos. Several different groups are included in the category of "Latino" or "Hispanic," including those that originate in Mexico, Puerto Rico, Cuba, and Central and South America. Their histories and locations in the United States social structure vary, as do their patterns of health. Latino groups have diverse migratory histories, assimilation processes, and geographical locations. These have produced socioeconomic, cultural, and health variations (Bean & Tienda 1987; Rogers et al. 2000; Vega & Amaro 1994). The following discussion uses the term *Latino* but includes both grouped U.S. health data (under the category "Hispanic") and information about specific groups.

Puerto Ricans' health patterns are influenced by their concentration at lower income levels. Puerto Ricans have poorer health and longevity, for example, than Mexican Americans. Cubans are more often middle class and higher income, and fare better in health. Latinos in general and Mexican Americans in particular do not share with African Americans the pattern of strong association between social class and health outcomes. Life expectancy for Mexican Americans is equal to or higher than for whites, despite their lower socioeconomic status (Markides & Coreil 1986). In this "epidemiologic paradox," Mexican Americans have longevity comparable to whites' despite their greater likelihood of being unemployed, low income, and without a high school degree (Rogers et al. 2000). In addition, Mexican Americans have experienced a long history of ethnic discrimination. The reasons behind their longevity are not fully understood but may be related to tightly knit families and communities, religiosity, diet, and additional health-promoting aspects of the culture.

First-generation immigrants have a health advantage compared to U.S.-born members of the same ethnic group. This "healthy immigrant effect" may be partially the result of self-selection of immigrants who are healthier and more motivated than their counterparts who remain at home. James (1993) proposes that Mexican immigrants also benefit from the cultural factors mentioned above, including a strong sense of belonging and obligation to extended family and community. For many, their support networks apparently buffer the difficulties of immigration; these benefits fade if immigrants become acculturated and also weaken with the next generation's acclimation to American culture.

Acculturation involves loss of many practices beneficial to health. These include decreased fiber consumption; decreased breast feeding; increased use of cigarettes and alcohol, especially in young women; driving under the influence of alcohol; and the use of illegal drugs (Vega & Amaro 1994).

Poverty, prejudice, and immigration difficulties affect Latinos' lives in serious ways. Latinos are two and a half times as likely to live in poverty and half as likely as non-Latino whites to complete college. Latino children are less likely than white children to receive the standard vaccinations before the age of three and twice as likely to have no regular source of health care (Centers for Disease Control and Prevention 1997, 1998.) Latinos are at heightened risk for diabetes and its serious complications, and they die at higher rates than the general population from drug use and violence (Weitz 2000). Due to higher rates of cigarette smoking, Latinos have higher death rates from hypertension and lung cancer. Young adults have higher risk of chronic liver disease, homicide, and HIV disease than whites; Latinos overall are twice as likely as whites to die from HIV disease (Rogers et al. 2000).

Migrant Mexican-American laborers have especially harsh living conditions and environmentally hazardous work in farming and meat-packing industries. As agricultural workers, they are exposed to toxic pesticides, herbicides, and fertilizers; must stoop and use repetitive motions for long hours; and have limited access to drinkable water and toilets (Gwyther & Jenkins 1998; Sandhaus 1998; Weitz 2000). Housing is poor and crowded, and health care is often unavailable or hampered by language differences, cultural differences, or fears of deportation. Women suffer higher rates of miscarriage, and infant mortality is several times higher than in the general population. As a result of all these factors, migrant workers have higher rates of chronic and infectious diseases (Gwyther & Jenkins 1998; Sandhaus 1998). As with low-income African Americans, migrant Mexican-American workers have health patterns influenced by both their social class and racism.

Native Americans. Native American peoples are diverse, with ancestry in 500 culturally different and geographically dispersed tribes. A federally financed program, the Indian Health Service is responsible for providing health care to Native Americans, both on and off reservations. Grouping together Native Americans to examine disease patterns reveals some differences from other ethnic groups. Infant mortality has been reduced in the second half of the twentieth century but is still greater than among whites (Kunitz 1996). Neonatal infant mortality (death within the first twenty-seven days) is equal to whites', but during the post neonatal period (from the twenty-eighth day to eleven months), infant mortality is twice as high among Native Americans as among whites (Weitz 2000). Causes of infant death include pneumonia and gastritis, which are related to poverty and are preventable with prompt medical care (Rhoades et al. 1987). Native Americans have lower cancer rates, in large part because they have shorter lives, dying from infectious diseases and accidents before cancers become fatal.

Alcohol use takes a heavy toll on Native American health. Indians are nearly three times more likely to die from liver disease and cirrhosis than are whites. They are also more likely to die from homicide and unintentional injuries, often related to alcohol use (Weitz 2000). Native American teenagers are at far greater risk of serious injury and death than other American teens. They have more fights and attempted and actual suicides; accidents contribute to a mortality rate twice as high as among American teens overall. For Native American *males*, the rate is three times as high (Weitz 2000; Blum et al. 1992).

Asian Americans. Asian Americans, taken as a group, have the lowest mortality rates in the United States. Asian Americans experience the same causes of death as whites, except for lower rates of cardiovascular disease. The latter is hypothesized to be related to dietary differences, including lower consumption of meat and dairy products. As with Latinos, the category "Asian Americans" obscures wide differences in country of origin, language, culture, immigration experiences, geographic location, and occupational status. The National Health Interview Survey (NHIS) data set used by Rogers and colleagues in *Living and Dying in the USA* (2000) includes Chinese, Filipinos, Asian Indians, Vietnamese, Japanese, and Koreans. An additional designation is Pacific Islander, which is included with Asians for some analyses. Like Latinos, a substantial proportion of Asian Americans are foreign born and also benefit from the immigrant advantage in their lower disease and death rates. At the turn of the twenty-first century, less than 20 percent of Asian Americans are U.S. born.

Since the end of the Vietnam War in 1975, many Southeast Asian immigrants have come to the United States to escape war conditions or out of fear of postwar reprisals. Not enough is known about how these groups are faring in the United States, but there is some evidence of higher mortality rates (Association of Asian Pacific Community Health Organizations 1997; Weitz 2000). For example, Southeast Asian Americans are more likely to have tuberculosis and hepatitis B than the general population, and the latter causes higher rates of liver cancer (Weitz 2000). Several factors contribute to lower levels of medical care, including cultural and language differences, and lack of medical benefits through employers.

There is not sufficient evidence to conclude that Asian Americans differ significantly from other ethnic groups in their rates of mental illness. However, Asian Americans troubled by mental disturbance receive less care than several other groups. This is partially because the stigma of mental illness prevents them from approaching professionals when symptoms appear (Goode 2001). And, from wartime experiences, Southeast Asian groups of Vietnamese, Cambodian, and Hmong Americans may indeed suffer higher rates of PTSD and other emotional distress. In addition to a cultural stigma, a stereotype among mental health professionals that Asian Americans are mentally healthier than other groups may also operate as a barrier to care.

Conclusion

Unfortunately, class and ethnic disparities in health are increasing, rooted in economic disadvantage and prejudice. These inequalities affect individuals throughout the life course (Hayward et al. 2000). Health campaigns to change behaviors such as smoking, drinking, diet, and exercise will improve health, but it is doubtful that they will reduce the health inequalities among social groups. Reducing inequalities in chronic diseases such as hypertension, heart disease, and cancer requires long-term structural changes. For example, improving educational opportunities and access to jobs that pay a living wage, along with more progressive taxation policies, could create greater equality. Programs for young children, such as the Head Start program in the United States, are steps in the right direction. In addition, expanding the federal government's Earned Income Credit to assist low-income families has the potential to raise the standard of living and reduce income inequality. And universal access to primary health care also has the potential to reduce health disparities. Such measures are needed if the widening gap of economic and health disparities is to be narrowed.

7

Mental Health: Social and Global Issues

Mental disorders are not simply symptoms of broader social conditions; nevertheless, poverty, lack of security, violence, the lack of healthy family relationships during childhood, and trauma or significant losses . . . are crucial factors for mental illness. Indeed, although mental illnesses can be categorized and diagnosed, they most often are found in constellations that bind together biological forces, social conditions, cultural responses, and particular illness forms.

—Robert Desjarlais et al., *World Mental Health: Problems and Priorities in Low-Income Countries*

In American and Western European cultures, mental and physical health have been regarded as somewhat distinct. Today, however, the trend in both cultures and in global public health is toward viewing physical and mental health as parts of a whole. There is strong evidence that neuropsychiatric disorders are biosocial; that is, they have both biological and social causes. For example, evidence strongly suggests that quality of the social environment influences the risk of suffering mental disturbance, the triggering of an acute episode of mental illness, and the likelihood that the illness will become chronic (Desjarlais et al. 1995, 263). Our emotional relationships with family members and close friends influence the course of a wide range of psychological stress, distress, and disorders. In particular, events early in life and in the months preceding the onset of symptoms play a major role in determining whether emotional distress will turn into chronic depression or an anxiety disorder (Neff 2001, 151).

Public health and sociological research has revealed that social conditions such as high unemployment, poverty, violence, and low access to education are implicated in poor physical and mental health. Risk behaviors such as smoking, excessive drinking, drug use, and reckless driving are also intricately connected to our social relationships and to mental and physical health.

There is a "mental health gradient" linking socioeconomic status to mental illness. For example, cross-national studies have found that mood disorders, anxiety disorders, and substance-use disorders all are associated with indicators of socioeconomic status (World Health Organization, International Consortium in Psychiatric Epidemiology 2000). Despite the biological roots of some forms of mental illness, such as schizophrenia, the presence or absence of resources and health-promoting circumstances influences the management of symptoms, likelihood of disease onset, and psychotic episodes. Similarly, vulnerability to the more frequently experienced mental disturbances of depression, anxiety, and other neuroses is influenced by the social environment, emotional relationships, and the ability to receive effective care.

We consider the following questions:

- What are the major forms of mental illness, as identified by mental health experts, today?
- What role do social factors play in the onset of mental disturbance and mental illness?
- Do such social factors affect individuals in developed and underdeveloped countries in the same ways?
- Does economic development increase or decrease mental illness, and what are current global trends?
- What policies can improve mental health?

Major Categories of Mental Illness

During the twentieth century, mental disturbances became medicalized; that is, defined and treated as biologically based diseases. During the last three decades of the twentieth century, psychiatry began to conceptualize mental illness as a set of discrete disorders that are acute or chronic in form and can be treated more or less successfully by specific drugs, psychosocial interventions, and rehabilitative care (Desjarlais et al. 1995, 39). Still controversial is the relative causal weight given to genetic and other biological causes as opposed to social and experiential causes. Considerable resources have been devoted to discovering genetic markers and other biological causes of mental illness. Desjarlais and colleagues (1995, 36) criticize this trend: "Since the 1970s, the 'brainless' social psychiatry of the 1950s has too often been replaced by a 'mindless' biological psychiatry, deflecting attention from the social factors so obviously important to understanding the burden of mental illness."

An example of medicalization of a behavioral pattern, perhaps for social control reasons, is the recent history of attention deficit/hyperactivity disorder (ADHD). The diagnostic criteria in the *Diagnostic and Statistical Manual (DSM IV)* are entirely *behavioral*, rather than identifying patterns of *psychological* dysfunction. For example, the diagnostic list in the *DSM IV* lists indications of inattention ("often fails to give close attention to details or makes careless mistakes in schoolwork, work, or other activities"), hyperactivity ("often fidgets with hands or feet or squirms in seat"), and impulsivity ("often blurts out answers before questions have been completed") (Eaton 2001, 31). It is not entirely clear whether this new "illness" is instead a function of a changing society in which many children receive inadequate nurturing and limit setting at home (and are thus less able to focus), larger school class sizes, and teachers who have trouble controlling their classrooms. In any case, the newly emerging medications during the 1960s and 1970s strongly influenced the spread of diagnosis of hyperactive children. Ritalin calmed them down, yielding its company 15 percent of its gross profits in 1971 (Eaton 2001, 32–33).

The cultural specificity versus the universality of mental illnesses is a matter of debate. Given these uncertainties, the following categories provide current Western definitions of mental illness and guideposts for its global investigation. They do not assume universal cultural interpretations of symptoms or illness.

Affective Disorders

This category includes disturbed moods or feelings, including primarily depression or elation. One major diagnosis within this category is bipolar affective (or manic depressive) disorder, which involves repeated swings in the individual's mood, energy level, and activity, between depressed mood and decreased energy, and periods of elation and overactivity (mania). There are normal periods, but the mood swings recur. Unipolar depressive disorder is the same but without the episodes of mania.

Depression may occur as one single episode in a lifetime, but that is relatively uncommon. More frequent are repeated depressive episodes, or episodes alternating with mania as part of a bipolar disorder. In addition to sadness and diminished pleasure in daily life, intense depression interferes with individuals' ability to function normally in work and interpersonal relationships. For some individuals and especially in some cultures, depression includes such physical symptoms as chronic pain, fatigue, and headaches. In addition, suicide is a risk of major depression. Depression results in a substantial proportion of requests for care in primary health care settings, perhaps as high as one-fifth to one-third of visits (Desjarlais et al. 1995; Almeida-Filho 1993). Clinical depression may be of moderate to severe intensity, and it is much more common than schizophrenia—occurring perhaps ten times more frequently (Robins & Regier 1992).

Depressed persons experience as much disability and distress as patients with chronic medical disorders such as heart disease, diabetes, or arthritis. However, only a minority are properly diagnosed and treated. Depression tends to run in families, and individuals may have some inherited vulnerability. Still, it is important to understand that depression is rooted in social conditions, emotional relationships, and biological dynamics, in both its origins and its relative responsiveness to recovery. Relapse is also common; therefore, the availability of care over a lifetime is essential if quality of life is to be enhanced.

Processes of modernization have been associated with increases in rates of depression. This has been documented in recent years in Taiwan, the United States,

Western Europe, Lebanon, and Puerto Rico (Cross-National Collaborative Group 1992). Rapid social change and uprooting of community ties is certainly one explanation, as they entail unemployment and weakened social support from kin. At the other end of the spectrum, specialization in the modern work force plays a role in the routinization of many jobs. Consequently, a lack of purpose often plagues workers, and job insecurity is increasingly an aspect of middle-class as well as working-class jobs. These issues will be examined further in the discussion of economic development below.

Anxiety Disorders

Anxiety disorders are characterized by feelings of anxiousness and avoidance of social situations that produce those feelings. They include panic disorder, phobias, obsessive-compulsive disorder, generalized anxiety disorder, and posttraumatic stress disorder. Anxiety disorders have a high prevalence, close to that of depression. However, particular communities may have especially high rates. In part of Bahia, Brazil, 14 percent of villagers were found to have anxiety disorders, and women had double the rates of men (Almeida-Filho 1993). Anxiety may vary in the way individuals experience physical symptoms, especially given cultural differences. Latino cultures may identify "nerves" (*nervios*), whereas in Iran, individuals may experience "heart distress," and in China, fatigue and dizziness (Desjarlais et al. 1995, 46).

Panic disorder includes episodes of intense fear or discomfort, which include shortness of breath, dizziness, sweating, and often a fear of dying or being crazy. Agoraphobia can be part of this syndrome. If a person is fearful of being without escape in such a state, he or she will stay isolated at home. Obsessive-compulsive disorder includes intrusive and repetitive thoughts and behaviors that are senseless, yet difficult to control. Generalized anxiety disorder manifests itself in fear and worry about misfortune, motor tension, and overactivity of the autonomic nervous system (for example, shortness of breath, palpitations, dry mouth). Posttraumatic stress disorder (PTSD) involves repeated and persistent response to a trauma or catastrophic event or experience. PTSD interferes with functioning to the extent that flashbacks and physiological symptoms intrude on work, sleep, and interpersonal relationships.

Schizophrenia

This category is composed of a group of severe mental disorders that first appear in late adolescence or early adulthood. They are devastating in their symptoms and behavioral aspects, as well as in the disruption caused within families. Schizophrenia is most closely aligned with the notion of "psychosis" or "madness" across cultures. This category is seen to have some genetic influence, but heredity accounts for less than half of the variance in occurrence of the disease. There is no single gene for schizophrenia, and its specific cause is unknown. Its manifestations and acute episodes are influenced by social and environmental factors, but there is controversy over the extent to which harsh physical and social living conditions bring on psychosis. In many cultures, the stigma as well as the behavior of the psychotic individual is feared, and often families attempt to "normalize" or explain away the behavior. But, as time passes and symptoms progress, family members are more likely to yield to recognizing the symptoms as mental illness. Some cultures subject psychotic individuals to brutal treatment, even caging or starving them (Desjarlais et al. 1995, 39). Acute episodes are characterized by delusions (false beliefs), hallucinations (disembodied voices or visions), jumbled and incoherent thoughts, moods out of harmony with thoughts, and lack of awareness of being ill. Chronic schizophrenia includes symptoms of underactivity, apathy, and social withdrawal.

Cultural variations in interpreting the meaning of serious mental illness influence the response and recovery of individuals exhibiting symptoms of schizophrenia. For example, the World Health Organization conducted two cross-cultural studies of schizophrenia and found that sufferers in low-income countries had recovered at higher rates at a two-year followup than had those in developed countries (Waxler 1977; World Health Organization 1979). This difference may be related to cultural differences. Where those around the person have lower expectations that he or she will recover, this may actually inhibit improvement. If the disease is considered constitutional, as part of the self ("the schizophrenic"), there probably is less of an expectation that the person will change. By contrast, if the strange behavior is seen as being caused by spirits temporarily controlling the person, then recovery may be expected (Desjarlais et al. 1995, 43). The latter does not bring about recovery but may set a social and relational scene that makes recovery possible. On the other hand, where symptoms of mental illness persist, financial resources make continued treatment and stabilization of the condition over time possible.

Mental health professionals as well as advocates for the mentally ill now emphasize the need for persons with schizophrenia to live in the community. Short-term hospitalizations may be needed periodically to stabilize a patient before he or she returns to life in the community. Followup care is needed for support and monitoring to help prevent relapses. Medications, including neuroleptic drugs, can reduce acute symptoms and allow individuals to function outside of institutional settings. Supportive family, friends, and health care help individuals maintain social ties. Communities that support and reach out, rather than ostracize and react punitively, can create environments conducive to mental health for all citizens, not just the mentally disturbed.

A Cross-National Study of Mental Illness: Clues to the Global Prevalence and Correlates of Mental Illness

The World Health Organization established the International Consortium in Psychiatric Epidemiology (ICPE) in 1998 to carry out comparative studies of mental disorders. Studies were conducted in seven countries, including Canada, the United States, Brazil, Mexico, Germany, the Netherlands, and Turkey (WHO, International Consortium 2000). In face-to-face sessions, interviewers administered the Composite International Diagnostic Interview Schedule, the World Health Organization's mental health measurement instrument. Germany's respondents were excluded from some of the analyses because they were limited to an all-student sample. The total sample size was 29,644 persons, based on general population probability samples (not patient samples or quota samples). Respondents were fairly evenly divided between males and females. The majority of respondents were urban, although some urban samples included semi-rural subjects (who lived on the outskirts of the cities). The study focused on three broad classes of disorders: anxiety, mood, and substance use. Anxiety disorders included panic disorder, agoraphobia, simple phobia, social phobia, and generalized anxiety disorder. Mood disorders included depression, dysthymia (chronic depression), and mania. The substance-use category included dependence on or abuse of alcohol or drugs. The comparisons across countries are not perfect because of sample imperfections and cultural differences; nonetheless, the comparisons provide clues to the prevalence of mental illnesses, demographic correlates, initial treatment, and patterns of service (WHO, International Consortium 2000, 415).

Lifetime prevalence estimates varied widely across countries. More than one-third of the overall sample had at least one disorder at some time in their life. The percentages were as follows for countries with at least one-third of the sample having at least one lifetime episode: Brazil (36.3 percent), Canada (37.5 percent), Germany (38.4 percent), the Netherlands (40.9 percent), and the United States (48.6 percent). Lifetime prevalence estimates were considerably lower in Mexico (20.2 percent) and Turkey (12.2 percent) (WHO, International Consortium 2000, 416). Table 7.1 shows prevalence by country for anxiety disorders, mood disorders, and substance-use disorder.

Among the three broad classes, anxiety disorders were the most prevalent in Brazil, Canada, the Netherlands, and Turkey. Mood and substance-use disorders were found in at least one-third of individuals with any estimated lifetime disorder in

TABLE 7.1 *Prevalence of Disorders Among Those with Any Estimated Lifetime Disorder (study samples from Canada, United States, Brazil, Mexico, Germany, the Netherlands, and Turkey)*

Disorder	*Prevalence*	*Countries*
Anxiety disorders	Found in ≥ 1/3 of country samples	All except Mexico and Germany
Mood disorders	Found in ≥ 1/3 of country samples	All except Canada
Substance-use disorders	Found in ≥ 1/3 of country samples	All except Turkey, where substance use is not measured

Source: Developed from World Health Organization, International Consortium in Psychiatric Epidemiology, "Cross-National Comparisons of the Prevalence and Correlates of Mental Disorders," *Bulletin of the World Health Organization: The International Journal of Public Health* 78 (2000): 416–417.

all countries; the exceptions were for mood disorders in Canada and substance use in Turkey, where substance use was not measured. The evidence suggested that the anxiety disorders were more likely than other disorders to be chronically suffered over an extended period of time by the survey respondents. Comorbidity—that is, having two or more lifetime disorders—was common overall. It was highest in the United States, where having two conditions was estimated to be even more common (56.3 percent of lifetime cases) than having a single disorder.

Anxiety disorders had the youngest ages of onset, with a median of fifteen years (ranging from twelve years in Canada to eighteen years in the Netherlands). Mood disorders had the oldest age of onset, with a median of twenty-six years (ranging from twenty-three years in Canada, Mexico, and the United States to thirty years in Brazil). Substance-use disorders had a median age of onset of twenty-one years, with a more narrow range from eighteen years in Canada and the United States to twenty-two years in Mexico. Cultural norms and medical practice regarding recognizing symptoms and seeking care probably influenced these ages.

Gender differences appeared, but not uniformly; for example, women had a significantly higher prevalence of comorbidity than men in the Netherlands, Turkey, and the United States, but no clear sex difference appeared in the other countries. Consistent gender patterns appeared, however, across the three broad classes of disorders. Women had consistently higher prevalence of anxiety and mood disorders, whereas men had higher prevalence of substance-use disorders (WHO, International Consortium 2000, 418). Married individuals were estimated to have lower rates of comorbidity than unmarried couples in all seven surveys; however, that relationship was not statistically significant in Germany, Mexico, or Turkey.

Vulnerability to mental illness was associated with lower socioeconomic status. For example, the highest estimated prevalence was found among those with the lowest levels of education in six of the seven countries (Germany's association was not statistically significant but involved a student sample). However, high education is not necessarily associated with low prevalence. There does not seem to be a uniform increase in positive mental health as one moves up the socioeconomic ladder, at least as measured by education. Thus a cab driver's doctorate does not protect him from mental illness, but a better-paying and higher-status job might. The study found a significant inverse relationship between income and incidence of mental illness in three of the four countries for which income was measured (Canada, the Netherlands, United States; Mexico was the exception). Unemployed respondents reported the highest prevalence in five of six countries (with Turkey being the exception; there were no unemployed respondents in the Brazilian sample). There is a weak but consistent relationship indicating higher levels of mental illness among urban respondents. Higher mental illness in urban areas is a concern, as technological, economic, and political developments around the globe are driving populations to more densely populated urban areas.

The United States had the highest rates of estimated lifetime disorder in all three categories. The higher rate of substance-use disorder was especially striking: 28 percent of the United States sample had substance dependency or abuse, as compared to the next highest, in Germany, with just under 22 percent. However, the German sample included only students and therefore does not provide the best comparison. The next closest was the Netherlands at 19 percent. Mexico had the lowest rate of substance-use disorder, with just under 10 percent (WHO, International Consortium 2000, 417). The U.S. anxiety disorders (25 percent) were substantially higher than Germany's (9 percent); however, this percentage may be low due to the student sample. The Netherlands sample was next closest to the United States, with a 20 percent rate of anxiety disorder. The Turkish sample had low rates of both anxiety and mood disorders (both 7 percent). Mexico's anxiety disorder rate was the lowest, with less than 6 percent.

The authors of the study found a "cohort effect" of increasing lifetime prevalence of mental illness among younger age groups. This means that, in more recent generations, there is increasing mental illness in all three classes of disorders. The highest rates are for depression (WHO, International Consortium 2000, 420).

Poverty, Unemployment, and Job Insecurity

Poverty affects mental health in many of the same ways that it affects physical health, including inadequate nutrition, housing, and primary health care. Income levels affect the resources and attention that parents are able to devote to their children and their education, the security of neighborhoods, and protection from accidents and violence. Poverty lowers the quality of everyday life and limits the resources that enhance health (money, food, housing, education, jobs). Poverty increases intrusions from and vulnerability to harmful people, institutions, and the natural environment. Poverty often harms infants' and children's neurological and cognitive development. Chronic stress in childhood lays the groundwork for later vulnerability to depression and harm-related behaviors, such as substance abuse and violence.

The threat of job loss is bad for individuals' mental and physical health; this has been demonstrated by numerous studies (Bartley et al. 1999, 90). Fear of job loss may disturb sleep, increase blood pressure, and bring on symptoms of depression and anxiety. Job insecurity causes increased emotional disturbance (Arnetz et al. 1988), physiological changes (Cobb et al. 1966), and increased need of medical care (Beale and Nethercott 1985, 1987). Insecure jobs are also harder on the mind and body generally; they are more likely to involve exposure to harmful chemicals, heavy lifting, accidents, and injuries (Robinson 1986). Those most likely to experience unemployment may also be more vulnerable to illness because of hardships experienced earlier in life (Bartley et al. 1999, 91).

During periods of high unemployment, populations become more vulnerable to health problems. Working-class skilled and unskilled workers in the United States have experienced major job losses since the mid-1970s due to the decline in the manufacturing sector. The more plentiful service-sector jobs do not offer the same opportunities for pay and benefits. Job insecurity is not limited to the manufacturing sector. In fact, it is becoming more and more a fact of life in postindustrial societies. As markets drive businesses up and down the ladder of success, more middle-class workers are experiencing job insecurities. Technological innovations progress rapidly for example, robotics for manufacturing, computer software and chips to drive various work and information processes. Workers are laid off and must attempt to find themselves another niche in the economy. Those who do find another niche often must retrain and accept lower wages, forgoing benefits and job security.

Large numbers of educated, unemployed, and disappointed workers may lead to a deterioration of mental and physical health in the society generally. This occurred in the case of Russia. The U.S. population is coping with the insecurities of a quickly changing society, in part through the use of antidepressant medications. Family and community relationships are more transient, and globally, many welfare states have trimmed back their social programs and safety nets. Rapid social change, urbanization, high numbers of refugees, job insecurity, and unemployment are likely to continue to contribute to higher rates of mental illness in less-developed as well as in technologically sophisticated countries.

Social Support and Mental Health

Emile Durkheim's nineteenth-century study of suicide revealed that socially isolated people have higher rates of suicide (1897/1966). Also, adults who lose a loved one suffer unexpectedly high levels of illness and death (Stansfeld 1999, 165), especially during the year following the death of a spouse (Parkes et al. 1969). The effects of loss are not uniform; however, there is a consensus among researchers that social support buffers the effects of loss and major life events (for example, births, deaths, migrations, job loss) on minor psychiatric disorders (Aneshensel & Stone 1982; Kessler & McLeod 1985). Social support has also been found to buffer the effects of chronic and acute stressors generally (Brown & Harris 1978).

Especially of interest in a social approach to mental health are prospective community studies of mental health, because they examine the buffering and interactive effects of social support on mental health over time. George Brown, a British sociologist, made major contributions to understanding the social influences on emotional distress—in particular, on depression among women. Brown et al. (1986) found that the presence of a close friend had a protective effect for single mothers prior to experiencing a life event, and the absence of "crisis support" for women resulted in greater depression. In addition, women expecting emotional support who were let down by its unavailability when they experienced a life event were at greater risk of developing depression than others in the study. In comparison to a control group of women who did not become depressed, during the three months prior to onset of depression, the depressed women experienced an excess of threatening life events. In addition, comparing women who experienced these threatening events, three factors were associated with the women who became clinically depressed: loss of the woman's mother before age eleven, having three young children at home to care for (in the present), and the absence of an intimate relationship with a partner or close friend.

Henderson's community study in Canberra, Australia (1981), found that individuals who were more weakly integrated into the community and more weakly attached to others had more neurotic symptoms. Men and women had somewhat different perceptions of supportive relationships; close relationships were more important for women, whereas more diffuse relationships were more important to men. Both men and women who perceived their relationships as inadequate along those lines were more likely to develop neurotic symptoms (Stansfeld 1999, 166).

The British civil servant (Whitehall) study discussed in Chapter 4 also found a protective effect of emotional support on mental health. Men who had emotional support from the closest person in their life generally had good mental health (Stansfeld et al. 1998). Women experienced a beneficial effect of social support on mental health when there was support from up to four close friends (Fuhrer et al. 1999). For those suffering from a psychiatric condition, such as schizophrenia, critical comments, hostility, and overinvolvement from the primary group were related to higher risk of psychotic relapse (Bebbington & Kuipers 1994).

In recovery from depression, supportive ties play a role. However, gender differences appear here as well. In one study, recovery was predicted by the number of primary group members named and contacted by women patients (Brugha et al. 1990). For men this was not the case; their recovery was associated with being married and having negative interactions with primary group members. What should we make of the negative interactions associated with men's recovery? Perhaps issues come to the surface of relationships when men are in clinical care for depression that otherwise remain unaddressed.

Throughout the life cycle, social support influences mental health in the present and also lays groundwork for the future. Although popular psychology often emphasizes the repetition of unhealthy patterns learned in childhood, substantial proportions of those with a troubled childhood learn new ways to carry out parental and marital roles, and in the process avoid clinical depression. For example, one-third of women who had experienced disrupted home environments and been "in care" during their childhood later demonstrated good parenting abilities themselves (Quinton et al. 1984). Positive modeling seemed to be gained from positive school experiences, good relationships with peers, and the later addition of a supportive marital relationship.

Mothers raising small children are more likely to be vulnerable to depression when they are socially isolated from other adults. Postpartum depression, for example, is influenced by cultural beliefs about mothers and their infants, as well as by the social organization of childrearing. Most traditional cultures share a communal life in which women share daily chores and the care of infants and children. This social life is a buffer against depression. Nineteenth-century Western European women became more isolated as the ideal of a private middle-class lifestyle took hold. This ideal spread to North America as well, although immigrant, Native American, and African-American groups continued to maintain closer community ties. Today, "mothers' groups" and "play groups" organized by women with small children provide company and mutual support to partially fill this gap. When depression does emerge, friends and family members can help buffer its effects and prevent the episode from becoming prolonged. Supportive community agencies and organizations can also provide support and mental health counseling (Stansfeld 1999, 167).

Alienation and Social Exclusion

Alienation has become a concept woven into the fabric of modern cultures, as even privileged individuals rarely feel a comfortable sense of belonging. Witness the addiction problems and high divorce rates of the rich and famous. The use of mind-altering substances (legal and illegal) is rampant in the United States, symptomatic of malaise on the one hand and the search for childlike happiness on the other.

According to Marx, psychological alienation is related to economic arrangements (as discussed in Chapter 2). Workers are alienated from their labor when they lose control over its process and products. They are exploited by owners of capital for the "surplus value" of their labor, which is siphoned off as profit. Owners and managers also may be alienated in their drive to extract profits from the work process. Max Weber (1946/1969) analyzed bureaucratic institutions, noting their callous and impersonal procedures, and blindness to personal problems and needs. The impersonal nature of the modern work force thus affects both working and middle classes.

Freud (1961), in *Civilization and Its Discontents*, noted the inherent lack of fit between the individual and the modern social world. According to Freud, individual psychology involves a struggle between the needs of the self (in the ego), instinctual drives (id), and the demands of the social world (superego). These three psychological players are always in dynamic tension, striving to reach some equilibrium and never at peace. Freud's psychodynamic model provides insight into the widespread prevalence of neurosis, from mild to extreme severity in modern (and modernizing) societies.

In addition to the psychological state of alienation, systematic processes of exclusion limit the opportunities of particular social groups. The concepts of discrimination, prejudice, and social exclusion help to describe the systematically differential treatment of particular groups. Competition over resources and distinguishing "us" from "them" shape the dynamics of inclusion and exclusion, with race and ethnicity often defining the lines of exclusion (as discussed in Chapter 6). However, a striking example from the Great Depression in the United States reminds us that just about any difference can become socially constructed as significant. During the 1930s, wearing of eyeglasses was used to weed out applicants for scarce jobs (Bartley 1987).

What do processes of exclusion have to do with mental health? A great deal, especially in cultures that encourage all to aspire to middle-class affluence and suggest that this is possible with hard work and "the right stuff." Disappointment and humiliation are inevitable. As Wilkinson describes, "To feel depressed, cheated, bitter, desperate, vulnerable, frightened, angry, worried about debts or job and housing insecurity; to feel devalued, useless, helpless, neglected, hopeless, isolated, anxious and a failure: these feelings can dominate people's whole experience of life" (1996, 215). Even the affluent may experience exclusion if they become displaced in a rapidly changing society, whether from jobs or from marriages. This may be especially jarring in middle age or the elder years. Plastic surgery, dieting, and hair coloring are just three of the remedies sought to avoid the exclusionary effects of no longer being young. In the Silicon Valley, plastic surgeons joined together in an information and referral line, 1-800-BEAUTIFY. A writer for the *Silicon Valley/San Jose Business Journal* explained, "Plastic surgery has become commonplace especially as more middle-aged employees go under the knife thinking they have to look as young as those twentysome-things pouring into the work force" (York 1996).

Unemployment is an aspect of exclusion and a problem in developed and under-developed countries. In developed countries, manufacturing workers are displaced into lower-paid service jobs or unemployment. Underemployment—that is, working fewer hours or below skill and capacity—is widespread. The distance between the working poor and the affluent widens under these conditions, and social exclusion becomes a more pervasive trend. White (1998) describes four aspects of social exclusion.

1. From participation in civil society through legal constraint or regulation (for example, for immigrants or those with criminal records)
2. From social goods and services (for example, for the disabled or homeless)
3. From social production, by not being able to actively contribute to society (for example, because of stigma or joblessness)
4. From economic and social consumption (adapted by Shaw et al. 1999, 223)

Unemployment may lead to social exclusion in any of these ways, leaving workers more vulnerable to emotional disturbances and onset of mental illness. In addition, mental illness itself may result in stigma, joblessness, and exclusion.

A homeless woman forages through trash. Exclusion from the main-stream of social life leaves individuals more vulnerable to mental and physical illness.

Homelessness and Mental Health

Even in the wealthiest of developed countries, with highly developed welfare states, there are homeless people. Homelessness is rampant in the cities of less-developed countries. For example, in Brazilian cities, it is at epidemic proportions and includes many children. Many welfare states have cut back social services, and there is evidence that homelessness is rising, even in the generous Netherlands (Schnabel 1992). Not surprisingly, the homeless have poorer physical and mental health than the general population. Tuberculosis is more common, as are rates of alcohol and drug dependence (Shaw et al. 1999, 229–231). Violence is often a daily threat to the homeless, who are also far more likely to be suicidal. Studies have found them twenty-five and thirty-four times more likely to kill themselves than the general population (Grenier 1997 and Keyes & Kennedy 1992, respectively).

> Suicide and suicidal feelings are likely to occur at all stages of homelessness: fear of losing one's home, sudden and unprepared moves, having no settled home, seeking accommodation, waiting for a home, and settling into a new home (in some ways similar to the challenges faced by migrants). (Shaw et al. 1999, 231)

A Global Perspective on Mental Health

The World Federation for Mental Health is the oldest nongovernmental mental health organization with official relations with the United Nations. Its 1948 founding document, *Mental Health and World Citizenship* (Brody 1987), defined mental health as a condition that permits the optimal physical, intellectual, and emotional development of the individual "insofar as this is compatible with that of other individuals" (277, cited in Brody 2001, 127). This perspective is similar to the United Nations 1948 Declaration of Human Rights. Both documents suggest that respecting human rights includes self-expression and self-determination and that violation of these rights can cause emotional distress and impaired mental health (Brody 2001, 127–128).

The burden of illness and disability from emotional distress, psychiatric illness, and behavioral disorders is enormous in developed as well as less-developed countries. With perhaps one-fifth of the global population living in poverty, a substantial proportion of children go without the living conditions that promote optimal mental and physical health. There is no strong evidence, however, that poverty per se increases the incidence of psychosis (Brody 2001, 129). Mental illness often does not kill people directly and therefore has been left on the sidelines of global or national health reporting. Public health data identify the most immediate cause of death (for example, from disease or accident), even though underlying causes may include alcoholism, drug addiction, or depression.

A major breakthrough in conceptualizing the harm from mental illness and behavioral disorders occurred when the World Bank and the World Health Organization began to calculate "DALYs" (disability-adjusted life years) in their global reports. This calculation revealed the tremendous loss of productive years due to a wide range of injuries and illness, from depression to lost limbs or liver failure. *The Global Burden of Disease* (Murray & Lopez 1996), the book version of the report by these two agencies along with the Harvard School of Public Health, provided a global survey of disease, injury, and death, using disability-adjusted life years as a prominent measure. Over 8 percent of DALYs lost are directly linked to mental health problems, and an additional 34 percent are linked to behavior-related illnesses (both communicable and noncommunicable) (Desjarlais et al. 1995, 5; World Bank 1993). Included in behavior-related years lost are a wide range of disabilities, including cirrhosis from excessive drinking, injuries to self and others from driving intoxicated, and injuries and diseases from drug injection. This allows the losses in quality of life and social productivity to be seen in public health data.

Dorothy Rice and colleagues found that, in the United States, the cost burden from depression is about the same as that from heart disease, a major killer and cause of disability and death (Rice et al. 1992). Total costs for mental illness were estimated at $148 billion, with $99 billion for alcohol abuse and $67 billion for drug abuse. Table 7.2 shows disability-adjusted life years lost to particular mental health problems.

The situation has only gotten worse since the early 1990s. The director general of the World Health Organization estimates that, worldwide, mental disorders accounted for about 12 percent of all disability-adjusted life years lost in 1998 (Brundtland 2000, 411). Five of the ten leading causes of disability are mental problems (major depression, schizophrenia, bipolar disorders, alcohol use, and obsessive-compulsive disorders). Major depression ranks fifth out of the ten leading causes of disability, or disease burden. Mental health problems in developed countries in 1998 were an even larger proportion of the total disease burden in high-income countries (23 percent) compared to those with low and middle incomes.

In addition to the World Health Organization, U.S. national policy has recently paid more attention to the extent of mental health problems. A 1999 White House

TABLE 7.2 *Percentage of Disability-adjusted Life Years (DALYs) Lost Globally from Mental Health Problems*

Problem	Percentage
Depressive disorders	17.3
Other	16.4
Self-inflicted injury	15.9
Alzheimer's/dementia	12.7
Alcohol dependence	12.1
Epilepsy	9.3
Psychoses	6.8
Drug dependence	4.8
Post-traumatic stress disorder	4.7

Source: World Bank, *World Development Report 1993: Investing in Health* (New York: Oxford University Press, 1993).

Conference on Mental Health brought attention to the issue, with impetus from Tipper Gore, Vice President Al Gore's wife (who had personal experience with depression). In 2001 David Satcher, the surgeon general, began to play an active role in speaking out about mental health problems. His office released a report on the mental health needs of children, and a supplemental report on the effects of culture, race, and ethnicity on mental health disparities was reported to be in progress. In his article in the *Journal of the American Medical Association*, Dr. Satcher (2001) called for better prevention programs, comprehensive health care systems that include mental health treatment as a full and equal partner, and assistance in research and care for developing countries.

Mental health, like physical health, is more clearly viewed in social context. A group of mental health researchers set out to develop a global analysis in *World Mental Health: Problems and Priorities in Low-Income Countries* (Desjarlais et al. 1995, 7), the result of a two-year collaborative research project by members of Harvard's Department of Social Medicine. Some of the overlapping clusters of problems in which mental health and illness are embedded are presented in Table 7.3.

This approach integrates the causes and effects of health problems and illustrates the social and behavioral aspects of ill health. Viewed in this way, mental health problems are better understood as woven into the fabric of social life, as opposed to the view that they are aberrations caused by biological forces alone. Attention deficit disorder, mentioned earlier in the chapter, provides a good example. The cause of ADHD is not well understood, but it is defined as a disease in psychiatry and psychology's diagnostic manual, the *DSM IV*. It is by no means clear that the medical approach being applied is more beneficial to those affected than would be social and counseling approaches (Eaton 2001, 33). Sociologist William Eaton predicts, "An upward trend in the use of medications and chemicals for increasingly minor complaints and behaviors, personality traits and social situations will continue" (Eaton 2001, 33). The interests of the pharmaceutical industry are a force behind this trend, according to Eaton: "The more prevalent the disease or diagnosis (in the population), the more lucrative the drug and the more intensive the promotion campaign" (33).

TABLE 7.3   *Clustering of Social and Health Problems*

Social Pathology	*Health Problem*	*Exacerbating Conditions*
Substance abuse	Heart disease	High unemployment
Violence	Depression	Poverty
Abuses of women	Stress-related conditions	Limited education
Child abuse	Behaviors contributing to chronic illness	Stressful work conditions
		Gender discrimination

Source: R. Desjarlais, L. Eisenberg, B. Good, & A. Kleinman, *World Mental Health: Problems and Priorities in Low-Income Countries* (New York: Oxford University Press, 1999), 7.

As with conduct disorders such as ADHD and antisocial personality disorder, eating disorders emerge in the context of family and social relationships, and are influenced by broader cultural trends. Anorexia involves resistance to eating, allowing the body to get increasingly thin, even to the point of starvation. Bulimia involves eating irregularly, with periodic binging and vomiting. These problems are found most frequently among adolescent girls and young women; they have been reported at earlier historical periods but have become more pervasive in North America in recent decades. These behaviors are virtually unheard of in other cultures, even where there is a tradition of fasting, as in India (Eaton 2001, 171). The cultural roots of these problems are evident. For example, the "ideal bodies" portrayed in advertising, beauty pageants, *Playboy*, and *Sports Illustrated*'s swimsuit edition are markedly underweight, often anorexic, and surgically modified with breast implants and other adjustments. Pressures to have the supposedly perfect body go hand in hand with messages to achieve academically and in the work world. The message, especially among the middle class, is: Be young, beautiful, skinny, and successful. Failure looms everywhere for the aspiring college-bound female who feels she must do it all. For many, the result includes a compulsive relationship with food and a preoccupation with the imperfections of the body. Research also suggests that intense family relationships (called "enmeshed" by family therapists) are associated with eating disorders (Minuchin et al. 1978).

Ironically, for those of us in countries with abundant food supplies, going without food becomes a sign of status. But globally the profile looks quite different. There is an increase in mental illness worldwide, caused mostly by the longer life expectancy of populations. Infant mortality has decreased, and more people are living to ages during which symptoms of depression, schizophrenia, dementia, and other chronic mental illnesses are likely to emerge (Desjarlais et al. 1995, 4). For example, numbers of persons with schizophrenia increased about 45 percent between 1985 and the year 2000 because of a 45 percent increase globally in the population between ages fifteen and forty-five (Kramer 1989). Dementia is also increasing, due to the increased number of people living beyond age sixty-five.

Poor living conditions and disrupted social ties also contribute to increased mental disturbance. Massive urbanization in recent decades has occurred without parallel improvements in standard of living for sizeable populations in Asia, Latin America, Africa, and the Pacific Rim. This has led to large poor populations living on the fringes of cities. Desjarlais and colleagues (1995, 22) note, "Almost half of the residents live in unplanned and illegal settlements, in substandard housing and environmental conditions. [They] . . . face uncertain prospects for employment . . . as well as lack of sanitation, clean drinking water, and basic hygiene." Many work in informal sectors of the economy, and there are high rates of unemployment. Community and kin ties are disrupted or lost, and substance use, crime, and violence increase.

The rise in depression is a large part of increased mental illness in recent decades: "Depression is now being seen at younger ages and in greater frequency in countries as different as Lebanon, Taiwan, the United States, and the nations of Western Europe" (Cross-National Collaborative Group 1992; Desjarlais et al. 1995, 6; Lin et al. 1969; Yeh et al. 1987). Depressive and anxiety disorders account for 20 to 30 percent of all primary care visits worldwide (Desjarlais et al. 1995, 9). To what extent has actual depression increased as opposed to increased awareness, screening, and diagnosis of the problem? The answer is unknown, but it is certain that depression is a serious and debilitating problem in a world that continues to change rapidly, with major disruptions in daily life and cultural milieu.

In terms of the overall health burden in less-developed countries, neuropsychiatric diseases make up nearly 7 percent of the global burden of disease. Mental illness is most concentrated among teens and premiddle-aged adults. For individuals aged fifteen to forty-four, neuropsychiatric diseases are 12 percent of the disease burden, but when intentional, self-inflicted injuries are added in, the total comes to about 15 percent for women and 16 percent for men (World Bank 1993). Also on the rise globally are alcoholism, drug abuse, suicide, and violence against women and children (Desjarlais et al. 1995).

Cultural Variations, Economic Development, and Mental Health

The director general of the World Health Organization suggests that "mental health depends on some measure of social justice, and . . . given its scale, must be treated at [the] primary level where possible" (Brundtland 2000, 411). This involves reducing poverty and violence to improve the quality of living conditions. Rapid social changes brought on by economic and technological developments, as well as civil strife and violence, have disrupted countless communities. Family and kin ties have been weakened or lost with social disruptions, leaving individuals poorly protected from the effects of poverty and violence.

The model of a political economy of health presented in Chapter 3 suggests that two factors—where a person is located in the global world economy (that is, whether the individual lives in a core, periphery, or semi-periphery country) and which social class he or she is a member of—set the stage for living conditions and life chances. In addition, rural life seems to be more conducive to good mental health than living in densely populated urban areas. However, this is only generally the case; there are many examples of harmful rural conditions. For example, access to drinkable water is better in urban than in rural areas.

Culture influences the level of mental suffering in various countries. For example, rates of rape are estimated to be ten times higher in the United States than in Japan. And women in abusive relationships endure emotional and physical suffering, and sometimes death, in wealthy as well as poor societies. However, we also know that women with access to jobs, money, housing, and social support (caring relatives, shelters, police intervention) have much better chances of escaping violent relationships.

Does development bring improved mental health to populations? It depends on the consequences for the majority of the population. Increased inequality and displacement threaten to increase all forms of social problems and mental illness (Desjarlais et al. 262). Development may bring a higher standard of living to a country, reducing disease and death rates. Yet, with the shift to longer life expectancy, more individuals may develop heart disease, depression, and schizophrenia.

Policies that drive development also vary in their methods. Development that exploits indigenous peoples' knowledge, moves them off their land, and destroys centuries-old ways of life is harmful and immoral. However, development that provides clean drinking water, seed, and fertilizer to farmers (of both genders) is constructive and humane. Globally, agricultural development has made subsistence farming less and less tenable. The "green revolution" modernized agriculture but displaced women and many men from farming. This version of "development" left women and often men without the means to feed their children. Under these conditions, gross national product grew, but so did migration to urban shantytowns. Deteriorating health is one of the costs of this kind of development.

The following are guideposts for examining the potential effects of development on mental health:

- *Poverty affects infant and child development.* Micronutrient deficiency in childhood, malnutrition, poverty, and dislocation lead to neurological deficits and brain dysfunction (Desjarlais et al. 1995, 263). This occurs among some of the poorest citizens of highly unequal affluent societies (the United States, Brazil, Russia) and with greater frequency in low-income countries on the periphery of the world economic system.

- *Lack of primary health care, including mental health care, prevents the normal social functioning of many individuals with mental health problems.* Neuropsychiatric conditions for which effective treatments are available often go untreated in low-income countries. For example, in several Asian and African societies, approximately 90 percent of individuals with epilepsy (which results from pathology in the brain) go untreated.

- *Trauma and major losses, especially during childhood, increase depression, and these types of losses are more frequent in less-developed countries.* Major depression involves the abnormal functioning of neurotransmitters and may affect persons in any social class or type of country. The loss of a parent and social dislocation due to war or other disruption increase lifelong vulnerability to depression. Civilians, including many children, are the most frequent victims of contemporary wars; about 90 percent as compared to the 5 percent of victims of World War I are civilians (Klare 1999). In addition to political strife, the AIDS pandemic is leaving thousands of orphans in less-developed countries and is devastating these countries' economies. The implications of this combination for impaired mental health are staggering.

- *Behavioral disorders and a range of other mental health problems are closely linked to harmful social and economic conditions.* Examples include the following:
  - The selling of young girls into sexual slavery in Thailand followed the modernization of agriculture, migration to cities by the rural population, and the development of the market for sexual tourism (Desjarlais et al. 1995, 263).
  - Drug addiction and alcoholism usually have their origins in adolescence; use of mind-altering substances is related to the culture that surrounds adolescents and also to their availability.
  - Interethnic strife, civil wars, state terrorism, and environmental disasters produce trauma that makes individuals more vulnerable to depression, anxiety, prolonged grief, posttraumatic stress disorder, despair, and suicide. When

these conditions are prolonged, the results become more serious and entrenched. Cambodian refugees living in camps along the Thai border for a
decade following the genocide by the Pol Pot regime suffered widespread
emotional problems. One study found that over 80 percent said they were in
fair or poor health, felt depressed, and had a number of somatic complaints,
despite good access to medical services. Over half had symptoms that resemble Western criteria for clinical depression, and 15 percent had symptoms of posttraumatic stress disorder (Mullica et al. 1990). The most frequently reported symptom was a depressive state called *bebotchit*, translated as
"a deep sadness inside oneself" (Desjarlais et al. 1995, 140).

- Social dislocations due to agricultural modernization and other forms of "development" (such as dam building) also cause emotional difficulties similar to those
experienced by refugees.

- Communities of poverty and violence reproduce clusters of social and mental
health problems, which in turn reinforce structural inequalities through discrimination, disability, and unemployment. This may occur in residentially
segregated class cultures in affluent, highly unequal societies and also in less-
developed countries, where the very rich live in close proximity to the very
poor. These clusters of conditions are not easily eradicated. For example, following the end of apartheid in South Africa, violence among Africans continued
to perpetuate impoverishment.

- Among the sectors of the population that experience the affluence of development, a variety of mental health problems may emerge. These include depression, substance abuse, eating disorders, and a variety of other behavioral patterns
that are damaging to health.

Mental Health Trends

The following is a summary of trends that will affect mental health well into the
twenty-first century:

- Mental illness will increase globally, especially in the fifteen to forty-four age
group (mainly as a result of declining infant and child mortality). Schizophrenia is
likely to increase as this age group reaches adolescence and young adulthood.

- Incidence of dementia and other mental disorders will increase as the global
population ages.

- Poverty among approximately one-fifth of the world's population will continue
to contribute to developmental deficits among children and to vulnerability to mental problems.

- Violence against women within and outside the family is likely to increase due
to continued social disruptions.

- Improvements will occur in girls' and women's literacy, economic independence, and control over fertility.

- Child survival will continue to improve. However, the effects of rural and urban poverty, as well as dislocation and social upheaval, will continue to make them vulnerable to malnutrition, exploitation, and violence.

- Children of the rural poor, disproportionately displaced by civil strife, are most apt to be drafted by warring groups and injured or killed by armed conflict (Brody 2001; Klare 1999).

- Refugees worldwide will continue to be "internally displaced," subjected to harsh living conditions and violence, and vulnerable to mental health problems. Symptoms of trauma (including widespread PTSD), anxiety, and depressive disorders will continue to be widespread among refugees and displaced persons.

- Interpersonal as well as collective violence will most likely remain high. The global abundance of small arms and hand-held, highly destructive automatic weapons helps to perpetuate the high level of violence (Klare 1999; Renner 1998, 1999).

- The AIDS epidemic will continue to cause major suffering and losses in less-developed countries, making populations more susceptible to depression and other mental disturbances. Orphans are of particular concern due to their developmental needs and vulnerabilities.

- Absolute and relative increases in substance abuse (including legal and illegal substances) are likely to continue; absolute growth is due to population increases, relative growth is due to the availability and attractiveness of mind-altering substances. Weakened family and community supportive ties and vigilance will provide fewer constraints against consumption of mind-altering substances and development of addiction.

- Depression, anxiety, and compulsive disorders will increase among groups in developed and developing societies, especially where there is high income inequality.

Initiatives for the Improvement of Global Mental Health

From decades of work on mental health and illness, British psychiatrist Julian Leff (2001) offers this perspective:

> My vision for the future of psychiatry is one that depends not on technical advances in making images of the brain or replacing bad genes with good ones, but on increasing our understanding of relationships between people. It has become starkly clear that industrialisation and urbanisation, those unstoppable forces of modern societies, destroy the extended family and bonds with neighbours which are the essence of traditional ways of life. With the loss of this natural support network, individuals are more vulnerable to psychiatric disorders and it becomes more difficult to restore their mental health. (151)

With these challenges to populations' mental health, we look to experts' advice. Several developments are needed in order to make effective interventions possible on a global scale. The following are the public policy recommendations from the authors of the two-year collaborative research effort organized by Harvard's Department of Social Medicine (Desjarlais et al. 1995, 271–277):

1. *A major initiative is needed to upgrade the quality of mental health services in Africa, Asia, Latin America, and the Middle East.* Needs include well-trained practitioners, medication, and well-designed psychosocial interventions. The human rights of the mentally ill need to be protected, and their care needs to be separated from social and criminal control agencies.

2. *Upgrading in the amount and quality of mental health training is needed at all levels of the health care delivery system, from physicians and nurses to village health workers.* A cadre of well-trained professionals must determine programs and initiatives that are needed for particular regions and for particular at-risk groups.

3. *State gender policies must be improved to prohibit violence against women and to spur movement toward empowering women economically.* These efforts are understood as an investment in the mental health of all members of society.

4. *Improvements and innovations in mental health services for children and adolescents are needed, including early detection and prevention of mental disorders and educational programs.* These services need to be integrated into all forms of health care. This investment will more than pay for itself, financially and in improved health.

5. *Policy makers, researchers, and treatment providers must assess the global burden of substance abuse, seek ways to reduce demand, and develop effective treatment and prevention programs.* This work must recognize the extent to which substance use is intertwined with economies, from government revenues from the sale of tobacco products to whole economies grown dependent on production of particular drugs (for example, cocaine in Colombia and heroin in Afghanistan).

6. *Broad initiatives are needed regarding the causes and consequences of collective and interpersonal violence.* Some of the most harmful effects of violence directly affect health-sustaining conditions, including disruption of local economies, shortages of food and drinking water, dislocation, and separation from family members (Desjarlais et al. 276).

7. *Within the field of health, a major effort is needed in the primary prevention of mental, neurological, behavioral, and psychosocial disorders.* The authors of *World Mental Health* recognize that, for these initiatives to move forward, an international movement is required to push a mental health agenda. As policy initiatives, they provide a focal point around which international and local groups can direct their efforts. There are, however, other competing interests. Consequently, only an activist stance will generate momentum in moving this agenda forward. Mobilized grassroots groups, nongovernmental organizations, professionals, and individuals and groups linked in electronic networks have the potential to apply pressure and improve conditions conducive to mental health.

Underdevelopment and Health

I heard rumors about assistance for the poor, but no one seems to know where it is.

—From a discussion group, Tanjugrejo, Indonesia

Sometimes I stay for long hours until I can see one of the doctors, then afterwards the nurse comes and tells me that he is not coming or he came but he will not be able to see me.

—Poor woman, El Mataria, Egypt

The two main causes of . . . health problems in the least developed countries are malnutrition and infections. Infections in developing countries can be ascribed to two broad causal factors: poverty and a warm climate. A warm temperature allows animal parasites . . . to complete the essential part of their life cycle outside [humans], while the complex of social and environmental factors that comprise poverty facilitate the transmission of very many infections.

—David Bradley, *Health, Environment, and Tropical Development*

The authors of a major study of the "global burden of disease" predict that there will be major improvements in life expectancies by 2020 (Murray & Lopez 1996). The biggest improvements, the authors project, will occur in countries that presently have the highest infant and child mortality rates. How those improvements will occur is not fully addressed, but it is assumed that poor countries will follow the path that is under way among other developing countries: As the gross national product grows, the standard of living will improve, and mortality rates will decline.

This chapter examines countries that have the poorest health and questions the assumption that they are destined for improvement without substantial assistance. Not surprisingly, the least healthy societies are also the poorest economically. The vast majority are located in Africa, but some are in Asia as well (for example, Cambodia and Afghanistan). There are also poverty and ill health in countries where development is under way, including societies in Latin America, Asia, Africa, and Eastern Europe.

We examine data on thirty-two countries with the lowest life expectancies (in Table 8.1), as well as some of the causes of their poor health. We look at a measure of "equality of child survival," which represents the likelihood that children will survive to age five across various groups within a country. An additional measure that provides clues to population health is the probability of dying between the ages of fifteen and fifty-nine (also in Table 8.1). Case examples are used to illustrate the causes of poor health and also how groups cope with difficult living conditions. And, finally, we consider the effects of international lending policies on population well-being and conclude the chapter by considering prospects for improvement. Throughout the chapter, we use the terms *underdeveloped, low-income,* and *periphery* interchangeably to identify countries in which a substantial proportion of the population lives in absolute poverty. We consider the following questions:

- Are the barriers to improved health caused by countries' location in the global economy?
- Do other characteristics of underdevelopment impede health improvements as well?
- What makes some countries far more inequitable in this respect than others?

Underdevelopment and Health

During 1998, many so-called developing countries did not develop at all. The World Bank's yearly report found stalled progress in education, health, and other quality-of-life measures. Sub-Saharan African countries were doing the poorest, with life expectancies of fifty-one years or less. The World Health Organization's 2000 report identifies thirty-two countries with disability-adjusted life expectancies below forty years.

Also alarming are rates of HIV infection, estimated to range between one-tenth and one quarter of adults in eighteen African countries. More than 90 percent of people infected with the AIDS virus are in the less-developed world; both low income and unequal distribution of income are strongly associated with HIV infection rates (Ainsworth & Semali 1998). In countries with the highest infection rates, such as Botswana and Zimbabwe, the epidemic has wiped out the health gains made during the past thirty years, pushing life expectancies that would have reached about sixty-four by 2015 back to forty-seven years (World Bank 1997). The World Health Organization notes the following developments in the AIDS epidemic:

- Of the 5.4 million people newly infected with HIV in 1999, 4 million live in sub-Saharan Africa, the hardest-hit region. There are now more women than men among the 24.5 million adults and 1 million children estimated to be living with HIV/AIDS in sub-Saharan Africa. Transmission among adults in sub-Saharan Africa is primarily through heterosexual intercourse (90 percent).

- Asia continues to have relatively low prevalence rates; there are an estimated 5.6 million adults and children living with HIV/AIDS in Southeast Asia.

- An estimated 1.3 million adults and children live with HIV in Latin America and the Caribbean; these are mainly men who have unprotected sex with other men or share needles in drug use.

- In 1999 Eastern Europe and Central Asia experienced the sharpest increase in HIV infections. Most of the 420,000 people living with HIV/AIDS in these countries have been infected through injection drug use (World Health Organization 2001).

We have seen in previous chapters that health improvements require adequate care of human needs and improved living conditions. Several African countries have not been able to achieve those goals. Partially responsible is the AIDS epidemic's devastating effects on underdeveloped countries' abilities to marshal resources to deliver primary medical care. Infectious diseases continue to plague poor countries due to malnutrition, unsafe drinking water, natural disasters, corrupt leadership, and violence.

During the past decade, sub-Saharan Africa had the least economic growth of any global region, the highest infant mortality rates, the lowest school enrollments, and the lowest access to safe water. Insufficient food, or "food insecurity," as experts call it, is a pervasive problem in low-income countries globally, one that poses especially serious threats to infants, children, and pregnant women. It results in widespread malnutrition, which increases vulnerability to infectious and chronic diseases and causes widespread anemia among pregnant women. Newborns enter the world already vulnerable to illness. Inadequate nutrition is therefore a major cause of lower life expectancies in the countries shown in Table 8.1.

Table 8.1 lists thirty-two countries with the lowest life expectancies at the turn of the twenty-first century (World Health Organization 2000). With disability subtracted from life expectancy at birth, populations in these countries have life expectancies of less than forty years (first column). Their life expectancies without the disability adjustment are under fifty years (second column). Also included is equality of child survival from birth to age five across the country's population (third column); the lower figures toward the top of the table signify lower equality among a country's social groups.

In rural African areas, less than 60 percent of the population has access to safe drinking water, and less than half has access to adequate sanitation (World Health Organization 1998, 168). In addition, there are insufficient numbers of trained health personnel in African countries, and those who are trained often leave to practice medicine under more favorable circumstances. Rural populations, where most of the poor live globally, are especially underserved. Less than half of African countries are able to provide health care to half of all newborns. Also of concern in poor countries are the higher numbers of adolescent smokers and traffic fatalities (World Health Organization 1998, 168). Car accidents and smoking-related illnesses are sympto-

TABLE 8.1 *Lowest Life Expectancy Countries (estimates for 1997 and 1999)*

Country	Life Expectancy (disability-adjusted)[1]	Life Expectancy at Birth (1999) Males / Females	Equality of Child Survival[2] to Age 5 (rank)	Percentage Probability of Dying Under Age 5 (1999) Males / Females	Percentage Probability of Dying, Ages 15–59 (1999) Males / Females
Sierra Leone	25.9	33.2 / 35.4	.433 (186)	32.6 / 29.8	59.9 / 52.7
Niger	29.1	37.2 / 40.6	.457 (184)	33.1 / 33.9	47.0 / 36.2
Malawi	29.4	37.3 / 38.4	.378 (187)	22.2 / 21.5	66.4 / 61.8
Zambia	30.3	38.0 / 39.0	.535 (171)	17.4 / 16.3	72.9 / 68.2
Botswana	32.3	39.5 / 39.3	.624 (146)	9.9 / 9.7	78.6 / 74.0
Uganda	32.7	41.9 / 42.9	.653 (138)	16.5 / 15.3	62.2 / 59.2
Rwanda	32.8	41.2 / 42.3	.437 (185)	18.9 / 16.3	60.2 / 58.1
Zimbabwe	32.8	40.9 / 40.0	.785 (98)	12.2 / 11.3	73.0 / 71.0
Mali	33.1	41.3 / 44.0	.489 (180)	24.0 / 22.9	50.0 / 43.2
Ethiopia	33.5	41.4 / 43.1	.510 (176)	18.8 / 17.7	59.6 / 54.5
Liberia	34.0	42.5 / 44.9	.245 (191)	21.4 / 19.6	51.3 / 46.1
Mozambique	34.4	41.8 / 44.0	.261 (190)	19.6 / 18.9	58.0 / 51.4
Burundi	34.4	43.2 / 43.8	.599 (154)	17.0 / 16.6	58.2 / 54.6
Burkina Faso	35.5	44.1 / 45.7	.654 (137)	18.2 / 17.1	53.2 / 48.6
Namibia	35.6	43.3 / 43.0	.529 (173)	11.3 / 11.2	68.2 / 64.9
United Republic of Tanzania	36.0	44.4 / 45.6	.530 (172)	15.7 / 14.8	56.8 / 52.5

Country					
Central African Republic	36.0	43.3 / 44.9	.301 (189)	15.3 / 14.3	60.8 / 55.5
Democratic Rep. of the Congo	36.3	45.1 / 46.5	.527 (174)	17.0 / 15.3	51.5 / 48.2
Somalia	36.4	44.0 / 44.7	.495 (179)	20.6 / 19.6	52.2 / 48.7
Madagascar	36.6	45.0 / 47.7	.544 (168)	17.9 / 15.7	48.6 / 44.0
Lesotho	36.9	44.1 / 45.1	.570 (164)	14.7 / 13.4	60.4 / 56.5
Guinea-Bissau	37.2	45.0 / 47.0	.510 (177)	20.7 / 19.6	45.7 / 41.1
Eritrea	37.7	46.6 / 46.5	.544 (167)	14.4 / 13.4	52.0 / 51.4
Afghanistan	37.7	45.3 / 47.2	.470 (182)	27.9 / 24.9	34.8 / 32.6
Guinea	37.8	46.2 / 48.9	.549 (166)	21.7 / 19.3	41.3 / 36.9
Djibouti	37.9	45.0 / 45.0	.543 (169)	16.9 / 16.2	55.6 / 52.4
Angola	38.0	46.3 / 49.1	.509 (178)	20.9 / 19.2	42.7 / 37.5
Swaziland	38.1	45.8 / 46.8	.645 (140)	10.7 / 9.7	61.2 / 56.8
Nigeria	38.3	46.8 / 48.2	.336 (188)	17.3 / 17.0	47.3 / 42.9
Kenya	39.3	47.3 / 48.1	.660 (135)	10.0 / 9.9	59.1 / 54.6
Chad	39.4	47.3 / 50.1	.520 (175)	18.4 / 16.5	43.9 / 38.6
South Africa	39.8	47.3 / 49.7	.685 (128)	8.5 / 6.7	60.1 / 53.3

[1] Disability-adjusted life expectancy represents expected years of life without disability.

[2] Equality of child survival is a measure based on the distribution of child survival across a country's population.

Source: World Health Organization, *The World Health Report 2000. Health Systems: Improving Performance* (Geneva, Switzerland: World Health Organization, 2000. Statistical Annex Tables 2 and 5. The correct value for any indicator is estimated to have an 80 percent probability of falling within the uncertainty interval, with chances of 10 percent each of falling below the low value or above the high one.

matic of the uneven aspects of development, in which new products and technologies are introduced, but their harmful effects are not prevented. Consequently, poorly maintained roads, fast driving, and the absence of buckled seatbelts cause high accident rates in less-developed countries. Sub-Saharan Africa has the world's highest rate of fatalities per vehicle (World Health Organization 2000, 6). Safer roads and campaigns to bring about the installation and use of seatbelts would help save lives.

Environmental degradation is a serious problem in poor parts of the world, and state officials worry that they cannot control the problems on their own. There is an increased volume of industrial and domestic waste, inadequate disposal systems, and risk of water contamination and soil degradation by chemical pollutants (World Health Organization 1998, 167). Although the effects are difficult to measure apart from other causes, all of these translate into higher levels of disease.

On the more encouraging side, in recent decades national health systems have been developed and consolidated, with greater attention to localized care. Countries have made greater investments in maternal and child health, and there is better delivery and management of high-priority services, such as immunization, control of diarrhea, and delivery of essential drugs and vaccines (World Health Organization 1998, 168). Such advances often occur with the assistance of international agencies, including nongovernmental organizations. Nonetheless, sub-Saharan African countries have a long way to go economically and socially to move through epidemiological transitions in which infectious diseases would be greatly reduced.

Underdeveloped countries have health profiles that correspond to their social and economic conditions. In international relations there is reason to call all low-income countries "developing" out of diplomatic courtesy, but in the study of health, such terminology obscures the real differences between underdeveloped and developing countries. In the terms of world systems theory, these are contrasted as periphery and semi-periphery countries, with economic and social conditions that are shaped by their position in a global economy.

Characteristics of Countries in the World Economic System

A world systems approach partially explains the stratified health status among nations. An economic world system is a multicultural territorial division of labor in which the production and exchange of basic goods and raw materials are necessary for the everyday life of its inhabitants (Wallerstein 1974a). This means that, around the world, culturally and politically diverse groups occupy different production, labor, and trade sectors within a global economy. Core countries and transnational corporations dominate trade relations. Semi-periphery countries have developed as well as underdeveloped sectors and are heavily influenced by the economic interests of transnational corporations and core countries. The elite of less-developed countries is attracted to the wealth that foreign investment brings, whereas the least privileged may not reap benefits.

According to world systems theory, periphery countries do not develop along the same paths taken by core countries in earlier periods, but instead are "structurally constrained to experience developmental processes that reproduce their subordinate status" (Chase-Dunn & Grimes 1995, 389). Periphery countries therefore do not advance by simply gaining access to the essential ingredients of modernity (such as industrial and electronic technologies, a bureaucratic state, and an extensive educational system). Rather, the periphery is intertwined with and subject to the interests of core and semi-periphery countries, according to the model. For this reason, in alliance with foreign firms, the state and business elites use their political influence and coercive abilities as needed to remove roadblocks to market objectives. However, there are occasionally opportunities in the periphery for development that benefits society more generally, sometimes propelling countries into the semi-periphery.

> The chronic impoverishment of the periphery prevents the typical periphery state from being able to finance programs of public welfare or infrastructural improvement (even if they wished to), so its popular legitimacy is low. It is thus always vulnerable to coups or popular insurrection. Yet despite these barriers, some states have managed gradually to improve their infrastructure and to combine these improvements with policies that encourage the key industries that seem the most promising in the world market. Occasionally, such policies pay off in upward mobility. Contemporary examples include Taiwan, Singapore, Korea, Hong Kong, and China, while Japan has achieved an upward trajectory since 1880. (Chase-Dunn & Grimes 1995)

Periphery countries have the following characteristics: specialized economies, weak internal political structures, a low standard of living for workers, high potential for class conflict and political instability, and repressive rulers or governing bodies. These are described here, along with the consequences for the standard of living and health.

Specialized Economies

This means that a country depends on the export of a very limited number of products to raise capital with which it can buy needed imports. It may export, for example, raw resources such as precious metals, minerals or crude oil, lumber, or a limited number of crops, such as coffee, cocoa, or fruit. This nondiversified economy leaves the country vulnerable to dramatic downturns in revenue when the prices of these commodities decrease on global markets. Farmers can suddenly become unable to buy seeds or fertilizer, and health agencies may not be able to afford medicines. The state may default on its debt payments or be burdened by servicing debt. For example, Niger spends more than twice as much on servicing debt as it does providing primary health care (World Bank 2001, 82). If food is diverted away from hungry populations, exports and markets become implicated in chronic malnutrition.

In times of crisis and also in order to finance development projects, periphery countries borrow money from the financial core of the world system through international financial institutions such as the International Monetary Fund (IMF) and

World Bank. The terms of loans or debt refinancing may require that periphery countries reduce their spending on education, health care, and state employees. These austerity measures hurt poor and low-income people the most and have the overall effect of worsening population health by lowering the standard of living. If they continue over time, population health and prospects for modernization and improved health further deteriorate. The World Bank's *World Development Report 2000/2001* (2001) has a new stated policy devoted to improving the lot of the poor. The coming years will reveal whether new loan and debt policies will alleviate harsh conditions in the periphery rather than contribute to them.

From the perspective of average people in a periphery country, an economy with few areas of growth and development means that state and financial institutions are unavailable for short-term loans to deal with emergencies or long-term loans to establish an enterprise. Low-income communities often practice a kind of informal insurance by sharing money or goods when in need. This system works well only when a whole community is not affected by the same economic shortfall or when money gets sent from a family member who has traveled elsewhere for work. For example, in Jamaica in 1997, 53 percent of households received gifts or loans from other individuals or households; in the poorest households the percentage was even higher, at 66 percent (Cox et al. 2000). In Nepal in 1996, the percentages were nearly as high, with 45 percent of all households and 58 percent of poor households receiving gifts and informal loans (Cox et al. 2000).

Weak Internal Political Structures

State agencies have only shallow traditions of governing the country as a whole, and they are weakly linked to sources of legitimacy in the society. Decision making is not well distributed through layers of agencies within a bureaucratized administration but is heavily concentrated among just a few leaders. The ruler is often autocratic; that is, a "strong man" exercising power without constraints from other branches of government. This top-heavy structure makes periphery countries vulnerable to capricious executive decisions and corruption unchecked by other branches of government. The rule of law is often not observed or is done so in only the most superficial way. For example, administrations often are prepared to use their police, military, or special forces to get their way when legal outcomes do not coincide with their agendas. Elections may be held if required by aid donors and to maintain favorable trading status with core countries. Critics sometimes term this "donor democracy." Leaders generally aim to rule for life, consolidating their power and building the personal wealth of their family and cronies. Investments in the country's infrastructure and social well-being often come in a distant second to autocratic, self-serving priorities. For these reasons, it is not hard to imagine why many periphery countries have a small, healthy elite amid the malnourished masses.

Another aspect of a weak state is the inability (and sometimes unwillingness) to alleviate poverty. In the states of the former Soviet Union, as state enterprises were privatized or discontinued and workers laid off, workers were left to fend for themselves. Women often were laid off first and in the greatest numbers, sometimes with the erroneous excuse that women's incomes were supplemental rather than essential to household survival (Horton & Mazumdar 1999). A study of six countries in transition from state-run to market economies found that, among workers with less than a secondary education, there was increasing poverty during the period from 1993 to 1995, ranging from 33 percent in Poland to 46 percent in Russia (Grootaert & Braithwaite 1998). The Russian and Polish states have been hard put to solve the problems of their increasingly low-income populations. For example, Russia has not found the funds or political will to build up its civic infrastructure of schools, hospitals, clinics, and job retraining programs.

Yet another aspect of weak states is the lack of trust they engender in their citizenry. Both affluent and poor classes are unlikely to put money and energy into plans (especially those with goals of greater equity) if state managers and operatives are known to be corrupt. And, if the ruling administration is seen as vulnerable to takeover by another faction, investments in social insurance programs with long-term benefits may be viewed as too risky.

Low Standard of Living for Workers

In countries on the periphery of the global economy, there is an oversupply of low-skilled labor and a shortage of opportunities for education, training, and skilled work. Jobs are in short supply, and the abundance of workers keeps wages low, with union and governmental protections of workers weak or nonexistent. Harsh working conditions include the danger of accidents, exposure to harmful substances, and child labor. Poor living conditions vary by urban and rural conditions. Urban environments for the poor tend to put children at risk for diarrhea from impure water, measles and other infectious illnesses from cramped housing, and accident and injury from unsafe conditions. In rural areas, the health risks are even greater, mostly due to much lower public health and infrastructure spending (Sinha & Lipton 1999).

Unemployment and underemployment also are high in less-developed countries. Workers sometimes migrate to jobs and live away from their families for extended periods of time, causing hardship to families. Developing countries also experience dramatic fluctuations in labor conditions. The Asian economic downturn of the mid-1990s had dramatic effects on jobs and real wages (that is, wages adjusted for inflation). Countries affected by the recession saw declines in nonagricultural jobs and real wages. For example, Indonesia's nonagricultural wages fell 42 percent between 1997 and 1998, and laid-off workers crowded into urban areas looking for informal-sector work (World Bank 1999). In Thailand, job loss in Bangkok slowed migration into the city from rural areas and caused some return to the countryside, adding to rural poverty (World Bank 1999).

An aspect of poor working conditions that has a major impact on health is the unpredictable, and usually temporary, loss of earnings. For example, a nine-year study of south Indian villages found that movement into and out of poverty was the norm for the vast majority of households (Gaiha & Deolalikar 1993). Similar findings seem to be the case in China, with half of the households experiencing movement in and out of poverty over time (Glewwe & Hall 1998; Jalan & Ravallion 1999; Maluccio et al. 2000). In India, where women and children make up 73 percent of the poor, women work in the informal labor market (Amis 1994). Children are often pulled out of school and put to work to alleviate periods yielding insufficient funds.

Income loss can be caused by a variety of problems, including illness, harvest failure (drought, flooding), policy shocks (taxation, forced labor), livestock illness and death, land expropriation, asset losses, war, theft, or violence (Dercon 1999). A study in south India found that, if illness struck during the peak of the harvest season, wage losses were heavy, especially on small farms (Kochar 1995). This situation usually required informal borrowing. An Ethiopian study found that the largest income shocks were from illness; the next largest were from damage to crops due to pests, animal damage, or weeds; and the next were due to crop damage from rain (Dercon & Krishnan 2000).

Crime and violence affect the poor most harshly. In developing countries, with extreme differences between rich and poor, the affluent hire security guards and fortify their houses. Especially among low-income households, high levels of crime and domestic violence have been shown to reduce earnings and the accumulation of capital (World Bank 2001, Chapter 4). In São Paulo in 1992, the rate at which adolescent males were murdered was eleven times higher in poor than in wealthy neighborhoods (Sinha & Lipton 1999). Difficult economic conditions in urban areas lead to deteriorating social conditions. A study of urban communities in Ecuador, Hungary, the Philippines, and Zambia showed that poor economic conditions led to declines in community involvement in organizations, weakened informal ties among residents, and increased gang violence, vandalism, and other crime (Moser 1998). Domestic violence is influenced by the degree of social acceptance of wife beating, but it is experienced at higher levels in poor households. For example, in Santiago, Chile, an estimated 46 percent of poor women and 29 percent of wealthy women suffered from domestic violence, and in Managua, Nicaragua, the comparable rates were 54 and 45 percent (Morrison & Orlando 1999).

Living conditions in old age are another factor that affects health and longevity. The quality of life during the older years varies substantially. For example, in many Latin American countries, 16 to 48 percent of people sixty-five and older remain economically active (Prescott & Pradhan 1999). The number of elderly in Latin America most likely will continue to increase if economic growth continues to improve living conditions for a majority of the population. Extended families may continue to be a resource to the elderly in Latin countries, but states will have to assist with a safety net. In Eastern European former Soviet countries, the elderly are experiencing higher rates of poverty than in Latin American countries (Grootaert & Braithwaite 1998). The majority are women, due to their longevity compared to men and also because very few have pensions or savings plans.

High Potential for Class Conflict and Political Instability

This condition results from the three already described: a weak state with little legitimacy, a vulnerable economy, and neglected workers. There may be considerable opposition to the government among the population, and within the elite there may be coups d'état organized by factions within the military or government. Because there is not a large middle class heavily invested in stability, class conflict and political instability may cause chronic instability, as the new leaders do not develop legitimacy in their rule. These conditions are not conducive to investment in education, jobs, health care, and other social needs that improve population health.

Repressive Rulers or Governing Bodies

Leaders of weak states often do not have the legitimacy to rule by divine inheritance or institutional democracy. Nor do they have a large middle class or citizens who have lent their support to an elected leader to represent their interests and protect their freedoms. Instead, leaders are devoted to staying in power, often for life. They rely on an elite in government offices—often performing few actual functions—to maintain power behind the façade of government rule. A free and open press is not tolerated. Regimes often rely on the police, military, and their own cadre of forces to intimidate, torture, imprison, or murder the opposition. They hold carefully scripted press conferences to communicate with the rest of the world, especially when they wish to attract aid or foreign investment. Health statistics are often not kept, and unfavorable data about their populations are suppressed. Mismanagement of the AIDS epidemic provides a sad example. Many leaders stifled discussion of the problem while the epidemic silently spread, in some countries reaching exponential increases in infection.

Inequality and Human Needs

Denny Braun's (1997) comparison of nearly all world countries monitored by the World Bank (1994) found a relationship between inequality, standard of living, and health indicators. Countries were divided into high or low *inequality*, not high and low incomes, according to their median household incomes (180). He examined eight indicators of well-being to see how countries' level of inequality matched up. The indicators included infant mortality; male child mortality; female life expectancy; use of contraception; access to safe water; percentage of households with electricity; relative government expenditures on housing, welfare, and social security; and secondary school enrollment.[1] For all indicators, the profile is more favorable for those countries with greater equality. More equal countries performed better on all measures of caring for human needs. For example, the countries with higher inequality had an average infant mortality of 45 deaths per 1,000 births, as compared to 36 among the lower-inequality half. Government spending on housing, welfare, and social security was half again as high in countries with more equally distributed incomes (Braun 1997, 181).

---

[1] Braun used Tables 10, 26, 27, 28, 29, 30, and 32 of the *World Development Report 1994* (World Bank 1994).

Health and Life Expectancy on the Periphery

Colonialism left a legacy of institutional relationships in which host countries and indigenous peoples often were left underserved and underdeveloped. Further degradation often took place if corrupt leaders did not develop resources to benefit their populations, but instead ran empty "shell governments" and siphoned off their countries' wealth. This was often accomplished in cooperation with core countries and transnational corporations. The infrastructure left by colonial regimes often was neglected and fell into disrepair (Ayittey 1998).

Colonial powers in Africa and Asia and governments in Latin America developed health services for their own administrations and expatriates; indigenous populations were excluded from care. African British colonial governments in some places had a second rung of services for Africans; charitable organizations and public health programs also provided some care (World Health Organization 2000, 14). Where it existed at all, health care to local people took place in urban hospitals and served only 10 to 20 percent of the population. Rural residents often were left entirely without care. Urban hospitals responded to the health problems of poverty, with the majority of hospital inpatient spending going for preventable and treatable conditions such as diarrhea, malaria, tuberculosis, and acute respiratory infections (World Health Organization 2000, 14). Resources generally were not available for preventive care and early treatment of infectious or chronic diseases.

Following a 1978 "Health for All" conference jointly sponsored by the World Health Organization and UNICEF, primary care using local health workers became an international goal. The campaign aimed to make preventive and basic care available in rural areas that had never before received modern health care. Where funding and training were adequate to provide primary care services, health improvements resulted. However, many programs failed due to shortage of funding, equipment, and training, and also because of the enormity of the task (World Health Organization 2000, 14–15).

As shown in Table 8.1, the greatest inequality of child survival is found in Liberia, Mozambique, the Central African Republic, Nigeria, and Malawi. Nigeria has a disability-adjusted life expectancy thirteen years longer than in Sierra Leone but has slightly lower equality of children's survival; this suggests that an elite in Nigeria has access to better nutrition and prenatal and postnatal health care. All countries in the table may be contrasted with countries such as Japan and Chile, which in the 1990s had nearly perfect equality (0.999) of child survival and decades-longer life expectancies. The last two columns in the table provide male and female probabilities of dying during two periods of life: from birth to five years and between the ages of fifteen and fifty-nine.

The countries listed in Table 8.1 have been left out of the economic, technological, and social benefits of industrial and postindustrial development. They are handicapped by lack of investment in their populations and infrastructure. Critics of some countries' stalled progress since independence attribute this state of affairs to ineffective and corrupt leadership (Ayittey 1998). Additional and often-related aspects of periphery countries' underdevelopment include natural disasters, colonial legacies, and civil wars. For example, the industrialization and improved living conditions that occurred in several Asian countries have not occurred in parallel fashion in Africa and other places in Asia (for example, central Asia, Southeast Asia). Consequently, the epidemiological transition that reduces infectious diseases has not fully emerged in periphery countries, where populations continue to die from diseases for which there are vaccines and effective treatments. Making matters worse, HIV takes advantage of suppressed immunity to infection via sexual intercourse, childbirth, and nursing. And, adding to the chaos and injuries, civil war and ecological hardship plague countries with violence, droughts, floods, and pests that spread disease.

Life is dramatically shorter in these countries than in most of the rest of the world. The most striking comparison is with Japan's life expectancy of nearly seventy-eight for men and eight-five for women. The Japanese disability-adjusted life expectancy is nearly seventy-five, and likelihood of child survival across social groups is nearly uniform (0.999). By contrast, Sierra Leone has the lowest life expectancy (twenty-six adjusted for disability and thirty-four nonadjusted), nearly four and a half decades shorter than Japan's. The likelihood of child death is highly unequal across various social groups in Sierra Leone, ranking 186th among 191 countries. Sierra Leone's low life expectancy is due mostly to high child mortality; nearly 33 percent of boys and 30 percent of girls die before reaching five years of age. In contrast, only 0.5 percent of Japanese boys and girls die before they are five years old. The probability of dying between the ages of fifteen and fifty-nine in Sierra Leone is also substantial (60 percent for males, 53 percent for females). In the late 1990s, Liberia, another country with poor health, had the greatest inequality of child survival of all 191 countries. Children had a roughly 80 percent chance of surviving to five years, but privileged sectors of the population had far higher infant and child survival rates.

In the countries listed in Table 8.1, girls and women prior to old age have better longevity chances than boys and men. The only exception is Niger, where girls fare slightly worse than boys, and both genders have only a two-thirds chance of surviving to five years old. A striking pattern in the table is the dramatically lower chances of surviving infancy and early childhood in these countries generally. The second important pattern is the relatively poor odds for adult survival into old age.

Causes of Underdevelopment and Poor Health: African Countries

There are historical, political, ecological, and economic causes for current conditions in the poorest African countries. Individually, many of these conditions are not unique to Africa. However, in combination, they present a unique set of obstacles. Periphery status in the world economic system, corrupt rulers, civil wars, ethnic strife, and colonial legacies are some of the causes of arrested development and poor health outcomes. Together they contribute to widespread disability, disease, and premature death.

Colonial and Cold War Legacies

The African slave trade from the mid-fifteenth to the late nineteenth centuries, driven by Arab, African, and European slave traders, caused enormous social upheaval on the continent.

> Arab slaving gangs cut deep into central Africa. In the west, slaving kingdoms and roaming warlords seized millions of men and women for sale in other parts of Africa and the Americas. In the south, the *Mfecane*, a massive movement of fleeing and marauding peoples, wiped out hundreds of other small communities and settled as the Zulu empire. ("Africa: The Heart of the Matter" 2000, 23)

In addition, European colonial rule ran roughshod over boundaries between ethnic groups and created new artificial boundaries where none previously existed. European colonial regimes undermined African institutions without integrating populations into a system of stable rule that could be inherited by African societies. Preparation of Africans for modernization was poor, with the best schooling devoted to expatriates and small African elites. African labor forces often were not prepared to staff and manage a developing economy. Professionals were not poised to become integrated into leadership positions or to serve as engineers, doctors, or other skilled workers. Consequently, when colonial powers withdrew, conditions were ripe for monopolization of power by African leaders whose subject populations could not easily mount organized opposition.

Independence came late to African countries but occurred fairly rapidly. Almost all countries were under colonial rule up to the end of the 1950s. During the 1960s, over thirty countries became independent, and during the 1970s, six more shed colonial rule. Zimbabwe (formerly Southern Rhodesia) achieved independence in the 1980s, and Eritrea, Namibia, and South Africa did so in the 1990s. In the post–World War II economic boom, it became less necessary to maintain colonial rule. Trade relations emerged to play the central role in relationships between core countries, corporations, and less-developed countries. Companies made arrangements with local elites to extract resources and, when possible, to create markets for the sale of commodities.

International financial agencies have played a role in African countries' development efforts and also in their failures. Following the oil crisis of 1979, the 1980s' economic reforms implemented by the International Monetary Fund and World Bank had objectives of reducing debt and increasing self-sufficiency. However, this is not what occurred. African rural poverty increased, spurring migration to urban areas and swelling the numbers of urban poor. By the 1990s, the negative effects of lower oil prices and economic reforms were clear: "Twenty-one countries had a lower real, as well as nominal, average growth rate in 1991–1995 than they had in 1980–1985" (World Health Organization 1998, 166).

Cold War powers' interference in African disputes caused further difficulties. In what were sometimes called "surrogate wars," the Soviet Union and the United States chose up sides and supplied arms, training, and funds to warring factions within or between African nations. This made the rebuilding of African states and industrialization an even more distant possibility. Cold War politics in Africa prolonged and expanded violent conflicts and encouraged dependence on foreign money and weapons. Those wielding guns were tough competition for groups that wished to move in more peaceful directions of developing political and economic institutions.

Ecological Deprivation and Hardship

African landscapes are dramatic and beautiful, but they pose challenges to human populations.

> The soils are often poor and thin, lasting only a few planting seasons. The sun burns and the rain either does not come at all (Ethiopia) or comes in floods that wash every-thing away (Mozambique). The beasts and bugs are big, and they bite. Diseases fatal to man—and to his crops and animals—thrive. ("Africa: The Heart of the Matter" 2000, 23)

Location in the tropical and desert belt around the equator is key to the "ecology of underdevelopment" and poor population health, whereas most temperate-zone economies are either rich, formerly socialist, or as in Afghanistan and Mongolia, geographically isolated (Sachs 1999, 17). Life expectancies are shorter for many reasons, but infectious diseases stand out as most damaging. Tropical countries are burdened with malaria, hookworm, sleeping sickness, and schistosomiasis, all associated with a warm climate. In addition, poor food production is due in part to geography and climate, and technological advances are most often aimed at temperate climates. Biotechnology has only sporadically put its expertise to work in the tropics. Most agricultural production in the tropics brings meager yields, reflecting the fragility of most tropical soils at high temperatures combined with heavy rainfall. Small gains in production are often overshadowed by larger population increases and periodic catastrophes. High productivity in the rain forest is possible only in small parts of the tropics, generally on volcanic soil (for example, on the island of Java, in Indonesia). In the wet-dry tropics, such as the vast savannas of Africa, agriculture is hindered by the burdens of unpredictable and highly variable water supplies. For example, drought and famine have killed millions of peasant families in the past generation alone (Sachs 1999, 19–20).

In addition, global warming may be taking its greatest toll on tropical countries. Rich countries contribute increasing concentrations of carbon to the atmosphere, and global warming may actually lengthen the growing season for colder parts of the world, such as Canada, the northern United States, and Russia. But, for the tropics, the heat stress is likely to make matters worse agriculturally. Stresses on plants and more severe weather disturbances may hinder improvements in agricultural yields.

David Bradley, an expert on the epidemiology of tropical diseases, has constructed a table (Table 8.2) identifying several possible relationships between health, the environment, and economic development. As Bradley's table makes clear, the relationship between development, the environment, and population health is complex and varied. Bradley notes that, in the planning stages of development, it is important to examine the potential effects on the distribution of disposable income. The goal

Latin American children gather polluted water. The combination of poverty, pollution, and tropical climate causes greater illness and premature death.

should be to promote equality, which in turn has multiple positive effects on environment, health, and development.

Technological Neglect by Corporations and Core Countries

Disease-fighting technologies and biotechnologies to increase agricultural yields are not focused on the tropics. For example, in tropical countries, there are hundreds of malaria-infective bites per person each year, but mosquito control is difficult or impossible. A malaria vaccine would save many of the approximately 2.5 million lives lost to the disease each year. However, pharmaceutical firms are focused primarily on medical treatments and "lifestyle drugs" for affluent societies. But there are a few efforts under way to develop a malaria vaccine. Anthony Stowers led a research team at the National Institute of Allergy and Infectious Diseases; their vaccine has been

TABLE 8.2   *The Possible Interactions of Health, Environment, and Development, with Examples*

Possible Interaction	Examples
Environment favors development	Irrigated desert
Environment impedes development	Erosion of soils
Environment favors health	Better domestic water
Environment impedes health	Schistosomiasis in irrigation
Development favors health	Reduction of poverty
Development impedes health	Loss of land by the poor
Health favors development	Development of tea plantations
Health impedes development	Abandonment of agriculture
Development favors environment	Terracing of fields
Development impedes environment	Deforestation
Health favors environment	More energy to tackle problems
Health impedes environment	River blindness causing neglect

Source: From David Bradley, "Health, Environment, and Tropical Development." In B. Cartledge (Ed.), *Health and the Environment* (Oxford, UK: Oxford University Press, 1994), 127. By permission of Oxford University Press.

tested successfully in monkeys, but how it will perform in humans is still uncertain ("Goat Milk Holds Key to Malaria Cure" 2001).

Colombian immunologist Manuel Patarroyo has also been conducting research on a malaria vaccine on an island in the Amazon River (Honigsbaum 2001). His research subjects are owl monkeys, whose immune system bears a resemblance to humans'.[2] He has also conducted some tests on human volunteers, finding protection rates of 60 percent or lower. However, in random double-blind trials sponsored by the World Health Organization in Gambia and Tanzania, the vaccine did not protect children under five. An additional, U.S. Army–sponsored trial in Thailand in 1966 found the same disappointing result. Patarroyo's research was criticized for methodological flaws, but he has continued efforts to construct a vaccine that will attack any strain of the malaria virus, making it effective anywhere in the world. He has turned down offers from drug companies to buy his vaccine, because if it is successful, he plans to donate it to the World Health Organization. Patarroyo wants a malaria vaccine to be given free to pregnant women and children in sub-Saharan African first, the area worst affected by the disease (Honigsbaum 2001).

The United States has withheld its dues from the United Nations and World Health Organization. This has made it difficult for the UN and WHO to carry out their mission to assist disadvantaged countries. In May of 1999, public health experts

[2] Owl monkeys are one of only three primate species that can be infected with a deadly malaria parasite that also attacks humans, SPf66.

David E. Bloom and colleagues (1999) urged *Science* readers to contact their congressional representatives and apply pressure for World Health Organization support.

> [W]e regret to note that the United States is over $35 million in arrears in assessed dues to the WHO. Furthermore, the U.S. position of resisting even nominal increases in its contribution to the regular budget of WHO compromises America's vital interest in global health, violates the spirit of American generosity, and represents the antithesis of global leadership. . . .
>
> The U.S. government has vigorously criticized international agencies for ineffectiveness and for failing to exercise leadership. . . . WHO is exemplary in this regard. For example, it has reduced its administrative costs this year by 15%. Given WHO's record of success and its new vision, it is incumbent upon us to pay our arrears and enlarge our financial contribution so that WHO can fulfill its global mandate. (Bloom et al. 1999, 911)

In February 2001, the U.S. Senate voted to support an agreement in which the United States would begin to pay its back dues to the United Nations (within which the World Health Organization is located). In return, the UN would reduce the U.S. share of the peacekeeping budget from 31 percent to 26.5 percent. The deal was helped along by a one-time donation of $34 million by media tycoon Ted Turner to cover much of the shortfall resulting from the lower U.S. contribution. The United Nations argues that, even with payment of the $926 million promised, if UN-promised bureaucratic and fiscal reforms are made, $500 million is still owed for missed payments at the past level of obligation.

The World Health Organization recently sponsored a study of how to improve the health of the world's poorest peoples. The Commission on Macroeconomics and Health, led by Jeffrey Sachs (former World Bank economist and architect of Russia's drastic market transition), has issued a report asking wealthy countries to spend an extra 0.1 percent of their economies on the health of the poor. This would add up to $38 billion a year in health spending by 2015 ("World's Poor Need More Money for Health" 2002). Echoing the similar argument made by David E. Bloom and David Canning in *Science* (2000), the commission's bottom-line argument is that, if the poor countries of the world are to develop economically, their health must improve.

The world's sixty poorest countries spend an average of $13 per capita on health; the WHO recommends that be raised to $34. The commission projects that, if poor nations spent more and improved health care systems, they would produce $360 in economic gains, lifting millions of people out of poverty ("World's Poor Need More" 2002). For example, the treatment to cure a case of tuberculosis is $15, but many countries can't afford this expense. Childhood immunizations are also a relatively small expense, which saves about 3 million lives a year. The Bill and Melinda Gates Foundation has chosen universal immunization of children as one of the projects it sponsors.

Political Instability, Corruption, and Violence

Periphery rulers often resort to strong-arm tactics to remain in power and to amass personal wealth, and those are tactics symptomatic of a weak state. Both Max Weber's theory of the state and Immanuel Wallerstein's (1974a) world systems model note that legitimate rulers and consent of the governed are signs of a strong state. Often legitimacy is based in the support of a literate, employed middle class.

A cause of weak states is the "big man" style of rule, in which leaders replace a colonial administration with their own exploitive regime. They maintain a show of power and conspicuous displays of wealth rather than investing in sustainable economic development and democratic traditions. In this scenario, new power elites replace colonial ones, abandoning both traditional models for reaching collective consensus and also avoiding modern Western models of democracy (Ayittey 1998). Rulers stay focused on consolidating their power and keeping it for life. Often they plan for a son or daughter to replace them when they are gone, much as in dynastic succession. In addition, core countries have rewarded some of Africa's most rapacious leaders, such as Mobutu Sese Seko in Zaire. Unfortunately, postcolonial foreign economic and political influences often weaken and destabilize rather than nurture political and economic development.

Case Examples. A few examples illustrate the ways in which the weak, unstable states of periphery countries prevent the development of healthy societies.

Cambodian society has been fraught with war and political instability for over three decades, with the population suffering high rates of death, illness, and trauma. From 1975 to 1979, between 1.7 and 2 million Cambodians (one in five) died from starvation, disease, overwork, or execution under Pol Pot's Khmer Rouge regime. Children ended up in prison along with their parents, because of a Khmer Rouge policy of sentencing entire families to death, intended to prevent family members from seeking revenge later ("Exhibit Portrays Victims" 2000).

Basic services, such as potable water, toilet facilities, and electricity, are not available to the majority of the population, and meeting basic needs takes considerable energy—tasks performed mostly by girls and women. Child labor in the formal economy is estimated at 10 percent, with girls estimated to compose more than half of that group. Lack of access to education, primary health care, immunization, and social welfare services has resulted in the high child mortality rate of 143 per 1,000 children up to five years old (World Bank 2001, Table 2). Cambodia has the highest maternal death rate in Asia, with high rates of anemia among pregnant women contributing to this problem.

In efforts to recover and reform the Cambodian economy, market policy was "liberalized" beginning in 1985, and following the Paris Peace Accord of 1991, this policy was expanded with a massive influx of foreign investments and growth of consumer markets to serve the development sector of the economy. Agriculture lagged behind, growing at a low 2.6 percent rate between 1990 and 1995, slightly below the rate of population growth. Rice production did not increase at all (Arcellana 1998). Rather than focus on enhancing sustainable agricultural production, the Cambodian government instead arranged with corporate investors to expand the harvesting of rubber plantations for export, which resulted in massive deforestation.

Demilitarization has only recently evolved. Cambodia achieved national peace for the first time in nearly three decades, in part by persuading the remnants of the Khmer Rouge military to join the national military ("Cambodia Embarks on Long-awaited Army Cuts" 2000). In 1997 Hun Sen seized power in a violent coup, and the country continued its downward slide of poverty, poor health, and low levels of education. In 1999 life expectancy for men was forty-six and for women, just under fifty (Central Intelligence Agency 1999). Cambodia's per capita GDP is between $300 and $400 ("Helping the Other Guys" 1999, 39). The Asian Development Bank's report found that Cambodian development is hampered by a poorly educated work force, poor health care, and poor water and sanitation. However, in May of 2000, Prime Minister Hun Sen offered promises to the International Monetary Fund to clean up corruption and shrink the military, in exchange for promises of $548 million in aid ("Upbeat Cambodian Leader" 2000).

The legacies of the Khmer Rouge regime continue to degrade Cambodia's social fabric. In a still highly militarized society, violence against women within households is reportedly common. No reliable census has been taken, but a survey in 1991 in the eleven most populous provinces found that one out of three children had lost one or both parents; among that group, 45 percent had lost both parents (Arcellana 1998). Men died by the thousands as soldiers, and women, children, the elderly, and nonmilitary men also suffered an enormous physical and emotional toll.

Women's ability to engage in subsistence agriculture to support their family was further degraded by development policies that excluded women and degraded the environment. Health and social well-being would have been better served by support for sustainable agriculture in tandem with technological modernization and economic diversification, and by hiring women as well as men in the modernizing sectors of the economy.

Sierra Leone has the lowest life expectancy in the world, in part because of ongoing civil war. The rebel forces of the Revolutionary United Front (RUF) attack civilians, government forces, and (when present) United Nations peacekeepers. They routinely cut off the hands and feet of their so-called enemies. The bandaged stumps for hands and feet are reflected in Sierra Leone's dismal "disability adjustments" in WHO life expectancy tables. The RUF's leader, Foday Sankoh, had been arrested by the Nigerian-led force fighting for the Sierra Leone government, tried, and sentenced to death. But he was released to sign a peace agreement forged by the United States ("Sierra Leone's Agony" 2000, 45). Instead of jailing him, the agreement brought Sankoh into the government as vice president, granting him immunity from prosecution for his crimes. Sankoh did not keep his part of the bargain; few of his forces were disarmed, and more abuses followed. In response to a peace march in Freetown on May 8, 2000, which included many of Sankoh's mutilated victims, his guards opened fire, killing eight people ("Sierra Leone's Agony" 2000, 45). A third power broker, Major Johnny-Paul Koroma, and his own forces, "the West Side Jungle Boys," allied with the RUF and the government at different points in time. As we can see, the end of colonialism did not bring an independent or stable rule.

Nigeria returned to civilian rule in May 1999, but a year later was still troubled by violence. More than 100 people died in ethnic clashes in Lagos in November 1999, and most likely over 1,000 died in religious riots in the northern city of Kaduna in February 2000 ("Nigeria: Making a Bad Cop Good" 2000, 46). Fighting broke out between two towns in the southwest in May 2000, resulting in 25 deaths. Crime and corruption are widespread. Nigerians complain that the police are corrupt, incompetent, and brutal. "The 135,000-strong force has an appalling record of arresting innocent people in order to extort money from them, while leaving known criminals to go free in return for a part of their criminal earnings" ("Nigeria: Making a Bad Cop Good" 2000, 46).

Angola has been plagued with a twenty-five-year-old struggle between UNITA rebels and the ruling MPLA. The ongoing violence has not only eliminated chances for stable rule, but has also left the country terrorized and poor. In territory controlled by UNITA, nonsupporters are killed. The government provides financial benefits to encourage support from its potential opponents among politicians, trade unionists, and journalists ("Angola: A Third Force" 2000, 46). The "Psychological Action Office" within the administration silences opponents with blackmail and violence. In addition, the MPLA funds a number of small opposition parties to keep up the façade of democracy. Despite these efforts to consolidate government power, a grassroots movement for change exists. President Jose Eduardo dos Santos, wishing to enhance his legitimacy, announced that elections would be held in 2001. In response, a new United Front for Change has organized an opposition devoted to ending the war and beginning fair elections. All of Angola's churches have joined together in a campaign for peace and national reconciliation. Together, the churches represent the largest base of support in the country, so there is cause for hope that they will exercise some leverage in the elections and thereafter.

Zaire, now renamed the Democratic Republic of the Congo, suffered under the "kleptocracy" of Mobutu Sese Seko for thirty-five years, until he finally died of cancer. Mobutu siphoned off the country's rich natural resources to his own coffers and to those of his kin and cronies. He invested his money abroad in lavish estates and foreign bank accounts, leaving his own country impoverished and undeveloped. Mobutu operated a "shell state," which appeared to have ministers and ministries. They actually conducted little or no government but operated as a privileged network with whom Mobutu shared Zaire's wealth ("The Heart of the Matter" 2000, 24). As a reward for friendly ties enabling export of valuable natural resources, the United States supported Mobutu generously.

Liberia under President Charles Taylor is also accused of operating a shell state. The president recently passed a law that gives him the right to dispose of all "strategic commodities" as he sees fit ("The Heart of the Matter" 2000, 24). These include mineral resources; natural forest products; all art, artifacts and handicrafts; all agricultural and fishery products; and anything else the president should decide to add to the "strategic" list. Foreign capital from export of these resources does not trickle down to improve the population's standard of living.

The Policies of the World Bank and the International Monetary Fund

Loans from international agencies have pulled governments out of fiscal crises. When loans contribute to economic growth, they potentially improve the standard of living and population health. However, debt strangles the economies of many African countries. Forced to borrow to finance debts and pay bills, countries are required by the lending agencies to tighten their spending, keep inflation down, lay off civil servants, and reduce social programs. The World Bank may refuse to continue loan payments if they decide to punish human rights abuses or if loan conditions are not being met by the debtor country. The International Monetary Fund also gives loans to poor and developing countries. The public in core countries often regards loans as "free aid," whereas analysis of where the money goes reveals that corporations and financial institutions based in core countries, and a small elite in the host country, benefit generously from these funds. Large projects require sophisticated technologies and equipment, providing lucrative contracts to transnational corporations and jobs to the privileged in both core and periphery countries. British sociologist Tom Bottomore (1964/1993) argues:

> [T]he policies of the World Bank and the IMF in particular have contributed massively to the impoverishment of a large part of the third world (and to the destruction of the natural environment), while at the same time creating or strengthening in these countries small, wealthy, and frequently corrupt elites. (84)

Gabriel Kolko (1999) argues similarly, drawing on the IMF's own review of all seventy-nine low-income "developing" nations. The IMF loan program failed at two of its key stated purposes: reducing poor countries' foreign debt and promoting economic growth. The conditions of the IMF loans require standard prescriptions for poor countries, including

> reducing government spending and involvement in the economy; prompting exports and removing trade restrictions; deregulating the economy; privatizing government-run enterprises; eliminating price subsidies, including on essentials like food and housing; and imposing consumption taxes. (Kolko 1999, 52)

Rather than aiding countries, these loans have the potential to cause further impoverishment and bring about low or declining economic growth, large increases in foreign debt, stagnation, and increased poverty (Kolko 1999, 53). Kolko's analysis supports a world systems interpretation of the role of the World Bank and IMF. Loan conditions require reductions in social spending, while the wealthiest portion of the population receives a disproportionately larger share of the funds for health and education. The mandates that come with the loans often require workers and the poor to pay the price for the infusion of cash. There is no mystery about how "economic discipline" causes a decline in health and education.

Senegal provides a case example of IMF involvement in worsening social conditions. The country experienced economic crisis through the 1970s and 1980s. The IMF is not to blame for the initial problems, but their loans came with severe austerity measures which worsened living conditions for the Senegalese. Initial problems included years of drought, falling revenues, economic mismanagement and corruption, and declining demand for groundnuts, the principal export crop. The social and economic consequences of painful structural adjustment policies deteriorated living conditions in the capital city of Dakar and other urban areas (Somerville 1997). Rural farmers also did poorly, as the prices paid for their agricultural goods decreased during the latter 1960s. Conditions spiraled downward, made worse by the droughts of the 1980s. Renewed IMF agreements were signed, and the government was required to remove subsidies on food items. The cost of all basic staples increased, but wages did not rise to compensate. There were massive layoffs in government-run enterprises, and male unemployment rose. Public funds were no longer available for services, so user fees were instituted for health care services (Somerville 1997, 25). Without money for upkeep and basic medical supplies, health services and infrastructure deteriorated; per capita spending on health fell by 20 percent between 1981 and 1988 (Weissman 1990,1629). Those with money can still visit private clinics, but those without money must go without or rely on traditional healers (Somerville 1997, 25).

A Reformed World Bank?

In response to criticisms that lending policies have had the effect of worsening the well-being of populations, the World Bank has begun to alter its directives to loan recipients. At the very least, economists agree, loan conditions should not worsen population health and readiness for development. The bank's *World Development Report 2000/2001* is devoted to "attacking poverty." The report encourages the evaluation of redistributive policies for their efficiency and the extent to which they benefit the most disadvantaged (for example, in Chapters 3 and 5 of the report). The bank report encourages policies that meet both of these goals and acknowledges that a strong role must be played by states. "Public financing of services is a core element of poverty reduction policy and practice," but the report warns that services to the poor are often of low quality and unresponsive to their needs (World Bank 2001, 81). The report acknowledges that subsidies to sectors of the population that are not poor are sometimes politically necessary to gain support for programs that alleviate poverty conditions.

The poor need assistance in accumulating the assets (tools, livestock, equipment for their own small businesses) that can make them more productive and economically independent (World Bank 2001, 78–79). The bank acknowledges that "markets do not work well for poor people, because of their physical isolation and because of market failures in the financial, health and insurance sectors" (79). However, it acknowledges that there is no guarantee that state policies will be effective in improving the assets of the poor. Nonetheless, the report offers examples of how the state can play an important role in improving health. For example, mosquito and other pest control, health education on basic hygiene, and nutrition are public health measures with immediate and life-saving benefits. Reducing water and air pollution, along with improved sanitation, dramatically reduce child mortality caused by diarrhea and respiratory infections in poor areas. Dirty water and air are major causes of death for poor children. For example, a World Bank study of 144 water and sanitation projects found that improved water and sanitation services were associated with a median reduction of 22 percent in the incidence of diarrhea and 65 percent in deaths from diarrhea (World Bank 2001, 78).

The bank encourages public-private partnerships in a variety of initiatives, from the goal of achieving universal immunizations, to rejuvenating India's forests, to making telecommunications services more accessible (Chapter 5 of the report). Evaluating the World Bank's programs, including loan and debt relief policies in coming years, will reveal more about the institution's involvement and relative success in reducing poverty and inequality.

Programs That Improve Quality of Life and Health for the Poor

The following are a few examples of programs that improve life for the poor. Such programs have a variety of supports. Some are state supported, others are community-government partnerships, and still others are joint programs between private individuals, organizations or businesses, and governmental agencies. Effective targeting of low-income groups is essential for programs to actually improve the lot of the poor. Government spending on education and health care generally is regressive; that is, it provides the greatest benefits to higher-income groups (World Bank 2001, Chapter 5). The following programs effectively target subsidies and benefits that improve the lot of the poor.

The Singapore Model of Catastrophic Health Insurance

Serious injury and illness cause harmful temporary and sometimes permanent loss of income to poor households. For that reason, catastrophic health coverage is an important poverty prevention measure. The Singapore government set up a three-tiered system of health insurance between 1984 and 1993 as part of its social security system. Medisave, Medishield, and Medifund are the three tiers, funded by payroll and employer taxes. Medisave is aimed at medium-level health risks and pays hospitalization expenses of up to $300 a day. Minor health care needs are to be paid out of pocket or through private insurance. Catastrophic health risks are paid through Medishield, for expenses exceeding the coverage provided by Medisave. Medifund provides subsidies to poorer individuals who are not able to cover expenses that are unpaid by the first two tiers of the program. In this way, the poor are not locked out of the system due to their inability to pay sufficient funds to receive benefits. The Medifund tier turns a health care insurance program that would be regressive (favoring those with the greater ability to pay) into a system that allows the poor to apply for additional coverage as needed. Financial need must be demonstrated through applications to local Hospital Medifund Committees (Prescott & Pradhan 1999).

SEWA: Self-Employed Women's Association of Ahmedabad, India

SEWA was established in 1972 as a trade union for women who work in the informal sector of the economy. It includes 220,000 members, including street merchants, domestic workers, and laborers (Lund & Srinivas 1999). The union provides a social security program that insures members' health, life, and assets. It also operates a bank that provides savings accounts and loans to members. These services are covered by premiums paid by members (which cover one-third of the costs) and by a grant from the German Technical Development Agency. The Indian Ministry of Labor provides additional subsidies in collaboration with two private insurance companies. This community-public-private venture combines micro lending and saving programs with worker protections. It has helped to raise the income of its members, and there are plans to include health and pension components (Lund & Srinivas 1999). This kind of organization helps to make self-employed women more self-sufficient and able to weather temporary losses. Benefits to these women's children come from stabilizing wages and providing a safety net for unpredictable work and health problems. Ideally, as wages improve, there will be less need for subsidies to support the trade union's services.

Mexico's PROGRESA

This program targets low-income households, providing subsidies to prevent child labor and to encourage the poor to keep their children in school through secondary education. The subsidies can be a significant source of household income, and the amounts increase with the age of the children to reflect their increased potential earnings. The grant for a child in the third year of secondary school equals approximately 46 percent of the average earnings of an agricultural worker (Prescott & Pradhan 1999). There are also health and nutrition components to the program, which target poor families with free health care and nutritional supplements.

Social Funds

These are agencies that help to finance small projects identified by poor communities. Social funds exist in approximately fifty countries, following a successful model set up by the Bolivian government in 1987 in response to economic recession. Most of the funds are located in Latin American and sub-Saharan countries, but funds are also being set up in Eastern European and central Asian countries. The earliest social funds offered temporary employment in times of economic hardship. Crises caused by Hurricane Mitch in Central America, civil wars in Cambodia and Angola, earthquake in Armenia, and drought in Zambia all have been assisted by the operation of social funds. In addition to crisis management, social funds help to develop infrastructure in ways that originate within communities. This provides an opportunity for communities to identify their primary needs for roads, water, and other projects. Finally, social funds have been used to improve the health and welfare of low-income communities by, for example, assisting with boosting school enrollments or health center use (Frigenti et al. 1998; Jorgensen & Van Domelen 1999).

The Eritrean Community Development Fund combines a public work program with a social fund to carry out community projects. Local committees supervise projects and monitor the community's contribution. In the process, community members and local government staff are trained in project design and management (Frigenti et al. 1998). The flexibility and the community-based nature of social funds make them a promising mechanism for support of projects that can have significant impacts on living conditions. Such improvements have the potential to improve the health and well-being of low-income communities.

Prospects for Improvement?

From a world systems perspective, the prospects for upward mobility for periphery countries are slim. Wallerstein (1974b) identifies three routes of upward mobility and provides examples, but emphasizes that upward mobility does not come easily and that downward mobility is the more common occurrence. The first method for moving up is *"seizing by chance"* in a contracting world economy. Examples are Russia and Italy in the late 1800s; Brazil, Mexico, and South Africa following the 1929 depression; and Korea in the 1950s, following the Korean War. The second avenue is *"by invitation"* in an expanding world economy. This involves collaboration with investors from the capitalist core, bringing about increased dependency. Examples include the Ivory Coast and Kenya during the late 1960s and early 1970s. The third opportunity for upward mobility comes from the strategy of *"self-reliance,"* with state-directed development and import substitution. The latter involves production of goods that otherwise would have to be imported. This strategy is an effort to achieve economic independence from reliance on other countries' goods and to resist dependency. Tanzania experienced success with this method during the 1960s, but that success has since vanished (Green 1970). The limits of this approach are many, and successes often succumb to the pressures of the global economy. Protectionism can backfire and result in increased dependence on foreign corporations and international financial institutions, and a weakened state (Wallerstein 1974b). A country may be forced to reverse its priorities, sacrificing social spending, food subsidies, and care of workers as a result of the "discipline" imposed by loans.

The periphery status of poor African countries is firmly entrenched at the beginning of the twenty-first century. However, the discouraging facts found in Table 8.1 are not intractable. There are real opportunities to improve health and to lower mortality rates in African, Asian, and Latin American countries, as well as in countries of the former Soviet Union. International institutions and nonprofit agencies can provide a health safety net coordinated by the World Health Organization. Public health infrastructure can be expanded to reduce communicable disease through immunization programs, prenatal and postnatal care, local primary care clinics, and health education programs. To maintain financial support, the WHO requires partnerships with national, corporate, and individual sponsors committed to improving the life chances of the world's poorest populations. Infusions of leadership and cash are needed to meet the goals of basic and preventive health care for all. In the meanwhile, the World Bank and International Monetary Fund are attempting to incorporate a more holistic model of social health into their economic policies. Coordination with the World Health Organization could ensure that social health is furthered by economic policies; this in turn will improve the prospects for economic and political development.

An example of a global effort to improve health is the Global Alliance for Vaccines and Immunization (GAVI). The partners involved include national governments, research institutions, the Bill and Melinda Gates Children's Vaccine Program, the International Federation of Pharmaceutical Manufacturers Associations, the Rockefeller foundation, UNICEF, the World Bank Group, and the World Health Organization (World Health Organization 2000, 83). This powerful lineup of institutions and resources aims to make childhood immunizations universal. Twenty-five of the thirty million nonimmunized children born each year live in countries that have per capita incomes of less than $1,000 U.S.. The program aims to deliver six basic vaccines identified by the World Health Organization (against poliomyelitis, diphtheria, whooping cough, tetanus, measles, and tuberculosis). In addition, it will expand the use of newer vaccines now in use in developed countries, such as those for hepatitis B and yellow fever. The alliance's goal for the year 2005 is to see that all countries achieve at least 80 percent immunization. It estimates that an additional $226 million is needed annually to reach this level of immunization with the six basic vaccines; an additional $352 million is needed for the two newer vaccines (World Health Organization 2000, 83).

The World Health Organization estimates that cost-effective interventions could save children under five from deaths caused by malnutrition or communicable diseases. Vaccines, rehydration treatments, and nutritional supplements are some examples. The cost would be an estimated $100 or less per disability-adjusted life year saved. Interventions could save children from ages five to fourteen from malnutrition and communicable diseases as well (World Health Organization 2000, 5). The organization predicts that death rates will decline by 2020, giving the poor of the world over four additional years of life (World Health Organization 2000, 5).

The priority of the World Health Organization is to care for those most burdened by disease and premature death. A revised World Bank health policy now states that it will give highest priority to improvements in the health, nutrition, and population status of the world's poor (World Bank 1997). The bank's 1990 "Global Burden of Disease" study provided the first global estimates of disease and found that, in 1990, *communicable* diseases caused 59 percent of deaths and disabilities among the world's poorest fifth of the population (Gwatkin et al. 1999; Murray & Lopez 1996). Among the world's richest 20 percent, *noncommunicable* diseases caused 85 percent of deaths and disabilities. Projections to 2020 suggest that an accelerated decline in communicable diseases would *decrease* the poor-rich health gap, while an accelerated decline in noncommunicable diseases would *increase* the poor-rich gap (Gwatkin et al. 1999).

A new kind of investing is needed, conceived in terms of long-term global well-being and stability. Significant gains are possible, given the enormous resources and technological sophistication in the world today. Providing inoculations and improving food security are a high priority. The commitment of wealthy nations, corporations, and individuals to develop and maintain this safety net is essential. Improvements may be carried out with multiple purposes and benefits, some altruistic and others self-interested. They may provide tax breaks and philanthropic satisfaction for the wealthy and contribute to global political and economic stability.

The World Health Organization estimates that, in poor countries, half of the household expenditures on health are spent on medicines (2000, 131). Within their governments' health budgets, pharmaceuticals are usually the second largest expenditure after wages. Governments and companies can make it a priority to ensure that essential medicines are available to those in need. Pharmaceutical companies can perhaps be persuaded to give back to the global community in the form of reduced-price medicines to countries that cannot afford them. The WHO admonishes all players in the international community to apply activist pressure in this effort (2000, 131). Perhaps tax breaks for donations of pharmaceuticals and medical technologies are one answer. In addition, whenever possible, the WHO should deal directly with local and international health organizations and agencies, so that corrupt officials cannot sabotage these important efforts. International stewardship by the World Health Organization is needed to coordinate efforts among governmental and nongovernmental organizations, universities, professional and consumer networks, religious bodies, and private providers.

9

Development and Health: Promise and Limitations

Economic growth is a means to an end—a better life for the masses. Unless economic growth raises general living standards, true "development" has not taken place.

—Glenn Firebaugh and Frank Beck, "Does Economic Growth Benefit the Masses? Growth, Dependence, and Welfare in the Third World"

Far too much of our analysis of the transitions [to democracy and a market economy] . . . neglects the raw emotional impact of these changes. The collapse of a moral order complete with childhood socialization, treasured symbols, accepted beliefs, and sentimental associations cannot be treated as a simple choice between past and future, better and worse living conditions, or even liberty and coercion. . . . In the final analysis, the success of the political and economic revolutions of the late twentieth century will rest with what they come to mean to those who must bear the cost of change.

—Miguel Angel Centeno, "Between Rocky Democracies and Hard Markets: Dilemmas of the Double Transition"

A definition of economic growth is an increase in the total value of goods and services produced in a nation. But, typically, "development" is used to refer to a diverse array of social and economic changes, such as transformations from an agrarian to an industrial economy or from a state-directed economy (such as former Soviet economies) to a market-driven economy with decisions made by corporations and major investors. Development also may refer to continued technological development and economic growth in affluent postindustrial societies. Democratic institutions may or may not emerge with transformations to a market economy. And it is also possible for more

169

civic-minded policies to evolve while economic transformations are heavily directed by the state (as in South Korea).

We recall from earlier chapters the association between increases in gross national product, improved standard of living, and life expectancy. Does increased national wealth always improve living conditions for the majority of the population? We know that greater equality makes healthier societies. And state policies play an important role; they have the potential to provide a safety net for displaced workers and ensure that people have adequate food, shelter, education, and health care.

In this chapter, we discuss six dynamics that affect the relationship between development and health. Case examples from Japan, South Korea, Botswana, Argentina, Brazil, and Chile illustrate the dynamics and the various combined elements that influence health outcomes. For most countries, a formula is presented showing the ingredients influential to that country's health. Before introducing the dynamics and case examples, a brief overview of three conceptual perspectives on development are presented. Readers may consider these perspectives as more or less applicable to the examples presented in the chapter. We consider the following question:

- Just how much does development improve population health?

Approaches to Development

The following are three perspectives on development that influence policies and shape debates among scholars and leaders.

The *liberal and neoliberal* perspective may be called the "free-market" perspective, in which the state theoretically plays a minimal role in directing market developments. Those who hold this perspective believe in the workings of a "laissez-faire" (hands-off) market: Left on its own, markets will move naturally toward what is most economically productive. For example, if a business cannot compete and is not profitable, it should lose out to its competitors. The neoliberal version of this perspective is updated from its eighteenth-century origins. In the more recent version, states play a more active role, setting rules for corporations and countries to follow in trade relations, ensuring that corporate interests are protected. Tariffs and other national barriers to trade are considered bad for free trade. In various regional trade agreements, countries make a pact not to levy tariffs on products entering their country from other countries in the agreement, establishing free trade zones. The North Atlantic Free Trade Agreement (NAFTA) between Canada, the United States, and Mexico is an example. Another example of neoliberal policies can be seen in less-developed countries where international lending agencies restrict social spending and sometimes require countries to "float" their currencies; that is, allow their currencies to devalue on an international market.

Dependency and world systems perspectives are by now familiar to the reader. The global economy is one system, with countries arranged in core, periphery, and semi-periphery positions. This perspective is critical of liberal and neoliberal acceptance of social inequalities between classes and among countries, which is seen as harmful to health. Dependency theorists dispute the idea that there are "free markets" and "laissez-faire" states, and ask why workers cannot move across borders the way that capital does. This perspective questions the reality of the laissez-faire ideology, pointing to the history of states' playing a central role in fostering and protecting the interests of capital and core countries. (Remember, in the fifteenth century, Queen Isabella of Spain financed Christopher Columbus's expedition to the New World.) States are not always generous and hard working toward the interests of labor and the poor, according to the world systems perspective. This perspective does not trust that "trickle-down" benefits accrue to the disadvantaged when capital reaps healthy profits. Export-driven development in periphery and semi-periphery countries distorts their economies, inhibiting their development of indigenous industries and sound infrastructures.

The *statist perspective* emphasizes the role of the state in directing economic as well as social policies. State managers are key economic actors in decisions on how to spend funds and set priorities. State managers support a development program that to varying degrees provides advantages to the elite and disadvantages to workers. The Chinese government is a good example, along with other developing Asian economies, such as South Korea, Malaysia, and Indonesia; Japan also developed earlier under a "capitalist development state" (Johnson 1982; Kerbo & McKinstry 1998). Leaders in these countries consider the state's role to be critical in controlling the direction of the economy and containing the pressures from labor for higher wages and better working conditions.

A variant on world systems and statist perspectives is a view that emphasizes the *importance of social movements* (Biggart & Guillen 1999). This perspective focuses on the inequities that emerge from economic transformations, which produce discontents and social movements. Popular citizen and worker uprisings often demand a greater share of a country's wealth, greater civil rights and freedoms, and representative democracy. For example, the authors of *Revolutions of the Late Twentieth Century* describe the role of social movements in explaining social changes and political revolutions (Goldstone et al. 1991).

Refining the "Wealth Equals Health" Formula: Six Dynamics

The following six dynamics influence the relationship between economic development and population health:

1. A country's readiness for development
2. Internal development processes
3. The extent to which the majority benefits from development
4. The extent to which inequality increases with development
5. The effectiveness of civic-minded state policies
6. The epidemiology of the country

1. A Country's Readiness for Development

A country's readiness for economic development determines its ability to respond to market opportunities. There is no one formula for readiness. It is influenced by conditions in the global economy at a particular point in time and is shaped by a country's organizational and developmental processes (Biggart & Guillen 1999). Japan and South Korea serve as examples of readiness and successful courses of development. In both cases, but especially in the case of Japan, dramatic health benefits are the result of its development and economic success, particularly after World War II, when inequality was dramatically controlled. Japan's post–World War II health successes can be properly understood only in social context. Japan has greater income equality, less crime, and fewer ethnic groups and immigrants compared to most other modern postindustrial societies (Kerbo & McKinstry 1998).

Japan: Healthiest Country in the World.

Nearly 150 years ago, during the Meiji Restoration, development was made a priority in Japan. Fearing colonization or economic exploitation by either Europeans or Americans, the new political elite and the Meiji government wanted rapid industrialization, so that they could hold their own economically and militarily against Western powers (Kerbo & McKinstry 1998). A new upper class of wealthy families called the *zaibatsu* dominated the economy prior to World War II. They created new industries and financial institutions in a highly integrated set of familial, political, and economic ties. Before the war, about ten *zaibatsu* families controlled about 75 percent of Japan's corporate assets. There were enormous gaps between rich and poor, considerable poverty, and extreme exploitation of labor (Kerbo & McKinstry 1998, 49).

Following World War II, wealthy corporate families had their assets taken away by U.S. occupational forces. However, interlocking groups of corporations, called *keiretsu*, reemerged following the war but resembled the old *zaibatsu* in many ways. In addition, land reform policies, externally guided by the United States, created many small land-owning farmers and mostly dismantled the feudal organization of Japanese agriculture, which had been aristocratically managed with peasants providing the labor. Japanese land reforms reduced the area under feudal tenancy (peasant laborers' farming sections of landowners' property) from nearly 50 percent to approximately 10 percent (Horowitz 1972, 293). Most farmers acquired land of their own in a relatively smooth transition, with minimal disruption of agricultural production. Military overseers lost political power to middle-sized farmers, which laid the foundation for local decision making and a more satisfying rural life (Horowitz 1972, 293–294). Land reform was also successful because other factors contributed to improvements in agricultural production, including industrialization, occupational specialization, and urbanization.

Japan led Asia for several decades in successful growth and development. Horowitz (1972) suggests that Japan's successful development process was due to the fusion of nationalist values with peasant demands, in combination with urbanization and industrialization (298).

An additional positive development was the narrowed income differences across the Japanese population during the postwar decades. Japan's development and income equality have paid off in a healthy population. For example, despite higher rates of smoking than in the United States, the Japanese experience one-third to one-half the number of lung cancer deaths. Their cardiovascular disease rates are also considerably lower. During the postwar decades, Japan also experienced substantial and long-term reductions in crime (Wilkinson 1996, 167). Japanese policing and criminal justice practices reflect its highly integrated social relations and its cultural emphasis on harmony. Police are considered moral guardians, and only 2 percent of crime convictions result in jail sentences. The goals of Japanese policing are markedly different from their American and British counterparts.

> An analogue of what the Japanese policeman wants the offender to feel is the tearful relief of a child when confession of wrong doing to his parents results in a gentle laugh and a warm hug. In relation to an American policeman, Japanese officers want to be known for the warmth of their care rather than the strictness of their enforcement. (Bayley 1976, 156, cited in Wilkinson 1996, 170)

Early in the twenty-first century, Japan is going through economic and social changes that may enhance inequality and erode health. Nonetheless, Japan still has the highest life expectancy in the world (seventy-seven for men and eighty-four for women), the highest level of income equality, and nearly perfect equality of child survival across its population.

Japan and Sweden have the lowest death rates in the world for children under five. Interestingly, the two countries' family structures differ markedly: Japanese families are overwhelmingly nuclear, with a low divorce rate; Swedish families are often single parent–headed or composed of a cohabiting couple. More than half of all Swedish births occur outside marriage (Wilkinson 1996, 166). What the two countries have in common is the relative absence of poverty and the highest levels of income equality. For example, only 2 percent of single-parent families lived in relative poverty (below half the average income) as measured in 1987, compared to 54 per cent in the United States and 21 percent among OECD (affluent, developed) countries (Hewlett 1993, cited in Wilkinson 1996, 167). In these comparisons, we find wealth and equality predicting favorable health outcomes. Higher inequality in affluent countries (such as the United States) detracts from quality of life and weakens the health benefits that come from development. We can summarize Japan's development-health profile in this formula:

> Successful development → Wealth + income equality + State policies and civic culture that favor egalitarian policies and social harmony → High life expectancy and low infant mortality

From the Japanese example, we add another principle to our list from earlier chapters.

Principle 9

Development is most able to improve health and life expectancy when it increases overall wealth and equality, and includes policies that place a high priority on civic life.

South Korea: Postwar State-directed Development and Recent Attention to Social Welfare.   Korea was annexed by the Japanese in the early twentieth century and administered as a colony until the end of World War II, when the Japanese surrendered to the Allies in 1945. Modest reforms following World War II increased the number of South Korean farmers who owned their own land; the number of owners and half-owners increased by 170 percent, resulting in approximately 26 percent of all cultivated land being owned by its tillers (Horowitz 1972, 294). Some analysts have attributed South Korea's later economic success partly to this creation of a small land-owning peasantry in the evolution away from feudal control (e.g., Berger 1991; Gold 1986). However, in the short run, land reform failed to greatly improve the conditions of tenancy and was not accompanied by a process of industrialization that might have ensured success (Horowitz 1972, 294–295). In the Korean War (1950–1953) the South, with support from U.S. and other international forces, fought off a Chinese and North Korean effort to establish Korea as a communist country. South Korean casualties were estimated at 415,000 dead and 428,568 wounded and missing. Following the war and throughout the 1950s, South Korea remained poorer than most of its neighbors and one of the poorest countries in the world (Suh 1998, 16). During the 1960s, Korea's authoritarian regime focused on building a market economy and left quality of life a low priority (Suh 1998, 107). This state-directed development was remarkably successful. During the thirty-year period from 1965 to 1995, Korea averaged a real growth rate of over 8 percent in gross domestic product (GDP), much higher than its East Asian neighbors, Latin American countries, and wealthy developed countries.[1]

A high level of education and literacy fueled South Korea's development. By 1985, approximately 99 percent of the age group for middle school were enrolled, and about 35 percent of the student age group attended colleges and universities; these are among the highest rates in the world. By 1997 adult literacy was up to 99 percent for men and 96 percent for women (World Bank 2000, Table 2).

Nonetheless, it is predictable that a highly educated, aspiring, affluent, and youthful population would become discontented with authoritarian-style government. Suh (1998) summarizes, "Korea's civil movement emerged in reaction to the unequal treatment of the population, the lack of democracy, and the state's attempt to define 'nationalism' as the whole population's support for economic growth" (108). Worker unrest also emerged with the Asian economic downturn of the mid-1990s. Tensions surfaced over workers' rights and employers' obligations. In South Korean producers' effort to move production offshore for cheaper labor and to lay off workers, the *chaebol* (large corporate conglomerates) used their influence to push through legislation that would release them from the traditional obligation to keep workers employed (Conforti 1999). This legislative effort occurred on December 26, 1996, and the response was a massive strike and demonstrations by hundreds of thousands (Conforti 1999).

---

[1] Divided into decades, South Korea's growth rate for 1960–1969 was 7.7%, for 1970–1979, 9.5%, for 1980–1989, 8.2% and 1990–1995, 7.6% (Suh 1998, 18). Growth of private consumption per capita from 1980–1997 averaged 7 percent per year (World Bank 2000, Table 2). Only Hong Kong exceeded Korea during the 1960–1969 period (Suh 1998, 18).

Major improvements in longevity, death rates, and infant mortality occurred during the decades of economic development following the Korean War. Life expectancy increased from fifty-one years for men and fifty-four years for women in the late 1950s to sixty-nine years for men and seventy-six years for women as of 1997 (World Bank 2000, Table 2). South Korea's "equality of child survival" figure was a high 0.947, indicating a high degree of child survival across social groups (World Health Organization 2000, Table 2).

There is no universal health care in South Korea, but the government initiated a private-public insurance plan that gradually incorporated the majority of the population. In 1977 the Ministry of Health and Social Affairs coordinated its plan with employers and private insurance firms to establish two programs. The Medical Aid Act gave basic medical care to low-income individuals and did not provide much service to rural areas (Suh 1998, 91). In the second program, oriented toward higher-paid workers, insurance was provided for employees and their families from private businesses of 500 or more employees. Employers and workers shared expenses. In 1979 the latter plan was expanded to businesses with 300 or more people, with subsequent reductions until only 16 employees were needed to implement the health insurance program. By the end of 1988, almost 79 percent of the population was insured. However, a contentious issue remained regarding differences in premium costs across various businesses, state-employed workers, and rural residents. The expansion of the program in the 1980s coincided with other policy initiatives to improve quality of life and social welfare (Suh 1998, 91).

Grassroots movements continue to mobilize around equality and health issues in South Korea. During the 1980s, movements demanded greater social equality, and a patients' rights movement in 1986 won passage of a Bill of Patients' Rights in response to a campaign led by the Citizens' Alliance for Consumer Protection (Kaur & Herxheimer 1994). Under this proclamation, every patient is deemed to have access to competent health care and equal treatment regardless of age, sex, ethnic origin, religion, political affiliation, economic status, or social class.

Korea's state-directed economy has brought affluence and at the beginning of the new century is at a juncture at which it can contribute to social development through a variety of policies and programs in education, health care, and taxation policies (Suh 1998, 103). To apply our analysis of health outcomes, we offer a formula in which development and affluence have played the greatest role in Korea's health improvements.

Economic growth → Improved living conditions →
Lower infant mortality and improved longevity

In comparison to Japan, we can see that there are fissures in the links between South Korea's economic development, relative social equality, and health outcomes. Greater income equality and more democratic processes could further enhance South Korea's health profile. If the country is able to ease its labor problems while satisfying the pressures of its well-educated and aspiring younger generation, then we could expect continued improvements in social welfare and health. Its relationship with North Korea is evolving, and reunification has been mentioned as a possibility. The North's dire economic problems have created some interest in movement out of its isolationism. For the South, reunification would increase both overall inequality and social tensions, despite the advantage of inexpensive labor from the North. Policy makers will have to attend to these issues if they wish to continue progress toward civic culture and improved health.

The case studies of Japan and South Korea illustrate internal processes that spurred development, allowing them to take advantage of regional and global economic opportunities. We continue discussion of "country readiness" here by noting the handicap of regional economic disadvantage.

The Case of Botswana.   In Chapter 8 we noted the dilemmas of countries in sub-Saharan Africa and noted the cumulative effects of social, political, and economic factors. We saw the disadvantages of being in a neighborhood of countries on the periphery of the global economy, where basic needs for food, water, medicine, and pest control are poorly met. Nonetheless, development is possible in underdeveloped regions.

Botswana, located in southern Africa, is currently mired in an AIDS crisis. However, prior to the onset of the epidemic, Botswana was in the process of remarkable economic and political development. At the time of its independence from Britain in 1966, Botswana went from being one of the poorest countries in the world to having an average GNP growth rate per capita of over 8 percent from 1965 to 1985 (Harvey & Lewis 1990). The growth rate was only slightly lower between 1985 and 2000. Employment in the formal sector grew over 9.5 percent per year from 1965 to 2000. Nonetheless, Botswana's reliance on a limited number of exports leaves its agricultural sector vulnerable to drought, and price drops for its diamonds in international markets dramatically reduce the country's income.

Botswana carried out successful national democratic elections between 1965 and 1984, in which the Botswana Democratic Party won large majorities against several others in its multiparty system. In stark contrast to some of its neighbors, its politics were not racialized or embroiled in ethnic disputes.

> Botswana had no political prisoners, maintained free speech, association, religion, and a free (if small) press, included a small number of its minority white population, as well as black citizens from a variety of the country's ethnic regions, in senior political and administrative posts without any system of quota representation. (Harvey & Lewis 1990, 1)

Botswana has a well-developed, government-funded health care system that has included a family planning program since the 1970s (Harvey and Lewis 1990). Before the AIDS epidemic, child mortality was low compared to that in most other African countries (88 per 1,000 children five and under, as of 1977; World Bank 2000, Table 2). However, the AIDS epidemic has wiped out the advances from health spending and the country's developmental success. Life expectancies dropped from a high of sixty-six years to forty-six years for men and forty-eight for women in 1997, and in 2000 overall life expectancy was below forty. In the World Health Organization's disability-adjusted life expectancy (which subtracts years of estimated disability), Botswana ranked dismally low at thirty-two years (World Health Organization 2000, Table 5). This, too, is caused mostly by the AIDS epidemic.

2. Internal Development Processes

Internal development processes are varied and complex, influencing the results of transitions to a market economy (Biggart & Guillen 1999). They have an impact on growth as well as on economic stagnation, on social improvements as well as on deterioration of quality of life and health. For example, consider the "immense differences between a transition from the communism of Eastern Europe, the neoliberal military authoritarianism of Latin America, and the authoritarian state-directed capitalism of East Asia" (Centeno 1994, 126). The transition to market capitalism may involve a variety of economic policies and programs, sometimes internally directed, at other times externally mandated (for example, in Japan after World War II or in contemporary countries developing with loans from the International Monetary Fund). Policies aimed at spurring rapid economic growth may variously include state fiscal austerity, tightening of credit, currency devaluation, trade liberalization (removing tariffs and subsidies), wage reductions (enabling capital accumulation and investment), and privatization of state-owned businesses, services, or natural resources.

What *is* the relationship between type of government and economic development? The question is an important one if we wish to understand the ways that policies contribute to improvements in quality of life and health. One view presupposes that democracy and transitions to a market economy are intricately connected (Passel 1993, 60, cited in Centeno 1994, 128). Another argues that a state-directed approach is a necessary first strategy for making the transition to a market economy. Later, democratic institutions can be developed (Bhagwati 1966, 204). However, studies comparing countries' political regimes have not found a clear relationship between development outcomes and any one form of government—democratic, authoritarian, state-directed, or mixed models. For example, one analyst did not find that authoritarian regimes economically outperform democracies, nor are they more likely to impose fiscal belt-tightening policies (Remmer 1986). Others found that authoritarian regimes were better at dealing with inflation and cutting budgets, but that transitional governments (toward or away from democracy) have the greatest difficulty making debt payments (Stallings & Kaufman 1989, cited in Centeno 1994, 128). We conclude that, although state policies and social institutions are key in shaping the development process, there is no one prescription for accelerating economic and democratic development.

For example, China's path has been a state-directed one. It has opened its previously closed and tightly controlled economy to Chinese entrepreneurial enterprises and foreign investors. However, its market transformation differs from the neoliberal path of rapid "radical restructuring" followed in post-Soviet countries under the tutelage of Western economists. The Chinese development process, including liberalization of prices, foreign trade, and investment plans, has been carried out more gradually, guided by state administrative decrees (Adam 1999, 7). Despite its new openness to foreign investment, China still proclaims that it is building *market socialism*, guided by the state, rather than capitalism or democracy. And yet China's urbanized, developing regions are experiencing some degree of westernization, culturally and economically. The enormity of its potential consumer markets has attracted billions in foreign investment, and high rates of production have also spurred economic growth. The Chinese economy grew very rapidly during the 1980s, and more rapidly still during the 1990s (with, for example, a growth rate of just under 9 percent in 1997).

We expect democratic countries with vibrant civic cultures to perform best in bringing about improved living conditions and better health. But democratic processes (whether in socialist or capitalist countries) are most closely associated with equity-enhancing policies that minimize income inequality, develop remedies to minimize poverty, and promote social welfare among all citizens. Democratic institutions and the rule of law need time to develop gradually; they are cultural developments as much as political ones, and never a fully attained ideal.

> None of the revolutions that produced the developed states of Western Europe and of North America originally established what today would be called a democracy. Even into the twentieth century large segments of these populations were excluded from voting for reasons of sex, class, or race. . . . The conflict between the economic and political imperatives facing contemporary states in Eastern Europe and Latin America would certainly be less problematic if a state had only to consider the wishes of 8% of the population, as was the case in Britain in 1867. (Centeno 1994, 135)

Indeed, economic development often poses challenges to democratically ruled countries. The need to accumulate and invest capital through taxes does not often coincide with the majority of constituencies' demands in a democracy. Therefore, there are tensions between the processes of economic development and democratic governance. Centeno (1994) suggests that solutions to the dilemmas of development within democracies involve the following: contracts (legal agreements among parties), mechanisms to enforce policies (laws, regulations, penalties), and trust in the viability of agreements (131). These dovetail with characteristics of working democracies, including the availability of spontaneous and voluntary participation by citizens, policy making, and a moral commitment by participants (Przeworski 1991).

Laws often involve explicit compromises and agreements that distribute resources in an acceptable manner to social groups. These may take the form of legislation that attempts to protect the interests of business *and* labor, including, for example, minimum wage guarantees, unemployment insurance, limited progressive taxation, financial incentives for business interests, or provisions allowing (but limiting) workers' striking rights.

But the "inequality and health" thesis holds that, as inequality between social groups increases, group participation, trust, and health deteriorate. Conversely, greater social equality fosters social trust and lowers stress on those at the lower end of the social hierarchy. From this perspective, greater equality would be predicted to prevent cardiovascular disease and to boost immune functioning generally in the population. Social trust enables economic and political change to move forward. It enables a climate of civility and greater consensus on principles of fairness. This "precontractual solidarity"

(Durkheim 1893/1973) comes easier when societies are culturally and ethnically homogeneous, with relatively equal distributions of wealth and income. Class relations in highly unequal societies are not as conducive to social trust as in more equal societies. For example, discussions of the market and democratic transitions in post-Soviet Eastern European and Latin American societies note the need for a return to "civil society" as integral to dismantling authoritarian regimes and developing democratic institutions (Centeno 1994, 137). That shift entails managing class relations with policies that prevent poverty and enhance overall quality of social life (for example, in schools, housing, health care, and protection of the environment). In reforms, state managers who promise higher wages and relatively stable food and housing prices must be able to carry through on those policies in order to maintain trust and hold onto power in a democratic framework.

Table 9.1 presents a measure of inequality for countries discussed in this and earlier chapters. The Gini Index is provided alongside the countries' per capita gross national product, infant mortality rate, and life expectancy at birth.

Argentina: The Limitations and Pitfalls of Development for Enhancing Health. After the second world war until the early 1980s, Argentina experienced political upheaval, much of which was associated with integrating the urban working classes into the social and political system (di Tella & Dornbusch 1989, 1). Just after World War II, Argentina had a per capita GNP second only to the United States' in the Americas, and ahead of Italy's and Spain's. However, the economy began to slip after that, and by the early 1980s, Argentina's per capita and total GNP was fifth in the Americas and also ranked behind Italy's and Spain's (di Tella & Dornbusch 1989, 1).

TABLE 9.1 *Gini Index, GNP per Capita, Infant Mortality Rate, and Life Expectancy for Selected Countries*

Country	Gini Index	GNP per Capita (1999 dollars)	Infant Mortality Rate, 1998	Life Expectancy at Birth, 1998
Japan	24.9/1993	32,230	4	80.5
Sweden	25.0/1992	25,040	4	79.5
South Korea	31.6/1993	8,490	9	72.5
China	40.3/1998	780	31	70.0
United States	40.8/1997	30,600	7	77.0
Chile	56.5/1994	4,740	10	75.0
Brazil	60.0/1996	4,420	33	67.5
Argentina	n.a.*	7,600	19	73.5
Botswana	n.a.	240	62	46.0

*Not available

Source: World Bank, *World Development Report 2000/2001: Attacking Poverty* (Washington, DC: World Bank, 2001), Tables 1, 2, 5, and 7.

Argentina's slide into increased poverty during the 1990s contrasts with its neighbor Chile's progress during that period (described below in a case study). In both countries, 22 percent of the population was in poverty at the start of the decade (as measured by the World Bank), but by the end of the decade, Argentina's rate had increased to 29, whereas Chile's remained at 22. During the 1990s, both countries were developing economically, but they charted different courses. Argentina developed rapidly but left much of its population untouched by any trickle-down wealth ("It's an Unfair World" 2000, 14). Argentina has a literate, highly educated, and urbanized population, with an average GNP per capita ($8,970 international dollars,[2] 1998) nearly double neighboring Brazil's ($4,570) and Chile's ($4,810). Its life expectancy is correspondingly higher as well, with seventy years for men and seventy-seven for women, compared with Brazil's sixty-three years for men and seventy-one years for women (World Bank 2000, Table 2). The real surprise, though, is that less-wealthy Chile's is higher than both countries', with seventy-two years for men and seventy-eight years for women.

Economically, Argentina has the dilemmas predicted by world systems theory for semi-periphery countries; it must produce beef and compete for sales in the global marketplace while purchasing consumer goods and oil at world prices. A World Bank survey of Argentine leaders found that they blamed worsening inequality and poverty on free market and privatization policies ("It's an Unfair World" 2000, 14). The United States and Britain have trade barriers against Argentine beef and sweets. For example, U.S. beef quotas, influenced by domestic beef interests, let in only a tiny bit of Argentine beef, which is still grass fed and would sell briskly with choosy consumers. Its soy meal faces a 10 percent U.S. tariff, whereas by comparison, American competitors enjoy a dollar-per-bushel government loan. Exports of sweets to Europe are tagged with a 10 percent tariff, plus sugar taxes that can bring the trade burden to 45 percent ("Anything Grows" 2000, 12). Argentina's own relative affluence and higher wages compared to its neighbors' result in higher underemployment and considerable inequality. *The Economist*'s description fits Argentina's semi-periphery status.

> Argentina today is a half-way house, a second-world country. On one level, it has to compete with rich countries, skilled and geographically favoured; on another, with next-door Brazil, its big market and competitor, barely out of the third world, with wages far below Argentina's, but a managerial elite just as clever. That is the economic conundrum. ("Getting from Here to There" 2000, 3)

Argentina's worsening inequality is a common problem among developing Latin American countries. Symptomatic of increasing inequality are the urban slums and homelessness that grow as people migrate (and are pushed) away from rural areas toward urban ones. But incomes in Buenos Aires are still double those in poor rural areas, even counting the slums on the outskirts of the city, with official urban unemployment above 12 percent from 1995 to 2000. The actual rate is presumed to be considerably higher.

---

[2] An "international dollar" is a measure of the World Bank that refers to dollars having the same purchasing power over gross national income (GNI) as a U.S. dollar has in the United States. Purchasing power parity GNI is gross national income converted to international dollars using purchasing power parity rates.

In the absence of policies that weave a safety net for those falling through the cracks of economic development, Argentine human services, including those for health, have deteriorated. People fare well if they have money to pay for services or if they have trade union coverage for medical care. For the rest, conditions are grim. Within the city, public hospitals are barely able to doctor the health problems of poverty, and medical personnel are paid meagerly.

> A typical tale of medical woe is that of the pediatrician who has to do three jobs to earn $1,600 a month. . . . [G]o to a big hospital in a poor district of Buenos Aires, and you are in another world. . . . Here poor people queue for hours: a hospital is their only source of free care. And outside the capital, the public health worries in the worst provinces really are like Africa's: malnutrition, dirty water, not enough sewers, ignorance and second-rate medical services to handle the results. ("It's an Unfair World" 2000, 15)

Argentina does not have a profile of economic and health failures; rather, it is a profile of slippage among competitive semi-periphery countries combined with debt, IMF pressures to lower government spending, and weak social welfare and health policies. Its relative wealth from development allowed Argentina to make improvements in lowering its under-five child mortality from 38 to 24 per 100,00 from 1980 to 1997. In contrast, the case study of Chile below reveals the greater health progress that is possible through good policies. Despite the fact that Chile's per capita GNP is nearly half Argentina's, its aggressive health policies produced a more impressive drop in child mortality, from 35 per 100,000 in 1980 to 13 in 1997.

Policies for a healthier Argentina must reduce inequality and provide a safety net for the poor. This must be accomplished following seventy years of rapid social change that included dictatorships, repeated military coups, Cold War intrusions by the United States, left-wing violence, and right-wing state terrorism. The country floundered for half a century following its turn-of-the-century economic ascendancy.[3]

A key challenge at the start of the twenty-first century is to continue reforms of the educational system, which so far have benefited mostly the private schools of the affluent and a small fraction of schools generally, favoring those involved in special government initiatives (Braslavsky 1998, 310). Reform of higher education, along with more sweeping educational reform at lower levels, "should play a fundamental role in any program of economic reform that considers international competition a dynamic element in growth" (Balan 1998, 283). Financially, this would be easier with debt forgiveness from the IMF, rather than pressures to pay down the debt in place of spending on social programs. Argentina is hard pressed to increase the grossly inadequate pay of public-sector professionals such as teachers and doctors. Its unemployment problems resulted from the early 1990s, when the economy expanded in capital-intensive rather than labor-intensive ways. This is the squeeze of the semi-periphery developing country: competitive markets, debt, a literate and culturally middle-class population with high expectations, and pinched social welfare spending.

---

[3] The period culminated during 1976 to 1983 when over 10,000 citizens "disappeared" at the hands of the military (Tulchin & Garland 1998, xi).

This leads to the "absence of absolute poverty" rather than "affluence" in our formulation. Second, there is high inequality and a high poverty rate, both of which bode ill for health. And, third, the Argentine government is not aggressively pursuing social welfare and health policies, in part due to debt pressures and in part due to poor political leadership. Consequently, despite its greater wealth, its infant mortality rate (18) is greater than Chile's (11), yet better than highly unequal Brazil's (40). Argentina's profile can be summarized in the formula

Absence of absolute poverty (amid economic development) → Improved mortality rates (compared to nonindustrial and underdeveloped countries)

Missing are

Relative income equality + State policies and civic culture that enhance social welfare → Maximized health outcomes

Argentina's inability to maintain a strong educational system and pay its state-employed professionals a living wage are warning signs that improvements are not just around the corner. "The task is to reconstruct civil society: to build a nation of both opportunity and equity, of democracy and good governance, able to quarrel, yet at peace with itself. Less Peru or Venezuela, more Switzerland" ("Getting from Here to There" 2000, 5). Whether Argentina will find the civic, political, and economic resources to accomplish this task remains to be seen. The answer lies in its internal development processes as well as in the configuration of regional and global forces.

3. The Extent to Which the Majority Benefits from Development

Dependency and world systems writers have argued that economic growth in developing countries often does not benefit the majority, and may even harm them. This perspective views the involvement of foreign firms as increasing the dependence of "host" developing countries, hampering the care of human and social needs and weakening their ability to truly develop. Development is often isolated to export-focused sectors of the economy, and profits are not used to build infrastructure, nor are they necessarily reinvested in the host country or allowed to trickle down to average citizens. An array of studies in the 1980s and 1990s focused on these dynamics.[4] They documented increased inequality and argued that the benefits of development are highly concentrated among the elite.

The counterargument to dependency theory rests on the observation that, in a growing economy, workers can lose *relatively* while gaining *absolutely* (Firebaugh & Beck 1994). Among even highly unequal developing countries, "the masses" do benefit

[4] Bornschier & Chase-Dunn 1985; Boswell & Dixon 1990; Braun 1997; Evans & Timberlake 1980; Jaffee 1985; London 1987, 1988; London & Robinson 1989; London & Smith 1988; London & Williams 1988, 1990; Stokes & Jaffee 1982; Wimberley 1990, 1991; Wimberley & Bellow 1992. A review and critique of the evidence of dependence is available in Firebaugh & Beck 1994.

With development, workers often gain in absolute wage increases, but also lose by experiencing greater inequality compared to higher paid workers.

from development, according to Firebaugh and Beck. Care of basic needs and overall living standards improve for the majority, and mortality rates decline. Inequality increases, while workers gain access to more jobs and increased wages; however, inflation often takes away some of these gains in spending ability. This line of argument takes the focus off inequality and places it on *gains in the standard of living*. It emphasizes that development produces improvements for workers despite increased inequality. Because a better standard of living improves health, we are interested in the evidence offered by this perspective.

Firebaugh and Beck (1994) investigated whether development benefits the masses in less-developed countries, especially where there is heavy dependence on foreign investment. They found that wages increase with production, with a high correlation ($r = .96$) between average incomes and average productivity for eighteen countries that have investment dependence above the median (Firebaugh & Beck 1994, 634, based on analysis of data from the World Bank 1990). However, Wimberly and Bello (1992) found contradictory results; their analysis found that dependence on foreign investment actually harmed the level of food consumption. Braun's (1997) analysis of quality of life indicators (described in Chapter 8) also found that the higher inequality that comes with development predicts poorer care of human and social needs.

Which perspective is correct? Firebaugh and Beck (1994) argued that Wimberly and Bello and other dependency researchers misinterpreted the data. Firebaugh and

Beck analyzed welfare measures from sixty-two nations, including longevity, infant survival, and caloric consumption (640). They found that caloric consumption per capita,
infant survival, and life expectancy improved most in less-developed countries from
1965 to 1988, and they argued that improvements were spread across the majority of the
population (640). This change is described as the epidemeologic transition in Chapter
4, for countries whose incomes rise above subsistence levels.

***Brazil: Case Example of Development and Health Improvements amid High
Inequality.***   Brazil is the most unequal country in the world, according to the World
Bank. The top fifth of the population in income earns twenty-seven times more than the
poorest-paid fifth of the population. Brazil's economy during the 1980s and 1990s experienced booms and busts. For example, the economy contracted with "negative growth"
during the 1997–1998 years (World Bank 2000, Table 1). During the 1990s, employment conditions worsened as better-paying industrial jobs were replaced with lower-
paying service jobs. During the 1990s, formal employment fell from 60 to 50 percent,
increasing the number of unemployed and informal-sector workers, who were excluded
from protective labor laws.

The *Real* Plan in 1994 (named after the country's new currency) was designed to
stabilize the Brazilian economy. It succeeded in increasing per capita income and
slightly reducing income inequality. The lowest-paid half of the population increased
its revenues by 1 percent, while the richest fifth's share decreased by 2 percent (Pan
American Health Organization 1999). Inflation was reduced to 10 percent in 1996,
down from earlier rates as high as 45 percent.

Brazil's health profile reflects both the improvements brought by economic development and the costs of high social inequality. Development brought an improved standard of living and moved the country through its epidemiological transition. For
example, malnutrition among children under five was reduced 60 percent between 1975
and 1989, and a further 20 percent by 1996 (Pan American Health Organization 1999).
Life expectancies in 1999 were sixty-three years for men and seventy-one for women
(Pan American Health Organization 1999). These figures are much higher than in
underdeveloped African countries but lower than in Honduras (sixty-seven and
seventy-two), which is a lower-income country than Brazil.

Literacy is 85 percent for both men and women, an aspect of Brazil's improved
standard of living. Infant mortality rates are still relatively high (33 per 1,000 live births
in 1998) and highest among the lower social classes. Compared to its neighbors', Brazil's
infant mortality is more highly concentrated among its poorest citizens. For example,
Brazil's poorest quintile accounts for almost 35 percent of all infant deaths, whereas the
richest quintile accounts for 10 percent. By contrast, Costa Rica has a GNP per capita
that is 60 percent of Brazil's, yet a lower infant mortality rate of 13 per 1,000 births in
1998. Costa Rica also has a more equal distribution of infant mortality, with the poorest
quintile accounting for approximately 25 percent of infant deaths and the richest quintile accounting for 15 percent (Pan American Health Organization 2000, 11–12; World
Bank 2001, Table 7).

Infant mortality rates, in Brazil and generally, are associated with the mother's
level of education (an indicator of social class), as shown in Table 9.2.

TABLE 9.2 *Brazilian Mothers' Years of Schooling and Infant Mortality*

Number of Years of Schooling	Infant Mortality per 1,000 Live Births
1	93
4	42
5–8	38
9–11	28
≥12	9

Source: Pan American Health Organization, *Brazil: Basic Country Health Profiles, Summaries.* Retrieved March 7, 2001, from http://www.paho.org/english/SHA/prfbra. htm, 4.

Despite its high inequality, Brazil's demographic profile reflects its developmental progress. The fertility rate and mortality rate decreased rapidly during the final decades of the twentieth century. Mortality declined most sharply among infants and children. Between 1980 and 1994, mortality in children up to age one, as a proportion of total mortality, decreased from 24 percent to 10 percent (Pan American Health Organization 1999). Between 1989 and 1996, the frequency of exclusive breast feeding increased eleven-fold for infants up to three months old and twenty-five-fold in infants four to six months old.

Brazil's disease profile indicates its passage through its epidemiological transition, as well as the ill effects of its high social inequality. The leading cause of death is circulatory disorders, accounting for 34 percent of the total during the 1990–1994 period (excluding ill-defined causes); these are highest in urban areas and typical of a profile of a wealthy country. The second most common cause of death is "external causes," including injuries, violence, and poisoning. Accidents and violence account for close to 15 percent of all deaths from defined causes. In the fifteen to nineteen age group, homicide ranks first among all external causes of death, accounting for close to 30 percent. Among all age groups, homicide increased 160 percent during the period between 1977 and 1994. This is surely related to Brazil's economic instability, social disruption, and increasing inequality (Pan American Health Organization, 1999). This parallels the finding for the United States, namely, that the association between income inequality, homicide, and violent crime rates is even stronger than that between income inequality and total mortality (Kaplan et al. 1996; Wilkinson 1996, 156). Traffic accidents, a side effect of development, are also an increasingly common cause of death, with dramatic increases in the 1980s and a leveling off in the 1990s.

The third most common cause of death in Brazil is malignant neoplasms (cancers), at 13 percent; the most frequent are stomach and lung cancer among men, and breast and cervical cancer among women. Drug use is a growing problem, especially among Brazilian young people. Alcoholism and drug use together account for close to 20 percent of all hospitalizations for mental disorders. This profile illustrates some of the social and health costs of rapid and uneven development.

Regionally, the highest rates of child mortality and death from ill-defined causes are found in the northeast, which has been relatively uninvolved in Brazilian development. Symptomatic of the region's greater absolute poverty, of all deaths among children under age one, half occur in the northeast, even though only 29 percent of the population lives there. The north is home to half of the country's indigenous population, composed of over 200 ethnic groups. There is no national policy or agency designed to serve the health and welfare needs of these indigenous groups.

Brazil's health improvements from development are unmistakable. Also clear, however, are the strikingly uneven benefits of its transition to a market economy. Both rural and urban groups that are peripheral to the development process have experienced little new wealth. However, the improvements in quality of life that result from development have made an impact across many social groups, as evident in improved infant and child survival rates. There remain overwhelming quality of life problems, however, evident in Brazil's high rates of poverty, unemployment, homelessness, accidents, substance abuse, violence, and crime.

4. The Extent to Which Inequality Increases with Development

We expect less dramatic health improvements in highly unequal developing countries. Affluence brings improvements in the quality of social life, yet these are influenced by cultural views about the fair distribution of resources. Should wealth be partially redistributed to achieve greater equality? Should social deviants and criminals be ostracized and incarcerated, or nudged and encouraged back into the fold? The differences between Japan and the United States are striking in this respect and partially explain Japan's more favorable health outcomes.

More research is needed in the area of health-enhancing cultures. Two brief comparisons provide examples. Hungary and Brazil have nearly equal per capita gross national products ($4,510 and $4,570 U.S., respectively), but Brazil is much more unequal than Hungary.[5] Hungary's under-five mortality rate per 1,000 was 12 in 1997, as compared with Brazil's 44. Hungary's life expectancies were also slightly higher (sixty-six for men and seventy-five for women, compared to Brazil's sixty-three and seventy-one). The high infant mortality rate suggests that inequality affects primarily the weakest; that is, infants and small children. Brazil has an illiteracy rate of 16 percent, whereas Hungary's is 1 percent. This crude comparison overlooks cultural and historical differences, but at minimum it invites further investigation into inequality's detrimental effects on social welfare and health.

A second illustrative comparison is between Japanese and U.S. smoking and lung cancer rates. Japan ranks first (with China) in having the highest smoking rate in the world, three times that of the United States. Yet the Japanese do not die of smoking-

[5] Hungary's Gini Index is 27.9, and Brazil's is 60.1; the higher number indicates greater inequality (World Bank 2001).

related diseases to the extent that Americans do. As stated earlier, lung cancer mortality rates are half to one-third of U.S. rates. Japan's high level of income equality in comparison to that of the United States is consistently associated with Japan's comparatively better health and longevity (Bezruchka 2000).

5. The Effectiveness of Civic-minded State Policies

Equality-enhancing state policies and civic-minded cultures enhance the potentially positive effects on health that development provides. By contrast, highly repressive regimes and cultures tolerant of high degrees of inequality cannot hope to reap the same quality of life and health benefits for their populations. As discussed above with internal development processes, a democratic state must balance populist demands for equality, or "the pull of distributive politics," against the need for accumulation of domestic capital to promote long-term investment (Centeno 1994, 136). The state's ability to maintain its efficacy amid these competing demands rests on cohesion among the elite, a merit-based bureaucracy, and effective organization (Evans 1989).

State policies and leadership may make human and social needs a priority or may place them below other spending, such as for the military. For example, during the 1990s, North Korea built up its military capabilities at the expense of its population's

Demonstration for universal health care in Albany, New York. Redistributive policies promote greater equality among populations through tax and benefit programs, support of public schools and health care, and promotion of democratic institutions.

well-being, even to the point of widespread malnutrition. By the late 1990s, droughts and floods had worsened agricultural failures and left the North Korean population in a state of near-starvation (Noland et al. 1999). In Zaire (now Republic of Congo) for three decades, Mobutu Sese Seko siphoned off the country's wealth for himself and a small elite. He left a country that was rich in natural resources underdeveloped and its people impoverished. The following case study of Chile's recent developmental history provides a contrasting policy model for balancing both economic and social priorities.

Chile: Improving Health Through Equality-enhancing Policies.   The dynamics of development in Chile illustrate the important role that state policies and civic values can play in improving health. Chileans have a relatively high life expectancy (sixty-nine years), which can be expected to increase over time if health in all age groups continues to improve. Chile's child survival rate (99.05) is comparable to Japan's (99.5 percent), and the level of equality of child survival across the population matches Japan's at nearly 100 percent. Chile's child health is remarkable, considering that Japan's GNP per capita is nearly seven times Chile's. Here we look more closely at the policies during the 1990s that brought about these exemplary health results.

Military dictator General Augusto Pinochet ruled Chile from 1973 to 1990. He imposed a state-directed, capitalist "free-market" system; kept taxes low for business and the wealthy; and spent minimally on social welfare. Neoliberal capitalist ideologies were used to justify a high level of social inequality and to neglect public welfare. A repressive labor code and prohibitions on collective bargaining beyond the firm level kept labor weak vis-à-vis business interests (Weyland 1997). A repressive regime punished political opponents and intimidated citizens from voicing opposition. The regime was notorious for the "disappearances" of thousands of Chileans who were imprisoned, tortured, and murdered by Pinochet's forces. And, despite its neoliberal economic program, the Pinochet regime brought about negligible growth, averaging under 2 percent per year from 1974 through 1989 (Ritter 1992, cited in Weyland 1997). Meanwhile, the gap between rich and poor grew, and poverty increased to 44 percent by 1987 (Weyland 1997).

Democratic rule came to Chile in 1990 with the election of Patricio Aylwin, who ruled until 1994. His rule and the one following it, under Eduardo Frei Ruiz-Tagle, were left-center governments supported by a coalition of political constituencies. In the transition to democratic rule, Aylwin charted a middle course between appeasing business and other elite interests, and responding to popular demands for greater equality (Weyland 1997). The plan of action for the new civilian government was to enhance economic growth while maintaining political stability by strengthening the base of political support (Weyland 1997). The Aylwin government's slogan was "Crecimiento con Equalidad" ("Growth with Equity"), and it negotiated its policies with business leaders, their government representatives, labor, and other organized constituencies.

The transitional government moderated but did not throw out neoliberal economic policies, nor did it purge politicians associated with the Pinochet regime. However, drawing on its legitimacy from the popular election, the Aylwin government cut back business and upper-class privileges and raised taxes for these groups. The government simultaneously dramatically expanded labor rights and greatly increased social spending, funded by larger taxes from the wealthy. The combination of tax and labor reform along with building up the social security net has reaped impressive results.

Neoliberal fears of economic downturn turned out to be unfounded: Investment soared to over 25 percent of the GDP in 1993, and growth averaged 6 percent per year under the Aylwin administration (Aninat Ureta 1994, cited in Weyland 1997). The return to democratic rule and the administration's goal of stability enhanced investor confidence as well. Health spending was dramatically increased—70 percent in real terms between 1990 and 1994. Primary care spending nearly doubled during the Aylwin administration, with an expanded web of health centers in urban and rural areas. Extended hours of services also made basic care more accessible (Weyland 1997). Large public investments revived public hospitals, built new ones, and raised salaries for medical personnel. The Frei administration further improved and expanded the Aylwin government's efforts. As a result, the 2000 World Health Organization report ranks Chile's health expenditures per capita twenty-third out of 191 member nations, and its overall health system performance ranks thirty-third (World Health Organization 2000, Statistical Annex Table 1, 152). These changes, as well as additional equity-enhancing policy measures, are mostly responsible for Chile's improved health.

Economic growth under Chile's democratic governments of the 1990s far exceeded that of the repressive Pinochet regime and increased the incomes of the poor (Weyland 1997). From 1990 to 1992, the poorest fifth of the population increased its share of national income slightly (0.4 percent), and with the monetary equivalent of public education and health care added, its share grew 0.5 percent (from 5.9 percent to 6.4 percent; Weyland 1997). The richest fifth of the population experienced a slight loss of income through reformed tax structures. All these measures improved the living and working conditions of poor and low-income Chileans. This experience runs contrary to the frequent *increase* in inequality during periods of economic growth.

Chile's health improvements during the 1990s are reflected in the under-five mortality rate: It dropped from 35 per 1,000 in 1980 to 11 per 1,000 in 1997 (World Bank 2000, Table 2). Infant mortality stood at 11 per 1,000 in 1999 compared to wealthier Brazil's 40 per 1,000. Chile has the first and last of three ingredients for positive health outcomes.

Absence of absolute poverty + State policies and civic culture that ensure preventive and primary health care → Good and improving health

Missing:

Relative income equality (with 1990s progress in this direction)

There is still much progress to be made, as Chile's income inequality is high (Gini Index = 56.5), and the poverty figure remained at 22 percent of the population at the close of the century. If its affluence continues to grow with further civic minded policies, we should expect overall quality of life and health indicators to continue to improve.

6. The Epidemiology of the Country

A healthy population is an asset in development. The epidemiology of a country affects disease and death rates, and also the amount of resources needed to respond to epidemics and other health problems. The most tragic example in the world today is the AIDS epidemic, which poses a serious threat to many less-developed countries.

The overall patterns of disease and health influence a country's developmental potential. An extreme example is HIV/AIDS rates' climbing exponentially in several sub-Saharan African countries. When accompanied by declining fertility rates, a country loses much of its present and future work force, and costs overwhelm the economy. The global trend is the shift from deaths at younger ages to deaths at older ages and greater frequency of chronic conditions, such as cardiovascular disease, cancers, and depression (Murray & Lopez 1996).

A healthy population is an asset (and essential) to long-term economic development (Bloom & Canning 2000). Without a healthy population, a country is hard put to make improvements in literacy, adopt new technologies, and maintain a skilled and reliable labor force. This dynamic goes in the opposite causal direction of the "wealth brings health" formula. A country's improved health allows for a work force that is sounder in mind and body, improving a country's economic prospects. Longer lives allow investments in health and education to pay off for more years, with longer careers and time to pass along social and cultural capital to future generations.

Recipe for Healthy Development: Mix in Social Welfare and Equality-enhancing Policies

Neoliberal advocates of economic restructuring often regard hardships for labor and the poor as necessary costs of jump-starting development. Advocates of state-centric approaches sometimes add that freedom of speech and the press are also luxuries that must wait until economies get their market transition under way. Not surprisingly, policy makers and economists who make such arguments perhaps see the world from an elite perspective, because they identify with elite interests. The affluent perhaps too easily accept the hardships visited on the less-privileged in the development process. As Centeno remarks,

> In much of the literature on the transition to the market, economic dysfunctions are generally described by examples of labor's "lavish" ability to consume, but the excesses of the rich are accepted as the inevitable costs of trickle down growth. . . . Policies calling for "social order with economic progress" often neglect to ask "progress for whom?" (Centeno 1994, 129)

In contrast to neoliberal ideology, a more critical perspective argues that labor and the poor should not have to wait for a social safety net and that it is unjustifiable to sacrifice their well-being to maintain profit margins for the wealthy.

Economic problems and precarious conditions for labor and the poor are not unique to less-developed countries. For example, an 80 percent increase in France's gross national product from 1973 to 1993 was accompanied by substantial increases in unemployment (Goldsmith 1994). This is cause for concern because, as we saw in Chapter 4, unemployment is associated with poor health and premature death. American industrial firms' attraction to inexpensive labor has brought a growing industrial zone to the Mexican-U.S. border. Companies close plants at home and set up subsidiary *maquiladoras* (factories and assembly plants) that pay six times less for jobs previously held by U.S. workers (Shaiken 1993, cited in McMichael 1996, 181). And workers in former socialist countries have not fared well either. At the turn of the twenty-first century, the World Bank found countries of the former Soviet Union to be doing poorly, with one in three people surviving on less than $4 a day. The number of people living in poverty increased ten times from a decade earlier.

From this chapter's analysis of the varied relationships between development processes, cultures, and policies, we have identified essential ingredients for health improvements.

- Affluence or the absence of absolute poverty
- Relative equality in income and wealth
- Cultures that value equality and allow redistributive policies
- State policies that ensure the care of basic human needs, enhance social welfare, and correct high inequality
- Countries' relatively promising epidemiological profiles

The six points discussed in this chapter refine the analysis of the relationship between development and health beyond the observation that economic growth brings better health. A country's institutional readiness and internal development processes have a major impact on the success of development and in bringing about improvements in the standard of living for a majority of the population. International data show that, even when a country's development increases the degree of inequality among social groups, economic growth brings health improvements. However, cultural beliefs, civic involvement, and state policies influence the pervasiveness of those improvements.

10

Policies for Building Healthy Societies

Loans should be provided when we still have rice to eat.

—A poor woman, Vietnam 1999

A woman with gangrene of the foot tried for seven years to get a disability pension. Three doctors composing the commission deciding on the issue of disability, after they learned she had a brother in Germany, determined a bribe in the amount of 3,000 German marks.

—Macedonia 1998, from D. Narayan, *Voices of the Poor: Can Anyone Hear Us?*

Governments have the power to lead, persuade, legislate, and carry out policies to improve health. They can protect population health by investing in human capital through education, literacy campaigns, and health care that is preventive, primary, and universal. Governments should also play the essential role of protecting the environment from pollution and depletion. Of course, states often do not meet these expectations, and in underdeveloped and developing countries, poverty and debt are often barriers to dramatic improvements in health. Among all countries, unemployment, relative poverty, and increasing inequality are harmful to pubic health.

This chapter provides three examples of the impact of social and governmental health policies. Next, the HIV/AIDS epidemic provides an example of varied community and policy responses; this section offers policy recommendations for countries struggling with the worst effects of the epidemic. The remainder of the chapter is devoted to global and U.S. national policy recommendations for improving health by reducing poverty and inequality, and by supporting public health programs and infrastructure. Finally, the chapter closes with a brief discussion of what we, as individuals, can do to improve our own and others' health.

We consider the following questions:

- How do communities and governmental policies affect population health?
- What policies are needed to fight the HIV/AIDS epidemic? To improve health generally?
- What can we do to improve personal and social health?
- Three examples of state policies and their health results (good, mediocre, and bad) are presented here to demonstrate the enormous difference that policies and leadership can make in improving or worsening health.

Kerala, India: A Healthy and Literate Society Despite Low Income

Kerala is a poor coastal state at the southern tip of India, remarkable for its health and literacy despite considerable poverty (Isaac et al. 1998). The "Kerala model" refers to both public policy and community mobilization that together produce an improved quality of life in the absence of economic growth. Despite insufficient caloric consumption among its population, Kerala has achieved low mortality, mass literacy, and agrarian reform. It has improved the status of socially and economically marginalized groups, including girls and women (Kumar 1993). Community involvement, civic-minded policies, and ethical leadership have made this possible.

Land reform was one of the ingredients of the Kerala model. It dramatically expanded ownership of land for rice growing and increased household garden ownership to 100 percent. Nearly universal preventive health care and literacy levels over 90 percent led to dramatic effects on Keralan health. Although infant deaths in India account for about 30 percent of Indian deaths countrywide, they account for only 10 percent in Kerala. Clinics are widely available to provide prenatal and infant care, nutritional supplements, and preventive immunizations for tetanus, polio, DPT, measles, and other preventable illnesses (Isaac et al. 1998). Nutritional supplements and preventive care are especially important because Keralans are an underfed population. Nearly 90 percent of Keralan babies and mothers have followup health care (Kumar 1993). Life expectancy in Kerala reached seventy years in 1986, up from forty-five during the 1951–1961 period; the state has significantly lower mortality levels than the rest of India. Improved health and longevity were achieved despite considerable unemployment and poverty.

The Keralan case points to the enormous difference that state and community policies can make. However, "to see the Kerala model as an outgrowth only of 'wise policies' is to miss its most significant feature: The organization, mobilization and active participation of ordinary people to bring about those policies" (Isaac et al. 1998, 17–18). State leadership and grassroots mobilization made possible a healthier society. This was accomplished without the advantages of abundant resources, advanced technologies, the latest medicines, or even a fully nourished population.

Declining Access to Health Care amid Affluence: The California Example

Amid a booming California economy, 23,000 Californians fell off the health insurance rolls each month from 1997 to 1998 (Brown 2000). At the end of 1998, this wealthy state had an uninsured rate of 24 percent compared to a 17 percent national average. E. Richard Brown, of UCLA's Center for Health Policy Research, authored a report about California's growing uninsured population and found that, by the end of 1998, about 7.3 million Californians, or one in four of the state's nonelderly residents, had no health insurance (Brown 2000). This is a rate one-third higher than the rest of the United States. Of those, nearly half had been uninsured for more than five years or had never been insured; they were most likely to be male, Latino, and poor. The uninsured are primarily workers and their families (82 percent), and 47 percent of those are full-time, year-round employees. A relatively small segment of the total uninsured is composed of nonworking families (18 percent).

Loss of MediCal (California's publicly funded health insurance) during the period of "welfare reform" (1995–1998) is one cause of the decreased coverage. Another is California's shifting job market, in which new jobs are mainly in the lower-paid service sector and lack health benefits. Consequently, despite growth in the California economy, job-based health insurance did not increase, and the uninsured rate among nonworking families rose from 26 percent to 40 percent. Half of all noncitizens are estimated to be uninsured, and a majority of uninsured children are Latino. The percentage of uninsured children in California rose from 17 percent in 1995 to 21 percent in 1998, while the rate in the rest of the nation was relatively stable at 14 to 15 percent. Latino children account for 62 percent of all uninsured California children who are eligible for MediCal or the Healthy Families program, which provides health coverage to low-income families.

Without health insurance, people do not benefit from preventive information, screenings, or regular care. When sick, the uninsured delay medical visits and rely on hospital emergency rooms when symptoms become serious. Even then, lack of insurance may prevent prompt care and followup treatment. Wealthy California has cutting-edge technology unparalleled in most of the world, yet its policies are often less civic minded than in other states and countries. E. Richard Brown attributes California's high uninsured rate to policies that decreased MediCal coverage. He recommends that the governor and legislature act to expand eligibility for MediCal and the Healthy Families program, and to simplify entry to these programs (Brown 2000). During 2001, under Gray Davis (who became governor in 1999), California made additional efforts to enlist children from low-income families in the Healthy Families program.

A political economy perspective on health and health care highlights the dynamics of the California case example. Its key elements are

- Location in a prime position in the global economy, which includes many lower-income and immigrant workers and a large service sector
- Class relations in which increasing numbers of lower-income workers do not receive health care insurance from employers or the state

- Welfare reform policy that removes welfare recipients from MediCal, placing them in low-paying jobs without health coverage (for which they may reapply)
- Public opinion shaped by Cold War ideologies about the dangers of social welfare programs, including health care, and a misconception that state-supported health care would serve primarily the unemployed rather than large numbers of working adults and their children
- A political climate and state leadership (under Governor Pete Wilson, 1991–1999) that, rather than expand access to health programs, blamed immigrants for the state's inadequate social services

Zaire: Rich in Resources, Distorted by Colonialism, and Impoverished by Corruption

Zaire (Congo in the 1960s and now Democratic Republic of the Congo), under decades of government under Mobutu Sese Seko (1960–1997), provides a stark contrast to the Kerala example. Mobutu ran a "kleptocracy"; that is, he used his power to steal his country's wealth. During more than three decades, Mobutu siphoned off millions from Zaire's precious minerals for his own and his cronies' wealth. (Mobutu's wealth in the mid-1980s was estimated at $4 billion U.S.) This graft entailed generous arrangements with foreign firms to haul off many of the country's natural resources, while the people of Zaire were left impoverished and the economy, underdeveloped.

Around mid-century, Congo was straining under Belgian colonial rule; it became independent in 1960. Patrice Lumumba, a progressive, became its first premier. However, nationalist Lumumba was deposed and then assassinated, events carried out by one of his officials (Mobutu Sese Seko) with assistance from the U.S. Central Intelligence Agency. Mobutu was installed as head of state and declared himself president in 1965. He received generous aid from the United States and other countries with a stake in Zaire's riches. Colonialist carving up of Africa and foreign exploitation of its riches set the stage for corruption, but Mobutu deserves the lion's share of the blame for decades of neglecting his country's needs. At his death from cancer, his people were left in the crossfire of a devastating civil war. Lauren Kabila overthrew Mobutu in 1997 but was assassinated after a brief rule. The Congo continues to be embroiled in a regional war with the bordering nations of Rwanda and Uganda, which are also eager to tap into Congolese natural resources. The violence is so rampant that international relief workers often cannot provide assistance.

With the Congolese government in such chaos, health statistics are unavailable, but the World Health Organization estimates that, for the years 1997 and 1999, life expectancy was 36 years. Women's lives were even slightly shorter than men's lives (36.2 versus 36.4, respectively) (World Health Organization 2000, Annex Table 5). In addition, disability considerably shortens years of able-bodied life. The World Health Organization estimates that men spend 8.7 years of their lives disabled, and women spend 10.3 years disabled. These poor health prospects testify to the legacy of social disruption and diminished life chances brought about by a corrupt state and helped along by exploitive core governments and corporations. High levels of injury and death to women and children indicate the rampant civilian casualties of the country's civil strife.

Indian men and women cooking food for earthquake victims. With development, workers often improve their wages and standard of living, but also lose from weakened community ties and protections, as well as from greater inequality among social groups.

These three case examples teach how governmental and community policies can enhance or deteriorate population health. Rulers and officials are instrumental in leading their countries or regions down the path of either health improvement or increased illness. Of course, such developments occur within a broader social and political context. Mobutu could not have sustained his corrupt rule without the cooperation and support of powerful countries and corporations. California Governor Pete Wilson could not have pursued his campaign of scapegoating immigrants without support from other political leaders and a significant proportion of California voters. Kerala's political leaders could not have produced favorable health and literacy outcomes without a motivated and involved citizenry.

Now we turn our attention to HIV/AIDS and consider how responses to the epidemic either slowed or sped up HIV infection.

Tackling HIV/AIDS

The central insight from a decade of hard work against AIDS is that societal discrimination is at the root of individual and community vulnerability to AIDS—and to other major health problems of the modern world. This links HIV/AIDS work to the larger global movement for health. (Mann et al. 2000, 310)

The HIV/AIDS epidemic has provoked a variety of community and policy responses, some much more successful than others. The epidemic is central to the topic of inequality and health because it strikes poor and socially marginalized groups the hardest. In addition, the disease itself carries a stigma and therefore worsens affected individuals' social status. AIDS is also of concern because it so often disables and takes the lives of those it infects, in the process leaving many children orphaned and many families without breadwinners. In countries hardest hit by the epidemic, the human losses and financial costs have been staggering. In Zimbabwe, Willard Tinet became the head of his household when he was ten years old, caring for his younger brothers, Joseph (nine) and Cloud (seven), when the boys' mother died of AIDS. Their father had left when his wife became ill. Five years later, they were still living in their house, more fortunate than the many homeless AIDS orphans of Zimbabwe (Sternberg 1999).

In the United States, it took costly time before public health officials came around to incorporating the social aspects of HIV transmission into prevention campaigns. Public health officials turned to epidemiologists to track the disease; however, prevention efforts required knowledge about at-risk populations' lifestyles and daily routines. This information had to come from within those communities. It is therefore not surprising that activists among San Francisco gay men's neighborhoods developed the first successful community-based model for changing sexual behavior and slowing HIV infection.

Other communities learned from this success and launched their own preventive campaigns. Local outreach workers frequented gay bars, "shooting galleries" (places where drug-injecting paraphernalia are used for a fee), sex-worker and drug-sale locales. Outreach workers became public speakers, visiting schools, substance abuse treatment programs, and community groups to talk about the epidemic and how to prevent infection. They dispensed condoms and information about sterile needles, HIV antibody testing, safe sex, and ways to talk with partners about risk.

A variety of medications are available that effectively keep the virus in check for many people infected with HIV. As of the year 2000, the U.S. Food and Drug Administration listed more than forty approved therapies that slow or disrupt HIV replication in the body, or treat opportunistic infections (Bloom & River Path Associates 2000). As a result of these treatments, AIDS deaths have fallen dramatically across Europe and the United States. In the United States, for example, deaths from complications of the virus fell from 49,895 in 1995 to 17,171 in 1998 (Bloom & River Path Associates 2000).

However, the ability to survive with an HIV infection is not spread evenly within populations or among countries. Individuals with private health insurance in developed countries have the best access to antiviral and infection-fighting medicines. And the stigma of AIDS continues to obstruct early diagnosis and treatment of HIV infection among certain groups, such as gay Latinos and African-American men and women. And, for those receiving treatment, after several years of antiviral regimens some patients are showing resistance to the drugs. Consequently, continued research on treatments, a vaccine, and prevention campaigns are as important as ever.

Many less-developed countries have been hit hard by HIV infection and related diseases. Malnutrition and lack of safe water weaken immunity and increase vulnerability to HIV infection. People in less-developed countries have more disease generally; therefore, a person's health deteriorates rapidly when infection occurs. For example, tuberculosis and AIDS interact as a "dual epidemic" among many poor and marginalized populations (Bloom & River Path Associates 2000).

Before he tragically died in a plane crash on his way to meetings of the World Health Organization, Jonathan Mann argued for a new way to approach the global AIDS epidemic—as a human rights issue. He proposed bringing together public health and human rights perspectives to arrive at a more comprehensive and practical framework for acting on the *social* causes of HIV's spread (Mann 1999, 223). Mann suggested that the human rights approach "provides both a common vocabulary for describing the commonalties that underlie the specific situations of vulnerable people around the world, and a clarity about the necessary direction of health-promoting societal change" (222). Mann pointed out that working from a human rights stance brings empowerment both to those working to prevent disease and to those susceptible to infection. This approach rests on

> an understanding of the importance of societal determinants of health, of the ways in which human rights helps us to analyze and respond to societal deficiencies that underlie vulnerability to preventable disease, disability, and premature death. The second requirement is equally critical: the belief, faith, and confidence that the world can change. (Mann 1999, 224)

Health services have been overwhelmed in countries where the epidemic has spread rapidly. In sub-Saharan countries where AIDS has hit hardest, difficult decisions are being made about health spending. Given meager budgets, is it better to spend on nutrition, disease prevention, treatments of infectious and sexually transmitted diseases, or AIDS-related illness (Bloom & River Path Associates 2000, 2171)? International help is essential for less-developed countries to even barely meet these many health needs. For example, UNICEF in Tanzania is helping with the widespread problem of grief over its staggering number of deaths. It prepared a training manual to assist communities in coping. Hundreds of adults have been trained in one- to two-day courses addressing topics such as grieving, secondary stress, and how to speak with children about loss. A fourteen-week program for orphans offers them the rudimentary skills to begin coping with their losses (Madörin 2002).

In recent years, a global debate has emerged over the pricing of HIV/AIDS–fighting drugs. In the United States, antiviral therapies can cost up to $20,000 per person for a year's treatment (Bloom & River Path Associates 2000). Critics of the pharmaceutical companies point to poor countries' inability to afford the drugs and also to differential pricing of these life-saving drugs across countries. South Africa responded by pricing AIDS-fighting drugs more cheaply. The U.S. government initially threatened sanctions to support pharmaceutical companies' legal challenge against South Africa. However, activists protested to the Clinton administration, and subsequently, a policy shift occurred in 2000. The United States initiated a discussion in the United Nations Security Council of AIDS as a global threat. President Clinton followed with an executive order in May 2000 promoting more accessible and affordable

HIV/AIDS–related drugs and medical technologies in sub-Saharan Africa, within the scope of the existing agreement, Trade-Related Aspects of Intellectual Property Rights (TRIPS) (Bloom & River Path Associates 2000).

The problem is not solved, but several major drug companies made a commitment to better distribution. Patients' advocates were not satisfied, however. Médicins Sans Frontières (Doctors Without Borders) criticized the pharmaceutical industry for offering too little, and the French government argued for an international fund for AIDS drugs, supported by private and pubic commitments. There is considerable agreement outside the pharmaceutical industry that some oversight of pricing and distribution is needed, using "trust but verify" mechanisms to monitor profit levels and research and development expenses (Bloom & River Path Associates 2000).

Better incentives are needed to increase research on diseases that affect the poor. Incentives could include tax breaks, programs to guarantee markets, and direct public investment. These changes would be hastened if U.S. taxpayers were better aware of their subsidization of pharmaceutical profits (Bloom & River Path Associates 2000). An active global task force on AIDS could monitor information and address problems in the pandemic; individuals would participate as experts rather than as representatives of particular countries or industries (Bloom & River Path Associates 2000). The task force could address the following issues: drug pricing and distribution, fair trade of pharmaceuticals, epidemiological trends, coordination of prevention efforts, and the collection of funds from foundations, corporations, countries, and nonprofits to fight the AIDS pandemic. Priority would be given to improving equality of access to medicines and care, so that social inequities do not continue to be reflected so dramatically in HIV/AIDS illness and death.

How Can Countries Scale Up Efforts to Fight the AIDS Epidemic?

Hans Binswanger (2000), of the African division of the World Bank, offers a plan based on rural development experiences and successful HIV/AIDS programs. He points to examples of programs in African countries as models in fighting HIV/AIDS. First, resources and organizations need to be scaled up to regional and national levels. Model programs thus far reach only a small fraction of affected populations. For example, in the Kagera region of Tanzania, the devastation of the epidemic is overwhelming. There are an estimated 200,000 AIDS orphans within Kagera's population of 1.9 million (Binswanger 2000). "Nothing is like before," says Joel Rwamulerwa, a gray-haired counselor.

> When we were children, we would be sent away if somebody died. Nobody spoke of death; it was kept away from us. Today, children mention that so and so died—of ukimwi or AIDS—even when they are playing. In former times our elders could not imagine that their sons and daughters would die before them. Today, here they are, alone with their grandchildren. (Madörin 2002)

Ten nongovernmental organizations (NGOs) offer HIV/AIDS services in Kagera, staffed by volunteers, but these efforts are sorely underfunded. Their services reach a mere 5 percent of the population in only two out of five districts. Three districts are left completely unserved. Other countries face similar circumstances. In the Ivory Coast, only two out of eight regions have any programs in rural areas.

In the city of Mutare, Zimbabwe, only 3 percent of housebound patients are visited by any helping agency (Binswanger 2000). But this is not to say that residents are passive. Visitors from Catholic Relief Services found that all the men in a village in Mutare had AIDS but were working daily to make improvements that would help life be sustainable for their children. They had planted Protea bushes, whose blooms could be sold for a good price in the city; they had set up beehives in the woods and a fishpond near the stream. They had planted marsh grass in the pond so that the fish could hide from predators and later be caught for food ("Community-based AIDS Prevention and Care in Africa" 2001).

AIDS programs can benefit from lessons learned from rural development projects (Binswanger 2000). Governments and national public health agencies play the role of setting policies and arranging cofinancing, training, monitoring, and evaluation. This may sound like overly centralized control at regional and national levels, but a major shift has occurred toward setting priorities and program needs at the local level. Local governments and development communities plan and carry out their own projects with local labor and materials. Local governments seek matching grants for their projects and seek training and technical services from governments, nongovernmental agencies, and the private sector (Binswanger 2000).

To scale up efforts, Binswanger recommends the following strategies, tailored to particular circumstances of each country and region:

1. *Build on available models to achieve behavioral changes.* For example, Thailand's "hundred percent" condom program achieved national scope. It was organized and delivered by the public health sector and police departments. National responses to the AIDS epidemic require varied prevention efforts, a protected blood supply, testing, health care, and social services. The most successful models are tailored to best suit local needs.

2. *Rely on community participation and local coordination.* Those working with the epidemic locally will best inform prevention and care programs. Local volunteers and staff will also help programs to survive and become institutionalized. An example is Kwasha Mukwenu, a program in urban Lusaka, Zambia, that coordinates a program for AIDS orphans. Each woman in the program adopts three to five families of orphans to look after. These are called her "caretaker families"; she ensures that the children attend school and have food, clothing, shelter, medical care, and attention from a caring adult. Uganda has also adopted a policy of encouraging local communities to take the lead in AIDS prevention and care. Community Counseling Aides are trained to visit all households and see if they have the correct information for AIDS prevention, as well as to help coordinate efforts for the care of those who are ill ("Mutare Diocese . . ." 2002).

3. *Start with existing capabilities and build them, "learning by doing."* Improving programs as they operate can be locally achieved with technical assistance from government and private agencies. Binswanger cites a Nigerian example of grassroots agricultural

development: "In the state of Kano in Nigeria, an action plan for the September to December 1999 period included the training of 30 agricultural extension agents, who in turn would work with 12 NGOs, who in turn would help create village volunteer groups to train an estimated 30,000 individuals" (2000, 2174).

4. *Generate essential funds.* Funds for supplies and training are needed from outside the local level, including from centralized governments, NGOs, international agencies, and private donors. The remainder of what makes programs work is locally generated and not based on financial abilities. This means that most communities and program participants, at least to start, have to rely on their own resources, time, and management abilities. Some local governments help by allowing civil servants to spend work time in HIV prevention and care efforts. Schoolteachers, health workers, police, agricultural extension agents, and religious leaders can all assist in community-generated AIDS projects. Funds are needed to sustain these efforts and to purchase essential supplies.

5. *Treat prevention as a first priority.* Community mobilization, rather than top-down efforts, have the greatest potential to change behavioral norms and slow the spread of HIV infection. Intensive, highly participatory approaches work well. Community groups must identify behaviors and settings in which the virus is being transmitted and identify potential community health outreach workers. Following training, these workers learn from their experience and train additional educators. In this way, prevention work is spread throughout communities.

6. *Allow for earmarking of HIV/AIDS funding in national and regional budgets.* This requires that government leaders publicly acknowledge the AIDS epidemic in their country or state, allocate resources to prevent its spread, and assist those who are affected.

7. *Make funds available locally, and do not allocate them in predefined categories.* This allows local committees to flexibly decide how funds should be divided up between programs and participating organizations.

8. *Promote accountability.* This helps to prevent corruption and diversion of funds. Budgeting, disbursement, and accounting should all be transparent at the local level. Additional and continued accountability is needed for funds distributed by government and NGO sources.

9. *Improve fiscal sustainability with additional national and local resource mobilization.* This is especially challenging in low-income countries, but strategies may include selling condoms wherever possible, having private-sector firms finance programs for their workers, and engaging in ongoing fund raising with the assistance of nongovernmental organizations.

10. *Start by covering an entire district or region.* Experience has shown that a program that can cover an entire region can also be expanded to the national level.

11. *Replicate the district or regional model across the country.* This was done in Guinea, where prevalence of HIV infection was estimated at 6 percent. Expanding prevention nationwide is critical at that level of infection, because other countries' experiences sug-

gest that HIV infections increase exponentially above that rate (Binswanger 2000). In the year 2000 the Guinea government was collaborating with twenty-three NGOs, with intensive prevention programs in the schools, the military, and youth programs. The majority of health workers became trained in the diagnosis and treatment of sexually transmitted diseases, and medications were made widely available. In an effort to bring about change in the views of the majority of the population, including in rural areas, several thousand traditional healers, birth attendants, teachers, community livestock workers, religious leaders, and elected officials were mobilized and trained as AIDS educators and prevention advocates. They formed local committees and developed action plans to be carried out in their own area (Binswanger 2000). This process scaled up efforts into a national HIV/AIDS campaign.

Many low-income countries tackled the AIDS epidemic only reluctantly; leaders remained silent during the early stages of the epidemic in hopes of not scaring away tourists or potential investors. Today, however, grassroots efforts, local leadership, and outside assistance all play critical roles in responding to the AIDS epidemic.

We now return to the general challenge of improving population health. What should the policy agenda look like locally and globally?

Making Societies Healthier

More people are living in absolute poverty today than at any time since World War II. They are located mostly in Asia and Africa, but there are also significant pockets of poverty in Latin America, Eastern Europe, and affluent countries. This occurs despite a "green revolution" in food production and continuous, breathtaking technological advances. Poor countries' social and economic distance from the developed world grows, despite globalizing economic trends and electronic communication. Within Britain and the United States, the chasm between rich and poor continues to widen, while other more homogeneous societies such as Japan and Sweden struggle to maintain relative income equality and lower poverty rates.

Many regions within Eastern Europe are experiencing social disruption, poverty, and declining health. The dissolution of the Soviet Union threw many countries into disarray, with some splintering into new states. Jobs and services were lost, and health declined with spreading poverty. Moldova, a newly independent Eastern European country located west of Romania and south of Ukraine, felt some of the consequences.

> Poverty has created rifts in communities . . . between former friends and neighbors. People are cynical, suspicious, and jealous of others' success, which they most often attribute to dishonest and corrupt behavior. In their own communities the poor feel ashamed and constantly humiliated in their encounters with former neighbors and friends who have prospered. This humiliation is poignant in the case of children and young people, who sometimes prefer to remain at home rather than risk their classmates' mockery at their old clothes. (from Narayan 2000, 223)

Individuals at the lower end of the social hierarchy are vulnerable to being shamed as well as verbally and physically attacked, arrested, and jailed. More often they smoke, are overweight, and have sedentary lifestyles. The effects of disadvantage start young—in the uterus, to be precise—and continue during early childhood, often within less nurturing social and physical environments. Over the life course, we see the "clustering and accumulation of psychosocial disadvantage" (Brunner & Marmot 1999, 41). This is not to say that, by contrast, the affluent uniformly provide a healthy developmental environment for their children, but that the clustering of harmful conditions is overwhelmingly concentrated among the poor.

In countries with absolute poverty, improvements in water, sanitation, food supply, education, and health care are the keys to a healthier society. In developed countries that have *relative* poverty, reducing inequalities through social welfare and redistributive policies and improving civic involvement make societies healthier. What should be done to correct the damaging health effects of relative disadvantage? Those of us who are now middle-aged in the United States grew up with the Cold War ideology that not much can be done about poverty and that redistributive socialist policies are doomed to failure and are even threats to democracy. Today, younger generations hear muffled versions of the same point of view. The historical record, on the other hand, suggests that such policies have effectively reduced poverty. The Social Security Act of 1935 instituted old age insurance and greatly reduced poverty among elderly Americans. President Lyndon Johnson's War on Poverty infused inner cities with funds, reduced urban poverty, and began to grow an African-American middle class during the mid-1960s. And a program to prevent teen pregnancy in the 1990s succeeded by 1998 to bring rates down from the highest among developed countries to the median (Garrett 2000, 559). These were successful policies that reduced social inequalities either directly or indirectly.

Current U.S. and global economic and policy trends foster the widening of social inequalities. In the absence of new policies, current developments foreshadow worsening disparities in health, both within wealthy developed countries and between wealthy and poor countries. Which policies could reduce inequalities? The following are policy suggestions from experts, blended with observations and evidence described in preceding chapters.

National and Global Policies for Healthier Societies

The Commission on Macroeconomics and Health proposes that we as global citizens have the ability to save 8 million lives a year. The commission was set up at the turn of the new century by the director general of the World Health Organization, Gro Brundtland. The funding is to come from both developed and underdeveloped countries: Wealthy countries would contribute an increased 0.1 percent of their gross domestic product, and poor countries would collectively contribute $35 billion ("The Health of Nations" 2001). The commission argues that tremendous *economic* benefits would come from improved health if this investment is made—an estimated gain of $186 billion per year. Gro Brundtland (2001) identifies four policy challenges to citizens, governments, and the private sector to improve global health. We use these to organize the following policy recommendations.

1. *Greatly reduce the disproportionate burden of disease and death suffered by the poor.* Greater investments in maternal health and childhood nutrition would bring progress in this direction. A woman's positioning in her family and the economy affects her ability to care for her children; that is, to see that her children are fed, clothed, and housed. Income from fathers plays a central role in accomplishing that goal; however, when a husband's income is unavailable, women must seek work outside the household, often relying on informal economies to make money. Increased economic and political independence for women enhances the welfare of households. This may be accomplished through micro lending programs, education and training, enforcing paternal financial obligations to children, or ensuring jobs that pay a living wage. Additional policies that protect well-being are police protection from domestic violence and shelter services. Worker rights in informal labor markets would also help women protect themselves and their children. In addition, enforcement of antidiscrimination policies allows women to receive resources (seeds, fertilizer, training, schools, jobs) and improve the standard of living for their household.

Watchdog organizations, citizens, and governments must ensure that public welfare is protected. Nongovernmental and grassroots organizations can help by continuing to lead in pressuring companies and governments to implement policies that protect people and the environment. The vigilance and activism of watchdog groups such as Amnesty International, Human Rights Watch, and Doctors Without Borders is essential to maintaining policies that protect health. The corporate forces invested in rolling back protections of workers and the environment are rich and powerful; therefore, constant effort is required to keep citizen groups mobilized.

2. *Counter potential threats to health resulting from economic crises, unhealthy environments, and risky behavior* (Brundtland 2001, 7). Tobacco use is one of the biggest threats to health, with over 80 percent of smokers located in less-developed countries. Promoting healthy lifestyles around the globe, including healthy diets and exercise, helps prevent disease and disability. This challenge also involves responding to emerging infections and addressing the problem of resistance to antimicrobial drugs. In addition, the health of the physical environment must be protected, safeguarding the air, water, soil, forests, and oceans. Universal sanitation and safer transportation are needed to protect health and the environment.

Loss of community ties can dislodge a whole way of life and threaten care of basic needs. For example, rural women in Ghana in 1995 noted the breakdown in social solidarity over a ten-year period, as people migrated out of their villages in search of employment.

> [In the past] men organized themselves in groups through communal labor to assist each other to build and roof houses. Women supported each other to do farm work such as sowing, weeding, and harvesting. A woman who had recently given birth to a baby was always supported by young girls who cared for the babies and by older women who brought firewood and even treated the babies when they fell sick. . . . Women would work in groups in search of food to feed their children. They went to the bush in groups to cut firewood and to burn charcoal to sell. (quoted in Narayan 2000, 219)

Grassroots organizations enable women to act collectively to improve living conditions and shape local policies. Social networks and communities provide practical and emotional support, and the "social capital" gained from trusting communities buffers individuals from the effects of traumatic losses and adjustments to major life events. Individuals do better when woven into a network of family and community ties, whether they are adjusting to the birth of an infant, the loss of an aging parent, a disability, a mental illness, or a new (or lost) job. The United Nations in recent years has taken extraordinary steps to include women from local collectives in dialogues about community development.

3. *Develop more effective health systems.* Revive public health infrastructures and budgets where they have been undermined and defunded (Brundtland 2001, 8). Despite the widening role played by private (for-profit and nonprofit) organizations, the role of governmental agencies is more important than ever in providing oversight, coordination, policy development, and dissemination of information and technology. Health systems need to work toward improving population health; reducing health inequalities; enhancing responsiveness to legitimate expectations; increasing efficiency; protecting individuals, families, and communities from financial loss; and enhancing fairness in the financing and delivery of health care (Brundtland 2001, 8). A regulatory role for governments in the private sector is important, for example, in protecting the environment, ensuring humane pricing of life-saving medicines within and across borders, and preventing abuses in delivery of health care services. An example of the latter comes from poverty-stricken Moldova.

> After receiving a heart operation, hernia surgery, and removal of gallstones in the course of two weeks, Valentina remained in hospital for four more weeks. During that time, most of her elderly parents' money was spent on her treatment and medication. Each of the nurses had to be paid 10 lei . . . otherwise they wouldn't have bothered to bring her meals . . . and 10 lei so they would be careful when they gave her injections. At the end of the treatment, the doctors demanded that Valentina's mother organize a dinner for them. She acquiesced, selling some household items to purchase the food, since she feared that Valentina might have to enter hospital again and would depend on the doctors' good will, if not their skill, which the mother felt was inadequate. (from Narayan 2000, 231)

4. *Invest in an expanding knowledge base as a foundation for making further health advances.* Low-income countries need assistance from the World Health Organization and international donors for technology and staff training. They need to collect and analyze population and health data in order to plan and effectively target programs. Much of the current health investment in research and development by corporations benefits primarily affluent populations. Vaccines and medicines for diseases that overwhelmingly affect the poor, such as malaria, are needed; the World Health Organization is set up to best coordinate these efforts.

Access to education for girls and women (in addition to boys and men) broadens their worldview, builds skills, and widens access to further training and jobs. Educating girls and women also increases knowledge that improves the care of children, including hygiene, nutrition, and vaccinations. Schooling develops literacy and skills that are useful in agriculture, business, and being active citizens.

Continued improvement in the global health profile, including reducing inequalities between the health of the rich and the poor, depends on private and public contributions. In this effort, the technology of the developed world is as essential as the mobilization of local communities. The Kerala model discussed above is neither perfect nor universally applicable, but it nonetheless offers a model as well as an inspiration for policy driven by social justice values. It includes the essential ingredients for a healthy society: civic participation and activism along with redistributive policies.

We now turn our attention to issues of protecting health over the life course.

Enhancing Public Health Throughout the Life Course

Protective as well as damaging health effects accrue over the life course; therefore, public health systems should not be designed only as safety nets, catching individuals only after they become ill (Blane 1999, 77). Affluent as well as low-income countries have opportunities to work toward optimal health for all members of their society. Recommendations for social policy and public health systems to reduce poverty and inequality, as well as mitigate their effects, include the following.

Make Childhood Development a High Priority.
Child development is a powerful influence on health throughout life. Developmental researchers have identified latency, pathway, and cumulative effects from being born poor—that is to say, the harmful effects may not show up right away but instead may appear over a lifetime. For example, longitudinal research shows that the most seriously antisocial adolescents and adults had behavior problems as children. Funds invested in at-risk families during the first three years of life reduce the prevalence and seriousness of problems that occur later on (Tremblay 1999). For this reason, investments in infancy and early childhood development are of major importance. Developmental researcher Richard Tremblay concludes, "It is clear that the prevention strategy will, within a 20-year period, reduce substantially the relative amount of resources needed for corrective interventions in the education, health, and justice systems" (1999, 71). Programs to address this need for early support and intervention include universal prenatal and postnatal care (including fathers and mothers), infant-parent programs, and preschool programs. In each of these settings there are opportunities to educate, support, and intervene to enhance and protect infant and child well-being. This is not a policy invented by the twentieth-century welfare state; Tremblay reminds us of Plato's advice in *The Republic* that care of early childhood should be a high social priority.

Maintain an Accessible and Strong Program of Preventive and Primary Health Care Services.
Preventive services and information are most needed at lower levels of the occupational hierarchy, where they are often least available (Adler et al. 1993). For example, employers offer programs such as stress management, smoking cessation, and exercise promotion most often to upper management and technical staff. Extending such programs to all workers could help prevent illness, especially among the most vulnerable workers.

Governments can increase public awareness of a variety of health issues (diet, exercise, smoking, drinking, driving) and thereby help prevent disease and disability.

Targeted programs can reach groups with special messages, such as preventing smoking and pregnancy among teens or preventing head injuries among bicyclists. Policy can also tackle the food industry, challenging its promotion of refined foods, heavy in fats and sugars, targeted toward children (Wilkinson 1999). Governments and workplaces can promote policies that reduce chronic stress (anxiety, insecurity, low self-esteem, social isolation, low control), especially for people lower on the social hierarchy (Brunner & Marmot 1999).

Maintain Funding for Public Health Infrastructure and Programs. The public should not assume that high-tech research and development are substitutes for preventive and primary health care. Research and development areas of human genetics and protein chemistry do not hold the solutions to population health today. In both wealthy and less-developed countries, funding should reflect the high priority of preventive, primary, and universal health care. The terrorist attacks of September 11, 2001, including the subsequent anthrax scare, revealed weaknesses in the public health infrastructure. Although no country could fully prepare for such horrific events, the erosion of U.S. public health systems from decades of meager support came into focus. Local health departments provide vaccinations, screenings, and treatment for a variety of conditions (including disease prevention for children and treatment of sexually transmitted diseases). Bioterrorism is a new threat to which the system must respond. Regulation of the pharmaceutical industry and cost caps on medicines are also issues facing U.S. public health policy makers.

Reduce Poverty and Inequality. The following are ways to accomplish this goal:

- Legislation to protect the rights of minority and migrant groups, especially regarding access to asylum, employment, and protection from discrimination
- Income support, food supplements, and housing programs for unemployed and low-income households, to provide an adequate standard of living
- Progressive taxation policies on income and inherited wealth, to reduce social inequalities
- Educational, training, and employment opportunities for the short-term and long-term unemployed
- Access to health care, mental health care, and social services for marginalized groups
- Followup community agency support for those leaving institutional care and substance abuse treatment
- Employment policies to preserve and create jobs
- Improved access to health and welfare services to immigrant and refugee populations (Shaw et al. 1999, 232–233).

The Earned Income Credit program in the United States could be expanded to reduce poverty. This program reduces taxes and pays out money to working families that fall below poverty levels. Expansion of this program would bring the United States more closely in line with other developed countries' social insurance programs. The Earned Income Credit benefits the whole society by reducing poverty and inequality.

An additional policy would increase tax incentives for the wealthy to contribute to national and global health programs, job creation and training projects, and other social programs that reduce poverty and reintegrate individuals who have been displaced by a rapidly changing economy. Following the lead of Bill Gates, wealthy individuals can make an enormous difference in improving global health by contributing to life-saving programs, such as vaccinations and rehydration therapies for children, or by creating safe water supplies and sanitation. Job creation and training programs also have enormous potential to improve health by reducing unemployment in both poor and wealthy countries.

What Can We Do as Individuals?

We can appreciate the impact of our behavior on others. In our communities, we can be better aware of whether we are contributing to social health or detracting from it. We can participate in local organizations, enriching the social capital of our community. We can take special interest in children and the elderly, especially those who are not fully cared for by their families. We can be good family members and partners by supporting loved ones' efforts to live meaningful lives. In an affluent, fast-paced society, it is easy to overlook the need for adequate sleep, nutritious food, physical activity, and nurturing relationships. Friends and loved ones can best remind us to pay attention to these quality-of-life ingredients.

Thousands of large and small organizations engage in work that improves living conditions; for example, Habitat for Humanity helps low-income people build their own homes. We can research these organizations, choose ones we think are valuable, and contribute with volunteer work or money. Whether such organizations run a camp for children with burn injuries, work against violations of human rights, or lobby for a clean air bill, our participation is essential. Contributing to these larger efforts also provides role models of commitment and participation for young people.

Regarding politics, we can examine leaders' records and cast our votes judiciously. We can support reforms of the electoral process so that individuals other than multimillionaires and those sponsored by corporate coffers can engage in public service at state and national levels. We can support candidates who support policies that protect average citizens and the environment from pollution and degradation, not only in our own backyard but also globally.

As consumers in an affluent society, we can look carefully at the global consequences of our spending. Are we buying clothing, shoes, soccer balls, or rugs that have been produced with child labor? in dangerous and exploitive working conditions? by a company that is dumping toxins into the environment? Often we can't learn this information in our morning paper (or anywhere in the mainstream media), so we must look further for information, typically gathered by watchdog organizations around the globe and available on the Internet.

We are not all blessed with optimal health and able bodies, but we can start with Plato's admonition to "Know thyself." From there, we can develop healthy personal boundaries that are permeable enough to allow trusting relationships, yet protective enough to prevent abusive treatment by others. Coping skills help us get out of depressing, anxious, and angry moods. Being able to listen, be patient, and tolerate others' differences is challenging, yet it allows us to experience connection and closeness to others. This practice goes against the grain of a fast-paced American culture that is preoccupied with the next accomplishment or acquisition. The present is a difficult place to focus, in a culture anxious about the future and preoccupied with the next quick steps to getting there. And yet, improving health and well-being must start with an awareness of where we are now, personally and globally. Linking our personal lives to broader social conditions can help us make decisions that are not only individually meaningful but also socially constructive.

Appendix

Principles of Sociological Health Patterns

1. Globally, the major factor determining whether individuals will live longer lives and experience less life-threatening illness is the availability of living conditions that meet basic human needs (Wilkinson 1996).
2. Overall, people in affluent countries have greater life expectancy than those in poor countries.
3. Improvements in material living conditions among populations below the epidemiological threshold result in significant improvements in health and longevity. Smaller improvements occur in developed countries, where living conditions improve as a function of affluence or reduction of social inequality (Wilkinson 1996).
4. Across societies, there is an association between the degree of social inequality and the rate of disease and death: Higher inequality results in higher disease and premature death (Rodgers 1979; Wilkinson 1996, 2000).
5. Social inequality affects health in direct and indirect ways. High inequality entails a larger proportion of the population living in relative poverty and governmental policies that neglect human investments (such as in education, health, and an array of services). Inequality also affects health indirectly through psychosocial factors related to our place in the social hierarchy. Social capital (trust and civic participation) declines with greater inequality.
6. Higher social class or socioeconomic status gives individuals greater health and longevity chances. Some of the causes are direct, such as through nutrition, but many are indirect, through psychosocial influences. Relatively poor people experience more illness and live shorter lives than affluent people.
7. Within societies or communities where women have more equitable political and economic status with men, and ample reproductive rights, women will be healthier, less often disabled, and longer lived compared with women who live in places with less gender equality.
8. Ethnicity and race have effects on health that are independent of social class.
9. Development is most able to improve health and life expectancy when it increases overall wealth and equality, and includes policies that place a high priority on civic life.

Glossary

absolute poverty   Occurs when basic human needs for water, nutrition, and housing are not adequately met.

agrarian   Dominated by or related to subsistence farming or rural life.

alienation   The experience of personal and psychological separation from social groups.

anemia   A decrease in or subnormal levels of hemoglobulin, red blood cells, or both.

anomie   A shortage of rules, laws, and norms to guide human behavior in a society (Durkheim).

antiviral treatments   Medications that disrupt the life or replication of viruses; many have been developed for HIV/AIDS and are credited with prolonging life for many infected individuals.

acquaculture   Cultivation of fish or shellfish; fish farming.

atherosclerosis   The scarring and lining of the arteries with plaque, developed over time and implicated in cardiovascular disease.

biopsychosocial   A model or perspective that recognizes a combination of biological, psychological, and social influences and causes.

biosocial   A model or perspective that recognizes biological and social influences and causes.

bubonic plague   An infectious disease caused by bacteria transmitted by fleas; appeared in the early 1330s in China and spread to western Asia and Europe; became known as The Black Death, killing one-third of the European population; did not disappear until the 1600s.

cardiovascular disease   Results from arteriosclerosis (also known as atherosclerosis); degenerative changes and plaque formation occur in arterial walls from accumulation of cholesterol, other lipids, and additional substances.

chaebol   South Korean corporate conglomerates clustered together around a holding company, usually controlled by one family; first arose in the 1920s and 1930s under Japanese colonial rule; the system was continued following Korean independence.

chronic disease   Illness that is prolonged, does not resolve spontaneously, and is rarely cured completely (e.g., cardiovascular disease, diabetes).

class consciousness   A view of the world from the perspective of a particular social class (Marx).

colonialism   A policy in which a country rules other nations or territories and develops business and trade for its own rather than the host country's benefit.

core countries   In a world economic system, countries that have the most power, diversified economies, strong and stable states, and large middle classes (Wallerstein).

coronary prone   Prone to anger and hostility, and therefore more susceptible to cardiovascular disease.

coup d'état   Overthrow of a ruling government by force.

demography   The study of statistical information about human populations, such as size, density, distribution, disease, and other vital statistics.

dependency theory   A perspective that views less-developed countries as exploited and kept dependent by more-developed countries and transnational corporations.

developing countries   Those with both developed (e.g., industrial, electronic) and underdeveloped (e.g., subsistence agriculture) sectors of their economy.

disability-adjusted life years (DALYs)   A calculation by the World Health Organization that assesses a population's loss of able-bodied years of life; the estimated average years lost to disability is subtracted from life expectancy at birth to arrive at the disability-adjusted life expectancy.

division of labor   The specialization of work tasks among various workers and occupations.

double day   Combining a paid job in the labor force with a nonpaid job at home managing a household and caring for children; also called "the second shift" (Hochschild).

egalitarian   Valuing human equality with respect to social, political, and economic rights and privileges.

environmental racism   The concentration of toxic dumps and poison exposure in low-income neighborhoods—for example, those populated by African Americans and Latinos.

epidemiological transition   A population shift from a preponderance of infectious diseases to chronic or degenerative diseases and causes of death.

epidemiology   The branch of science that deals with the incidence, distribution, and control of disease in a population.

excess mortality   Higher-than-expected death rates, given a population's demographic characteristics; found in societies with relatively more inequality.

Gini Index   A measure of income inequality that gauges the distance away from a perfectly equal distribution of income in a population; the higher the score, the greater the inequality.

global apartheid   A concept suggesting an international system of minority rule by the wealthy and powerful, structured by race and place.

glucocorticoids   Chemicals activated during the stress response; an oversupply causes a wide variety of harmful effects on the body.

green revolution   An increased yield in food grains from the introduction of high-yield varieties, use of pesticides, and new management techniques.

gross domestic product per capita (GDPpc)   The value of all goods and services produced in a national economy, divided by the population.

gross national product (GNP)   A measure of the incomes of residents and companies within a country, including income they receive from abroad, but subtracting payments made to entities outside the country.

health gradient   Linear association between income levels and rates of morbidity and mortality.

healthy worker effect   Evidence in the United States of better health among working as opposed to nonworking adults; thought to be associated with a sense of self-worth and accomplishment from paid work.

immunity   The body's defense against a variety of toxins, malformed cells, bacteria, and foreign antigens.

indigenous peoples   Peoples who have originated in and lived naturally in a particular region or environment.

individualistic   Emphasis on separate individuals as opposed to social groups, communities, and their interconnections.

infanticide   Killing of an infant.

infectious disease   Illness transmitted from one person or organism to another (e.g., malaria, flu, HIV, tuberculosis).

inoculation   A substance injected into a person to create resistance to a disease.

international dollars   A measure used by the World Bank that refers to dollars that have the same purchasing power over gross national incomes as a U.S. dollar has in the United States. Purchasing power parity GNI is gross national income converted to international dollars using purchasing power parity rates.

keiretsu   A network of businesses that own stakes in one another as a means of mutual security, especially in Japan, and usually including large manufacturers and their suppliers of raw materials and components.

life chances   Structural constraints on an individual's economic and occupational opportunities, choices, and life trajectories (Weber).

longevity   Duration of life.

malaise   A general feeling of illness or depression without one specific cause; the absence of well-being.

malnutrition   Insufficient amount and variety of food in the diet or an excessive intake of unhealthy food, leading to physical harm.

market socialism   An economic strategy claimed by the Chinese government that embraces state-controlled development and participation in the global economy.

maquiladoras   Industrial-zone factories, located mostly in Mexico close to the southwestern border of the United States; subsidiaries of transnational corporations.

medicalized   A social process in which a condition (e.g., menopause, domestic violence, hyperactive children) becomes defined and treated medically as a biologically based disease.

morbidity   The number or rate of disease cases that occurs at a given time or in particular groups.

mortality   The number or rate of deaths that occurs at a given time, in a given group, or from a given cause.

neonatal infant mortality   Death within the first twenty-seven days of life.

paradigm   A model, pattern, or typical example of something.

peer cultures   Distinctive subcultures among friends, coworkers, or other social groups.

periphery countries   Countries with underdeveloped economies; their natural resources and inexpensive labor are often extracted by core and semi-periphery countries (Wallerstein).

personality factors   Personal factors that influence health and health-related behaviors (e.g., pessimism versus optimism, degree of anger and hostility).

political economy   A perspective that includes global and political forces, including the state, government, social classes, policy making and administration, and the distribution of resources among and between social groups.

postindustrial societies   Societies that have undergone an economic transition from being dominated by manufacturing to being dominated by services, along with the growth of professional and technical occupations, and the central role of knowledge and information; occurs within a global marketplace.

privatization   To change a business or industry from public (state) ownership to private control or ownership.

proletarian   A member of the working class.

psychological distress   Discomfort and upset that is rooted in ideas, feelings, and experiences.

psychosocial   Relating to psychological as well as social influences or causes.

racial profiling   Systematically different treatment of persons of color (while driving, shopping, or engaging in other public activities) by agents of the state, businesses, or other officials.

relative poverty   Groups experiencing poorer incomes and living conditions relative to other social groups; high degrees of inequality having damaging effects on population health.

residential segregation   The clustering and cordoning off of marginalized racial and ethnic groups in certain neighborhoods; results from discrimination and a greater preponderance of low incomes among groups of color.

self-efficacy   The sense of being in control of one's life.

semi-peripheral   As part of the world economic system, countries that have semi-diversified economies and weaker political institutions than core countries (Wallerstein).

social capital   Two distinct meanings in sociology: (1) the educational, social, and cultural advantages that accrue to people from upper classes. (2) As (used in this text), social assets (e.g., trust, civic participation, cohesion) that a community or society accumulates over time; fostered by low levels of inequality, emphasis on community (as opposed to individualism), and social institutions that foster participation and cooperation.

social cohesion   Within a community, closely knit social ties and a sense of connection, trust, and solidarity.

social Darwinism   Assertions of cultural superiority by colonial powers, adapted from Charles Darwin's biological theory of evolution.

social networks   The web of social interactions and connections among people; social network analysis is focused on uncovering the patterning of people's interaction.

stigma   A mark or characteristic of shame or dishonor.

stratification systems   Processes and institutions through which individuals and social groups are located at various positions of wealth, power, and status in social hierarchies.

style of life   Choices we make regarding personal tastes and activities, within the constraints of our life chances.

subsistence-level countries   Countries reliant primarily on widespread small-scale agricultural production; associated with low levels of infrastructure and higher population growth, infant mortality, illiteracy, and unemployment.

surplus value   The difference between the value of work done or of commodities produced by labor and the wage paid by the employer (Marx).

vital statistics   Statistics of human births, deaths, diseases, marriages, and divorces.

world systems theory   Immanuel Wallerstein's model of interconnections among core, semi-periphery, and periphery countries in a modern world economic system (from the sixteenth century to the present).

zaibatsu   The family-controlled banking and industrial powers of modern Japanese society; called *keiretsu* following World War II; the leading *zaibatsu* are Mitsui, Mitsubishi, Dai Ichi Kangyo, Sumitomo, Sanwa, and Fuyo.

Abbreviations

ADHD   attention deficit/hyperactivity disorder

AIDS   acquired immunodeficiency syndrome

CDCP   Centers for Disease Control and Prevention

CHD   coronary heart disease

CHIP   Child Health Insurance Program (California)

CIA   Central Intelligence Agency

DALYs   disability-adjusted life years

DSM IV   *Diagnostic and Statistical Manual* (4th edition)

GAVI   Global Alliance for Vaccines Immunizations

GDP   gross domestic product

GNP   gross national product

HIV   human immunodeficiency virus

ICPE   International Consortium in Psychiatric Epidemiology

INS   Immigration and Naturalization Service

IMF   International Monetary Fund

NAFTA   North American Free Trade Agreement

NGO   nongovernmental organization

MPLA   Angolan ruling party and forces

OECD   Organization for Economic Cooperation and Development

PAHO   Pan American Health Organization

PTSD   posttraumatic stress disorder

SES   socioeconomic status

RUF   Revolutionary United Front, rebel forces in Sierra Leone

TNCs   transnational corporations

TRIPS   trade-related aspects of intellectual property rights

UNICEF   United Nations Children's Emergency Fund

UNITA   Angolan rebel forces

USAID   United States Agency for International Development

WHO   World Health Organization

References

Adam, J. (1999). *Social costs of transformation to a market economy in post-socialist countries: The cases of Poland, the Czech Republic and Hungary*. New York: St. Martin's.

Adler, N., Boyce, W. T., Chesney, M. A., Cohen, S., Folkman, S., Kahn, R. L., & Syme, S. L. (1994). Socioeconomic status and health: The challenge of the gradient. *American Psychologist, 49*, 15–24.

Adler, N., Boyce, W. T., Chesney, M. A., Folkman, S., & Syme, L. (1993). Socioeconomic inequalities in health: No easy solution. *Journal of the American Medical Association, 269*(24), 3140–3144.

Africa: The heart of the matter. (2000, May 13). *The Economist*, pp. 22–24.

Ainsworth, M., & Semali, I. (1998). Who is most likely to die of AIDS? Socioeconomic correlates of adult deaths in Kagera Region, Tanzania. In M. Ainsworth, L. Fransen, & M. Over (Eds.), *Confronting AIDS: Evidence from the developing world*. Luxembourg: European Commission.

Alleyne, G. A. O. (2001). Latin America and the Caribbean. In C. E. Koop, C. E. Pearson, & M. R. Schwarz (Eds.), *Critical issues in global health* (pp. 21–28). San Francisco, CA: Jossey-Bass.

Almeida-Filho, N. (1993). *Becoming modern after all these years: Social change and mental health in Latin America*. (Working Paper, International Mental and Behavioral Health Project.) Boston: Center for the Study of Culture and Medicine, Harvard Medical School.

American Management Association. (1997, November). *Corporate downsizing, job elimination and job creation: Summary of key findings*. Chicago, IL: American Management Association.

Amick, B. C., & Lavis, J. N. (2000). Labor markets and health: A framework and set of applications. In A. R. Tarlov & R. F. St. Peter (Eds.), *The society and population health reader: A state and community perspective* (pp. 178–210). New York: New Press.

Amis, P. (1994). Indian urban poverty: Labor markets, gender, and shocks. *Journal of International Development, 6*(5), 635–643.

Anderson, J. W., & Moore, M. (1993, February 14). Born oppressed: Women in the developing world face cradle-to-grave discrimination, poverty. *Washington Post*, p. A1.

Anderson, N. (1989). Racial differences in stress-induced cardiovascular reactivity and hypertension: Current status and substantive issues. *Psychological Bulletin, 105*(1), 89–105.

Anderson, N., & Armstead, C. (1995). Toward understanding the association of socioeconomic status and health: A new challenge for the biopsychosocial approach. *Psychosomatic Medicine, 57*, 213–225.

Anderson, R. N., Kochanek, K. D., & Murphy, S. L. (1997). Report of final mortality statistics, 1995. *Monthly Vital Statistics Report, 45*(11), supplement 2. Hyattsville, MD: National Center for Health Statistics.

Aneshensel, C. S., & Stone, J. D. (1982). Stress and depression: A test of the buffering model of social support. *Archives of General Psychiatry, 39*, 1392–1396.

Angola: A third force. (2000, May 13). *The Economist*, p. 46.

Aninat Ureta, E. (1994). *Exposicion sobre el estado de la hacienda publica*. Santiago, Chile: Santiago Ministerio de Hacienda.

Anything grows [Survey of Argentina Insert]. (2000, June 6). *The Economist*, pp. 10–12.

Arcellana, N. P. (1998). Cambodia: Watered by women's sweat and tears. *Women in Action, 1*, 72–74.

Arnetz, B. B., Brenner, S., Hjelm, R. Levi, L., & Petterson, I. (1988). *Stress reaction in relation to threat of job loss and actual unemployment: Physiological, psychological and economic effects of job loss and unemployment* (Stress Research Reports No. 206). Stockholm, Sweden: Karolinska Institute.

Association of Asian Pacific Community Health Organizations. (1997). *Taking action: Improving access to health care for Asian Pacific Islanders*. Oakland, CA: Association of Asian Pacific Community Health Organizations.

Asvall, J. E., & Alderslade, R. (2001). Europe. In C. E. Koop, C. E. Pearson, & M. R. Schwarz (Eds.), *Critical issues in global health* (pp. 37–46). San Francisco, CA: Jossey-Bass.

Ayittey, G. B. N. (1998). *Africa in chaos.* New York: St. Martin's.

Balan, J. (1998). Higher education reform: Meeting the challenge of economic competition. In J. S. Tulchin & A. M. Garland (Eds.), *Argentina: The challenges of modernization* (pp. 283–296). Wilmington, DE: SR Books.

Balcazar, H., Denman, C., & Lara, F. (1995). Factors associated with work-related accidents and sickness among maquiladora workers: The case of Nogales, Sonora, Mexico. *International Journal of Health Services, 25*(3), 489–502.

Bandura, A. (1977). Self-efficacy: Toward a unifying theory of behavior change. *Psychological Review, 84,* 191–215.

Barefoot, J. C., Larsen, S., von der Lieth, L., & Schroll, M. (1995). Hostility, incidence of acute myocardial infarction, and mortality in a sample of older Danish men and women. *American Journal of Epidemiology, 142,* 477–484.

Bartley, M. (1987). Unemployment and health, selection or causation: A false antithesis? *Sociology of Health and Illness, 10*(1), 41–67.

Bartley, M., Ferrie, J., & Montgomery, S. M. (1999). Living in a high-unemployment economy: Understanding the health consequences. In M. Marmot & R. G. Wilkinson (Eds.), *Social determinants of health* (pp. 81–104). New York: Oxford University Press.

Batliwala, S. (1983, March 17–18). *Women in poverty: The energy, health and nutrition syndrome.* Paper presented at a workshop on Women and Poverty at the Centre for Studies in Social Sciences, Calcutta, India.

Bayley, D. H. (1976). *Forces of order: Police behavior in Japan and the United States.* Berkeley: University of California Press.

Beale, N., & Nethercott, S. (1985). Job loss and family morbidity: A study of a factory closure. *Journal, Royal College of General Practitioners, 35,* 510–514.

Bean, F. D., & Tienda, M. (1987). *The Hispanic population of the United States.* New York: Russell Sage Foundation.

Bebbington, P., & Kuipers, L. (1994). The clinical utility of expressed emotion in schizophrenia. *Acta Psychiatrica Scandinavica, 89,* 46–53.

Bell, C. (1997). Stress-related disorders in African-American children. *Journal of the National Medical Association, 89*(5), 335–340.

Berger, P. (1991). *The capitalist revolution: Fifty propositions about prosperity, equality, and liberty* (2nd ed.). New York: Basic Books.

Berkman, L. (1995). The role of social relations in health promotion. *Psychosomatic Medicine, 57,* 245–254.

Berkman, L. (2000). Social networks and health: The bonds that heal. In A. R. Tarlov & R. F. St. Peter (Eds.), *The society and population health reader: A state and community perspective* (pp. 259–277). New York: New Press.

Bezruchka, S. (2000). Is globalization dangerous to our health? *Western Journal of Medicine, 172,* 332–334.

Bhagwati, J. (1966). *The economics of underdeveloped countries.* New York: McGraw-Hill.

Biggart, N. W., & Guillen, M. F. (1999, October). Developing difference: Social organization and the rise of the auto industries of South Korea, Taiwan, Spain, and Argentina. *American Sociological Review, 64,* 722–747.

Binswanger, H. P. (2000, June 23) Scaling up HIV/AIDS programs to national coverage. *Science, 288,* 2173–2176.

Blane, D. (1999). The life course, the social gradient, and health. In M. Marmot & R. G. Wilkinson (Eds.), *Social determinants of health* (pp. 64–80). New York: Oxford University Press.

Blauner, R. (1969). Internal colonialism and ghetto revolt. *Social Problems, 16,* 393–409.

Bloom, B. R., Bloom, D. E., Cohen, J. E., & Sachs, J. D. (1999, May 7). Investing in the World Health Organization. *Science, 284,* 911.

Bloom, D. E., & Canning, D. (2000, February 18). The health and wealth of nations. *Science, 287,* 1207–1209.

Bloom, D. E., & River Path Associates. (2000, June 23). Something to be done: Treating HIV/AIDS. *Science, 288,* 2171–2173.

Blum, R. W., Harmon, B., Harris, L., Bergeisen, L., & Resnick, M. D. (1992). American Indian–Alaska Native youth health. *Journal of the American Medical Association, 267,* 1634–1644.

Blumberg, R. L. (1978). *Stratification: Socioeconomic and sexual inequality.* Dubuque, IA: William C. Brown.

Blumberg, R. L. (1984). A general theory of gender stratification. In R. Collins (Ed.), *Sociological theory* (pp. 23–101). San Francisco, CA: Jossey-Bass.

Booker, S., & Minter, W. (2001, July 9). Global apartheid. *The Nation, 273*(2), 11–17.

Bornschier, V., & Chase-Dunn, C. (1985). *Transnational corporations and underdevelopment.* New York: Praeger.

Boswell, T., & Dixon, W. J. (1990). Dependency and rebellion: A cross-national analysis. *American Sociological Review, 55*, 540–549.

Bottomore, T. (1964/1993). *Elites and society*. New York: Routledge.

Bourdieu, P. (1984). *Distinction: A social critique of the judgement of taste*. London: Routledge.

Bourdieu, P. (1986). The forms of capital. In J. G. Richardson (Ed.), *Handbook of theory and research for the sociology of education* (pp. 241–258). New York: Greenwood Press.

Bowman, J. (1994). "Water is best": Would Pindar still think so? In B. Cartledge (Ed.), *Health and the environment* (pp. 85–125). Oxford, UK: Oxford University Press.

Bradley, D. (1994). Health, environment, and tropical development. In B. Cartledge (Ed.), *Health and the environment* (pp. 126–149). Oxford, UK: Oxford University Press.

Brains v. bugs. (2001, November 10). *The Economist*, pp. 6–8.

Braslavsky, C. (1998). Restructuring the Argentine educational system, 1984–1995. In J. S. Tulchin & A. M. Garland (Eds.), *Argentina: The challenges of modernization* (pp. 297–314). Wilmington, DE: SR Books.

Braun, D. (1997). *The rich get richer: The rise of income inequality in the United States and the world*. Chicago: Nelson Hall.

Brenner, J., Ross, J., Simmons, J., & Zaidi, S. (1999). Neoliberal trade and investment and the health of *maquiladora* workers on the U.S.-Mexican border. In J. Y. Kim, J. V. Millen, A. Irwin, & J. Gershman (Eds.), *Dying for growth: Global inequality and the health of the poor* (pp. 261–290). Monroe, ME: Common Courage Press.

Brody, E. B. (1987). *Mental health and world citizenship: The view from an international, nongovernmental organization*. Austin, TX: Hogg Foundation for Mental Health.

Brody, E. B. (2001). Mental health. In C. E. Koop, C. E. Pearson, & M. R. Schwarz (Eds.), *Critical issues in global health* (pp. 127–134). San Francisco, CA: Jossey-Bass.

Brown, E. R. (2000, May). California's growing uninsured population and options to expand coverage. *UCLA Center for Health Policy Research and UCLA School of Public Health*. Retrieved December 18, 2001, http://www.healthpolicy.ucla.edu

Brown, G. W., Andrews, B., Harris, T. O., Adler, Z., & Bridge, L. (1986). Social support, self-esteem and depression. *Psychological Medicine, 16*, 813–831.

Brown, G. W., & Harris, T. O. (1978). *The social origins of depression: A study of psychiatric disorder in women*. New York: Free Press.

Brown, L. (1997). Facing the prospect of food scarcity. In L. R. Brown, C. Flavin, & H. French (Eds.), *State of the world 1997* (pp. 23–41). New York: W. W. Norton.

Brugha, T. S., Bebbington, P. E., MacCarthy, B., Sturt, E., Wykes, T., & Potter, J. (1990). Gender, social support and recovery from depressive disorders: A prospective clinical study. *Psychological Medicine, 20*, 147–156.

Bruhn, J. G., & Wolf, S. (1979). *The Roseto story*. Norman: University of Oklahoma Press.

Brundtland, G. H. (2000). Mental health in the 21st century. *Bulletin of the World Health Organization, 78*(4), 411–534.

Brundtland, G. H. (2001). The future of the world's health. In C. E. Koop, C. E. Pearson, & M. R. Schwarz (Eds.), *Critical issues in global health* (pp. 3–11). San Francisco, CA: Jossey-Bass.

Brunner, E. (1996). The social and biological basis of cardiovascular disease in office workers. In E. Brunner, D. Blane, & R. G. Wilkinson (Eds.), *Health and social organization* (pp. 272–302). London: Routledge.

Brunner, E., & Marmot, M. (1999). Social organization, stress, and health. In M. Marmot & R. G. Wilkinson (Eds.), *Social determinants of health* (pp. 17–43). Oxford, UK: Oxford University Press.

Cambodia embarks on long-awaited Army cuts. (n.d.). *CNN World News*. Retrieved May 8, 2000, http://www.cnn.com

Carter, J. (2001). Foreword. In C. E. Koop, C. E. Pearson, & M. R. Schwarz (Eds.), *Critical issues in global health* (pp. xix–xxi). San Francisco, CA: Jossey-Bass.

Cartledge, B. (1994). Introduction. In B. Cartledge (Ed.), *Health and the environment* (pp. 1–6). Oxford, UK: Oxford University Press.

Centeno, M. A. (1994). Between rocky democracies and hard markets: Dilemmas of the double transition. *Annual Review of Sociology, 20*, 125–147.

Centers for Disease Control and Prevention. (1997). Vaccination coverage by race/ethnicity and poverty level among children aged 19–35 months—United States, 1996. *Journal of the American Medical Association, 278*, 1655–1656.

Centers for Disease Control and Prevention. (2000). HIV/AIDS surveillance report. In A. J. Lemelle, C. Harrington, & A. J. LeBlanc (Eds.), *Readings in the sociology of AIDS* (pp. 33–35). Upper Saddle River, NJ: Prentice Hall.

Central Intelligence Agency. (1999). *CIA world fact-book—1999.* Washington, DC: Central Intelligence Agency.

Central Intelligence Agency. (2000). *CIA world fact-book—2000.* Washington, DC: Central Intelligence Agency.

Chase-Dunn, C., & Grimes, P. (1995). World-systems analysis. *Annual Review of Sociology, 21,* 387–417.

Chen, L., Huq, E., & D'Souza, S. (1981). Sex bias in the family allocation of food and health care in rural Bangladesh. *Population and Development Review, 7,* 55–70.

China steps up "one child" policy. (2000, September 25). *BBC News Online.* Retrieved February 9, 2002, http://news.bbc.co/uk/hi/english/world/asia-pacific/newsid_941000/941511.stm

Christianson, S. (1998). *With liberty for some: 500 years of imprisonment in America.* Boston: Northeastern University Press.

Cobb, S., Brooks, G. W., Kasl, S. V., & Connelly, W. E. (1966). The health of people changing jobs. *American Journal of Public Health, 56,* 1476–1481.

Cockerham, W. C. (1998). *Medical sociology* (7th ed.). Englewood Cliffs, NJ: Prentice Hall.

Cockerham, W. C. (1999). *Health and social change in Russia and Eastern Europe.* London: Routledge.

Coleman, J. S. (1988). Social capital in the creation of human capital. *American Journal of Sociology, 94* (Suppl.), S95–S120.

Collins, R. (1975). *Conflict sociology: Toward an explanatory science.* New York: Academic Press.

Collins, R. (1988). *Theoretical Sociology.* San Diego, CA: Harcourt, Brace, Jovanovich.

Collins, R., & Coltrane, S. (1995). *Sociology of marriage and the family* (4th ed.). Chicago: Nelson Hall.

Community-based AIDS prevention and care in Africa: Building on local initiatives, case studies from five African countries. (n.d.). *Population Council.* Retrieved February 27, 2002, http://www.popcouncil.org/ebert/wellbriefing.html

Community organizing to change conditions inside a worksite: Omaha together one community. (1998, June–July). *Organizing, 10.* Omaha, NE: Center for Community Change. Retrieved February 9, 2002, http://www.communitychange.org/organizing/OTOC10.htm

Conforti, J. M. (1999, Winter). The China model of Korean reunification. *East Asia: An international quarterly, 17*(4), 55–77.

Connell, R. W. (1987). *Gender and power.* Stanford, CA: Stanford University Press.

Cooper, R. (1984). A note on the biological concept of race and its application in epidemiologic research. *American Heart Journal, 108*(3, part 2), 715–723.

Cooper, R. S., Steinhauer, M., Schatzkin, A., & Miller, W. (1981). Improved mortality among U.S. blacks, 1968–78: The role of antiracist struggle. *International Journal of Health Services, 11,* 511–522.

Council on Ethical and Judicial Affairs, American Medical Association. (1990). Black-white disparities in health care. *Journal of the American Medical Association, 263,* 2344–2346.

Cox, D., Galasso, E., & Jimenez, E. (2000). *Inter-country comparisons of private transfers.* Washington, DC: World Bank.

Cross-National Collaborative Group. (1992). The changing rate of major depression. *Journal of the American Medical Association, 268,* 3098–3105.

Danziger, A., & Gottschalk, P. (1993). *Uneven tides: Rising inequality in America.* New York: Russell Sage.

Defo, B. K. (1997). Effects of socioeconomic disadvantage and women's status on women's health in Cameroon. *Social Science Medicine, 44*(7), 1023–1042.

de la Fuente, J. R., Alvarez Del Rio, F., Tapia-Conyer, R., & Ares de Parga, A. R. (2001). Mexico. In C. E. Koop, C. E. Pearson, & M. R. Schwarz (Eds.), *Critical issues in global health* (pp. 91–100). San Francisco, CA: Jossey-Bass.

Department of Health and Social Security. (1980). *Inequalities in health: Report of a research working group (The Black Report).* London: Department of Health Social Security.

Dercon, S. (1999, September). *Income risk, coping strategies and safety nets.* Background paper for the World Development Report 2000/2001. Oxford, UK: Center for the Study of African Economies, Oxford University.

Dercon, S., & Krishnan, P. (2000). Vulnerability, seasonality and poverty in Ethiopia. In B. Baulch & J. Hoddinott (Eds.), *Economic mobility and poverty dynamics in developing countries.* London: Frank Crass.

Desjarlais, R., Eisenberg, L., Good, B., & Kleinman, A. (1995). *World mental health: Problems and priorities in low-income countries.* New York: Oxford University Press.

di Tella, G., & Dornbusch, R. (1989). Introduction: The political economy of Argentina, 1946–83. In G. di Tella & R. Dornbusch (Eds.), *The political economy of Argentina, 1946–83* (pp. 1–15). Pittsburgh, PA: University of Pittsburgh.

Dobash, R. E., & Dobash, R. (1979). *Violence against wives*. New York: Free Press.

Dohrenwend, B. P., & Dohrenwend, B. S. (1969). *Social status and psychological disorder*. New York: Wiley.

Dressler, W. W. (1993). Health in the African American community: Accounting for health inequalities. *Medical Anthropology, 7*, 325–345.

Durkheim, E. (1893/1973). Organic solidarity and contractual solidarity. In R. Bellah (Ed.), *Emile Durkheim on morality and society* (pp. 86–113). Chicago: University of Chicago Press.

Durkheim, E. (1897/1966). *Suicide*. New York: Free Press.

Eaton, W. W. (2001). *The sociology of mental disorders* (3rd ed.). Westport, CT: Praeger.

ElderCare skill builders: Overcoming isolation. (2000). *ElderCare Online*. Retrieved February 9, 2002, http://www.ec-online.net/Knowledge/SB/SBisolation.html

Eller, T. J. (1994, February). Household wealth and asset ownership: 1991. *U.S. Bureau of the Census, current population reports*. (DHHS Publication No. SB/94–2, pp. 70–134). Washington, DC: U.S. Government Printing Office.

Embracing Afghan refugees. (2001, September 19). *Christian Science Monitor, 93*(207), 10.

Engels, F. (1884/1972). *The origin of the family, private property and the state*. New York: International Publishers.

Evans, P. (1989). Predatory, developmental, and other apparatuses: A comparative political economy perspective on the third world state. *Sociological Forum, 4*, 561–587.

Evans, P., & Timberlake, M. (1980). Dependence, inequality, and the growth of the tertiary: A comparative analysis of less developed countries. *American Sociological Review, 45*, 531–552.

Exhibit portrays victims. (2000, April 21). CNN Web.

Farley, R., & Allen, W. (1987). *The color line and the quality of life in America*. New York: Oxford University Press.

Firebaugh, G., & Beck, F. D. (1994, October). Does economic growth benefit the masses? Growth, dependence, and welfare in the third world. *American Sociological Review, 59*, 631–653.

Foucault, M. (1973). *Madness and civilization: A history of insanity in the age of reason*. New York: Random House.

Foucault, M. (1978). *The history of sexuality*. New York: Pantheon.

Foucault, M. (1979). *Discipline and punish: The birth of the prison*. New York: Random House.

Francis, D. R. (2000, January 5). Russia's growing health crisis. *Christian Science Monitor, 92*(30), 9.

Freedberg, L. (2000, October 1). Insuring California's children. *San Francisco Chronicle*, p. 2.

Freud, S. (1961). *Civilization and its discontents*. (J. Strachey, Ed. and Trans.). New York: W. W. Norton.

Frigenti, L., Harth, A., & Huque, R. (1998). *Local solutions to regional problems: The growth of social funds and public works and employment projects in sub-Saharan Africa*. Washington, DC: Water and Urban 2 Division Africa Region, World Bank.

Fuhrer, R., Stansfeld, S. A., Hudry-Chemali, J., & Shipley, M. J. (1999). Gender, social relations and mental health: Prospective findings from an occupational cohort (Whitehall II Study). *Social Science Medicine, 48*, 77–87.

Fukuyama, F. (1995). *Trust: The social virtues and the creation of prosperity*. New York: Free Press.

Gage, T. B. (1994, May). Population variation in cause of death: Level, gender, and period effects. *Demography, 31*, 271–296.

Gaiha, R., & Deolalikar, A. (1993). Persistent, expected and innate poverty: Estimates for semi-arid and rural India 1975–1984. *Cambridge Journal of Economics, 17*, 409–421.

Garrett, L. (2000). *Betrayal of trust: The collapse of global public health*. New York: Hyperion.

Geronimus, A. T. (1992). The weathering hypothesis and the health of African-American women and infants: Evidence and speculations. *Ethnicity and Disease, 2*, 207–221.

Gerth, H., & Mills. C. W. (Trans. and Eds.) (1969). *From Max Weber: Essays in sociology*. New York: Oxford University Press.

Getting from here to there [Survey of Argentina Insert]. (2000, June 6). *The Economist*, pp. 3–5.

Gezairy, H. A. (2001). Eastern Mediterranean region. In C. E. Koop, C. E. Pearson, & M. R. Schwarz (Eds.), *Critical issues in global health* (pp. 28–36). San Francisco, CA: Jossey-Bass.

Ghastly domestic abuse: Burning women. (1997, February 2). *CNN World News*. Retrieved February 14, 2002, http://www.cnn.com/WORLD/9702/10/pakistan.women/index.html

Giddens, A. (1991). *Modernity and self-identity*. Cambridge, UK: Polity Press.

Glewwe, P., & Hall, G. (1998). Are some groups more vulnerable to macroeconomic shocks than others? Hypothesis tests based on panel data from Peru. *Journal of Development Economics, 56*, 181–206.

Goat milk holds key to malaria cure. (2001, December 18). *Ottawa Citizen*, p. A13.

Gold, T. B. (1986). *State and society in the Taiwan miracle*. Armonk, NY: M. E. Sharpe.

Goldsmith, J. (1994). *The trap*. New York: Carroll & Graf.

Goldstone, J. A., Gurr, T. R., & Moshiri, F. (Eds.). (1991). *Revolutions of the late twentieth century*. Boulder, CO: Westview Press.

Goode, E. (2001, August 28). Minorities' care for mental ills is called inferior. *New York Times*. Retrieved December 18, 2001, http://www.nytimes.com/2001/08/27/national/27MENT.html?todaysheadlines

Green, R. H. (1970). Political independence and the national economy: An essay on the political economy of decolonization. In C. Allen & R. W. Johnson (Eds.), *African perspectives* (pp. 273–324). Cambridge, UK: Cambridge University Press.

Greenberg, M., & Schneider, D. (1994). Violence in American cities: Young black males is the answer, but what was the question? *Social Science Medicine, 39*, 179–187.

Gregorio, D., Walsh, S., & Paturzo, D. (1997). The effects of occupation-based social position on mortality in a large American cohort. *American Journal of Public Health, 87*(9), 1472–1475.

Grenier, P. (1997). *Still dying for a home: An update of Crisis' 1992 investigation into the links between homelessness, health and mortality*. London: Crisis.

Grootaert, C., & Braithwaite, J. (1998). *Poverty correlates and indicator-based targeting in Eastern Europe and the former Soviet Union*. (Policy Research Working Paper No. 1942). Washington, DC: World Bank.

Gwatkin, D. R., Guillot, M., & Heuveline, P. (1999). The burden of disease among the global poor. *Lancet, 354*, 586–89.

Gwyther, M. E., & Jenkins, M. (1998). Migrant farmworker children: Health status, barriers to care, and nursing innovations in health care delivery. *Journal of Pediatric Health Care, 12*, 60–66.

Hahn, R. A., Eaker, E., Barker, N. D., Teutsch, S. M., Sosniak, W., & Krieger, N. (1995, September 5). Poverty and death in the United States—1973 and 1991. *Epidemiology, 6*, 490–497.

Hartmann, H. (1981). The family as the locus of gender, class, and political struggle: The example of housework. *Signs, 6*, 366–394.

Harvey, C., & Lewis, S. R., Jr. (1990). *Policy choice and development performance in Botswana*. New York: St. Martin's.

Haub, C. (1994). Population change in the former Soviet Republics. *Population Bulletin, 49*. Washington, DC: Population Reference Bureau.

Hayward, M. D., Crimmins, E. M., Miles, T. P., & Yang, Y. (2000). The significance of socioeconomic status in explaining the racial gap in chronic health conditions. *American Sociological Review, 65*, 910–930.

The health of nations. (2001, December 22). *The Economist*, pp. 83–84.

The heart of the matter. (2000, May 13). *The Economist*, pp. 22–24.

Heise, L. (1993). Violence against women: The missing agenda. In M. Koblinsky, J. Timyan, & J. Gay (Eds.), *The health of women: A global perspective* (pp. 171–195). Boulder, CO: Westview Press.

Helping the other guys. (1999, February 27). *The Economist*, p. 39.

Henderson, A. S. (1981). Social relationships, adversity and neurosis: An analysis of prospective observations. *British Journal of Psychiatry, 138*, 391–398.

Hewlett, S. A. (1993). *Child neglect in rich nations*. New York: UNICEF.

Hogue, C. J. R., Buehler, J. W., Strauss, L. T., & Smith, J. C. (1987). Overview of the national infant mortality surveillance (NIMS) project: Design, methods, results. *Public Health Report, 102*, 126–138.

Holmes, T. H. (1956). Multidiscipline studies of tuberculosis. In P. J. Sparer (Ed.), *Personality, stress, and tuberculosis*, (pp. 65–152). New York: International Universities Press.

Honigsbaum, M. (2001, November 24). The monkey puzzle. *The Guardian* (London), p. 32.

Horowitz, I. L. (1972). *Three worlds of development: The theory and practice of international stratification* (3rd ed.). New York: Oxford University Press.

Horton, S., & Mazumdar, D. (1999, October). *Vulnerable groups and labor: The aftermath of the Asian financial crisis*. Paper prepared for World Bank/International Labor Organization (ILO)/Japan Ministry of Labor/Japan Institute of Labor Seminar on Economic Crisis, Employment and Labor Market in East and South-East Asia, Tokyo, Japan.

House, J. S., Landis, K. R., & Umberson, D. (1988, July). Social relationships and health. *Science, 241*, 540–545.

Institute for Women's Policy Research. (1996). *The status of women in the states* (Library of Congress Card Catalogue Number 96-79874). Washington, DC: Institute for Women's Policy Research.

Isaac, T. M., Franke, R. W., & Raghavan, P. (1998). *Democracy at work in an Indian industrial cooperative: The story of Kerala Dinesh Beedi*. Ithaca, NY: Cornell University Press.

It's an unfair world [Survey of Argentina Insert]. (2000, June 6). *The Economist*, pp. 14–15.

Jackson, J. S., Brown, T. N., Williams, D. R., Torres, M., Sellers, S. L., & Brown, K. (1996). Perceptions and experiences of racism and the physical and mental health status of African Americans: A thirteen year national panel study. *Ethnicity and Disease, 6*(1,2), 132–147.

Jaffee, D. (1985). Export dependence and economic growth: A reformulation and respecification. *Social Forces, 64*, 102–118.

Jalan, J., & Ravallion, M. (1999, July). *Income gains to the poor from workfare: Estimates for Argentina's Trabajar Program.* (Policy Research Working Paper No. 2149). Washington, DC: World Bank.

James, S. A. (1993). Racial and ethnic differences in infant mortality and low birthweight. *Annals of Epidemiology, 3*, 130–136.

Jaynes, G., & Williams, R., Jr. (1989). *A common destiny: Blacks and American society.* Washington, DC: National Academy Press.

Jenkins, J. C., & Scanlan, S. J. (2001, October). Food security in less developed countries, 1970 to 1990. *American Sociological Review, 66*, 718–744.

Johnson, C. (1982). *MITI and the Japanese miracle.* Stanford, CA: Stanford University Press.

Jorgensen, S. L., & Van Domelen, J. (1999, February 4–5). *Helping poor manage risk better: The role of social funds.* (Social Protection Discussion Paper No. 9934). Paper presented at the Inter-American Development Bank Conference on Social Protection and Poverty, Washington, DC.

Kaplan, G. A., & Lynch, J. (1997). Whither studies on socioeconomic foundations of population health? [Editorial]. *American Journal of Public Health, 87*(9), 1409–1411.

Kaplan, G. A., Pamuk, E., Lynch, J. W., Cohen, R. D., & Balfour, J. L. (1996). Inequality in income and mortality in the United States: Analysis of mortality and potential pathways. *British Medical Journal 312*, 999–1003.

Karoly, L. (1993). The trend in inequality among families, individuals, and workers in the United States: A twenty-five year perspective. In S. Danziger & P. Gottschalk (Eds.), *Uneven tides: Rising inequality in America* (pp. 19–98). New York: Russell Sage.

Katz, J. (1999). *How emotions work.* Chicago: University of Chicago Press.

Kaur, S. R., & Herxheimer, A. (1994, January 15). Recognizing patients' rights: Patchy progress. *Lancet, 343*(8890), 132.

Kawachi, I., & Kennedy, B. P. (1997). Health and social cohesion: Why care about income inequality? *British Medical Journal, 314*, 1037–1040.

Kawachi, I., Kennedy, B. P., Gupta, V., & Prothrow-Stith, D. (1999). Women's status and the health of women and men: A view from the states. In I. Kawachi, B. P. Kennedy, & R. G. Wilkinson (Eds.), *The society and population health reader: Volume 1, Income inequality and health* (pp. 474–491). New York: New Press.

Kawachi, I., Kennedy, B. P., Lochner, K., & Prothrow-Stith, D. (1997). Social capital, income inequality, and mortality. *American Journal of Public Health, 87*(9), 1491–1498.

Kawachi, I., Levine, S., Miller, S. M., Lasch, K., & Amick, B. (1994). *Income inequality and life expectancy: Theory, research and policy.* (Working Paper No. 94–2, Joint Program on Society and Health). Boston: New England Medical Center.

Keith, V. M., & Herring, C. (1991). Skin tone and stratification in the black community. *American Journal of Sociology, 97*, 760–78.

Kennedy, B. P., Kawachi, I., & Brainerd, E. (1999a). The role of social capital in the Russian mortality crisis. In I. Kawachi, B. P. Kennedy, & R. G. Wilkinson (Eds.), *The society and population health reader: Volume 1, Income inequality and health* (pp. 260–277). New York: New Press.

Kennedy, B. P., Kawachi, I., Lochner, K., Jones, C. P., & Prothrow-Stith, D. (1999b). (Dis)respect and black mortality. In I. Kawachi, B. P. Kennedy, & R. G. Wilkinson (Eds.), *The society and population health reader: Volume 1, Income inequality and health* (pp. 465–473). New York: New Press.

Kennedy, B. P., Kawachi, I., & Prothrow-Stith, D. (1996). Income distribution and mortality: Test of the Robin Hood Index in the United States. *British Medical Journal, 312*, 1004–1007.

Kerbo, H., & McKinstry, J. (1998). *Modern Japan.* Boston: McGraw-Hill.

Kessler, R. C., & McLeod, J. D. (1985). Social support and mental health in community samples. In S. Cohen & S. L. Syme (Eds.), *Social support and health* (pp. 219–240). Orlando, FL: Academic Press.

Kessler, R. C., & Neighbors, H. W. (1986). A new perspective on the relationships among race, social class, and psychological distress. *Journal of Health Social Behavior, 27*, 107–115.

Keys, S., & Kennedy, M. (1992). *Sick to death of homelessness.* London: Crisis.

Kim, J. Y., Shakow, A., Bayona, J., Rhatigan, J., & Rubín de Celis, E. L. (2000). Sickness amidst recovery: Public debt and private suffering in Peru. In J. Y. Kim, J. V. Millen, A. Irwin, & J. Gershman (Eds.), *Dying for growth: Global inequality and the health of the poor* (pp. 127–153). Monroe, ME: Common Courage Press.

King, G., & Williams, D. R. (1995). Race and health: A

multi-dimensional approach to African American health. In S. Levine, D. C. Walsh, B. C. Amick, & A. R. Tarlov (Eds.), *Society and health: Foundation for a nation* (pp. 93–130). York: Oxford University Press.

Klare, M. (1999, January/February). The Kalashnikov age. *Bulletin of the Atomic Scientists, 5*(1), 18–22.

Knudsen, C., & McNown, R. (1993). Changing causes of death and the sex differential in the USA: Recent trends and projections. *Population Research and Policy Review, 12*, 27–42.

Knust, A. E., & Mackenbach, J. P. (1994). The size of mortality differences associated with educational level in nine industrialized countries. *American Journal of Public Health, 84*, 932–937.

Kochar, A. (1995). Explaining household vulnerability to idiosyncratic income shocks. *AEA Papers and Proceedings 85*(2); 159–164.

Kochar, A. (1999). Smoothing consumption by smoothing income: Hours-of-work response to idiosyncratic agricultural shocks in rural India. *AEA Papers and Proceedings, 85*(2), 159–164.

Kohn, M. L., & Clausen, J. A. (1955). Social isolation and schizophrenia. *American Sociological Review, 20*, 268–273.

Kolko, G. (1999). Ravaging the poor: The International Monetary Fund indicted by its own data. *International Journal of Health Services, 29*(1), 51–57.

Koop, C. E., Pearson, C. E., & Schwarz, M. R. (Eds.). (2001). *Critical issues in global health*. San Francisco, CA: Jossey-Bass.

Kramer, M. (1989). Barriers to prevention. In B. Cooper and T. Helgason (Eds.), *Epidemiology and the prevention of mental disorders* (pp. 30–55). London: Routledge.

Krieger, N., Rowley, D., Herman, A., Avery, B., & Phillips, M. (1993). Racism, sexism, and social class: Implications for studies of health, disease, and well being. *American Journal of Preventive Medicine, 9*(6), 82–122.

Kumanyika, S. K. (1987). Obesity in black women. *Epidemiologic Review, 9*, 31–50.

Kumar, B. G. (1993). Low mortality and high morbidity in Kerala reconsidered. *Population and Development Review, 19*(1), 103–121.

Kunitz, S. J. (1996). The history and politics of U.S. health care policy for American Indians and Alaskan natives. *American Journal of Pubic Health, 86*, 1464–1473.

Kwast, B. E. (1989). Maternal mortality: Levels, causes and promising interventions. *Journal of Biosocial Science, 21*(Suppl. 10), 51–67.

Lacey, R. (1994). An abundance of cheap eggs, fish, and meat: The consequences. In B. Cartledge (Ed.), *Health and the environment* (pp. 46–84). Oxford, UK: Oxford University Press.

LaFraniere, S. (2001, August 28). Russian men living lush, but short, lives. *Washington Post*. Retrieved February 2, 2002, http://seattletimes.nwsource.com/html/nationworld/134334356_dying28.html

Lappé, F. M., Collins, J., & Rosset, P. (1998). *World hunger: Twelve myths* (2nd ed.). New York: Grove.

LaVeist, T. A. (1989). Linking residential segregation and infant mortality in U.S. cities. *Sociology and Social Research, 73*, 90–94.

LaVeist, T. A. (1992). The political empowerment and health status of African-Americans: Mapping a new territory. *American Journal of Sociology, 97*, 1080–1095.

Lee, M. A. (2001, March 5). The globalization of sexual slavery. *San Francisco Guardian*. Retrieved February 9, 2002, http://www.commondreams.org/views01/0305–06.htm

Leff, J. (2001). *The unbalanced mind*. New York: Columbia University Press.

Lenski, G. E. (1966). *Power and privilege: A theory of stratification*. New York: McGraw-Hill.

Lin, T. Y., Rin, H., Yeh, E. K., Hsu, C. C., & Chu, H. M. (1969). Mental disorders in Taiwan, fifteen years later. In W. Caudill & T. Y. Lin (Eds.), *Mental health research in Asia and the Pacific* (pp. 66–91). Honolulu, HI: East-West Center Press.

London, B. (1987). Structural determinants of Third World urban change: An ecological and political economic analysis. *American Sociological Review, 52*, 28–43.

London, B. (1988). Dependence, distorted development, and fertility trends in noncore nations: A structural analysis of cross-national data. *American Sociological Review, 53*, 606–618.

London, B., & Robinson, T. D. (1989). The effect of international dependence on income inequality and political violence. *American Sociological Review, 54*, 305–308.

London, B., & Smith, D. A. (1988). Urban bias, dependence, and economic stagnation in noncore nations. *American Sociological Review, 53*, 454–463.

London, B., & Williams, B. A. (1988). Multinational corporate penetration, protest, and basic needs provision in noncore nations: A cross-national analysis. *Social Forces, 66*, 747–773.

London, B., & Williams, B. A. (1990). National politics, international dependency, and basic needs provision: A cross-national study. *Social Forces, 69,* 565–584.

Lucas, A. O. (2001). Africa. In C. E. Koop, C. E. Pearson, & M. R. Schwarz (Eds.), *Critical issues in global health* (pp. 12–20). San Francisco, CA: Jossey-Bass.

Lund, F., & Srinivas, S. (1999, November). *Learning from experience: A gendered approach to social protection for workers in the informal economy.* Paper prepared for International Labor Organization (ILO)/Women in Informal Employment Globalizing and Organizing (WIEDO) Seminar on Social Protection for Women Workers in the Informal Economy, International Labor Organization, December 6–8, 1999, Geneva, Switzerland.

Lurie, N., Ward, N. B., Shapiro, M. F., & Brook, R. H. (1984). Termination from Medi-Cal—does it affect health? *New England Journal of Medicine, 311,* 480–484.

Madörin, K. (2002). When parents die of AIDS: The children of Kagera, Tanzania. *Novartis Foundation for Sustainable Development.* Retrieved February 27, 2002, http://www.foundation.novartis.com/social_development/children_aids_tanzania.htm

Maluccio, J., Haddad, L., & May, J. (2000, August). Social capital and household welfare in South Africa 1993–1998. *Journal of Development Studies, 36*(6), 54–81.

Mandinger, M. O. (1985). Health service funding cuts and the declining health of the poor. *New England Journal of Medicine, 313,* 44–47.

Mann, J. M. (1999). Human rights and AIDS: The future of the pandemic. In J. M. Mann, S. Gruskin, M. A. Grodin, & G. J. Annas (Eds.), *Health and human rights* (pp. 217–226). New York: Routledge.

Mann, J. M., Tarantola, D., & Netter, T. W. (Eds.) (1992). *AIDS in the world.* Cambridge, MA: Harvard University Press.

Mann, J. M., Tarantola, D., O'Malley, J., & Global AIDS Policy Coalition. (2000). Toward a new health strategy to control the HIV/AIDS pandemic. In A. J. Lemelle, C. Harrington, & A. J. LeBlanc (Eds.), *Readings in the sociology of AIDS* (pp. 302–310). Upper Saddle River, NJ: Prentice Hall.

Markides, K. S., & Coreil, J. (1986). The health of Hispanics in the southwestern United States: An epidemiological paradox. *Public Health Reports, 101*(3), 253–265.

Marmot, M. G. (1986). Social inequalities in mortality: The social environment. In R. G. Wilkinson (Ed.), *Class and health: Research and longitudinal data* (pp. 21–34). London: Tavistock.

Marmot, M. G. (2000). Inequalities in health: Causes and policy implications. In A. R. Tarlov & R. F. St. Peter (Eds.), *The society and population health reader: A state and community perspective* (pp. 293–309). New York: New Press.

Marmot, M. G., Rose, G., Shipley, M., & Hamilton, P. J. S. (1978). Employment grade and coronary heart disease in British civil servants. *Journal of Epidemiology and Community Health, 32,* 244–249.

Marshall, G. (1997). *Repositioning class: Social inequality in industrial societies.* London: Sage.

Massey, D. (1996). The age of extremes: Concentrated affluence and poverty in the twenty-first century. *Demography, 33*(4), 395–412.

Maurstad, D. (2000, January 24). *Memorandum: Review of working conditions in Nebraska meatpacking plants.* Retrieved February 9, 2002, http://gov.nol.org/Johanns/billrights/ltgovmemo.htm

McDonough, P., Duncan, G. C., Williams, D., & House, J. (1997). Income linked to health and mortality. *American Journal of Public Health, 87*(9), 1476–1483.

McGinnis, J. M. (2001). United States. In C. E. Koop, C. E. Pearson, & M. R. Schwarz (Eds.), *Critical issues in global health* (pp. 50–90). San Francisco, CA: Jossey-Bass.

McGinnis, J. M., & Foege, W. H. (1993). Actual causes of death in the United States. *Journal of the American Medical Association, 270,* 2207–2212.

McKinlay, J. B., & McKinlay, S. J. (1977). The questionable effect of medical measures on the decline of mortality in the United States in the twentieth century. *Milbank Memorial Fund Quarterly, 55,* 405–428.

McMichael, P. (1996). *Development and social change: A global perspective.* Thousand Oaks, CA: Pine Forge/Sage.

Merchant, K. M., & Kurz, K. M. (1993). Women's nutrition through the lifecycle: Social and biological vulnerabilities. In M. Koblinsky, J. Timyan, & J. Gray (Eds.), *The health of women: A global perspective* (pp. 63–90). Boulder, CO: Westview Press.

Millen, J. V., & Holtz, T. H. (2000). Dying for growth, Part I: Transnational corporations and the health of the poor. In J. Y. Kim, J. V. Millen, A. Irwin, & J. Gershman (Eds.), *Dying for growth: Global inequality and the health of the poor* (pp. 3–10). Monroe, ME: Common Courage Press.

Miller, J. E., & Korenman, S. (1994). Poverty and children's nutritional status in the United States. *American Journal of Epidemiology, 140,* 233–243.

Minuchin, S., Rosman, B. L., & Baker, L. (1978). *Psychosomatic families: Anorexia nervosa in context.* Cambridge, MA: Harvard University Press.

Morris, J. K., & Cook, D. G. (1994). Loss of employment and mortality. *British Medical Journal, 308,* 1135–1139.

Morrison, A., & Orlando, M. B. (1999). In A. Morris & M. L. Biehl (Eds.), *Too close to home: Domestic violence in the Americas* (pp. 51–80). Washington, DC: Inter-American Development Bank.

Moser, C. (1998). The asset vulnerability framework: Reassessing urban poverty reduction strategies. *World Development, 26*(1), 1–19.

Moss, N., & Krieger, N. (1995). Measuring social inequalities in health: Report on the Conference of the National Institutes of Health. *Public Health Reports, 110*(3), 302–305.

Mullica, R. F., Donelan, K., Tor, S., Lavelle, J., Elias, C., Frankel, M., Bennett, D., & Blendon, R. J. (1991). Repatriation and disability: A community study of health, mental health and social functioning of the Khmer residents of Site Two. (Working Paper). Boston: Harvard Program in Refugee Trauma, The Harvard School of Public Health, and the World Federation for Mental Health.

Mullica, R. F., & Son, L. (1989). Cultural dimensions in the evaluation and treatment of sexual trauma: An overview. *Psychiatric Clinics of North America, 12,* 363–379.

Mullings, L. (1989). Inequality and African-American health status: Policies and prospects. In W. A. VanHome & T. V. Tonnesen (Eds.), *Twentieth century dilemmas—twenty-first century prognoses* (pp. 154–182). Madison: University of Wisconsin Institute on Race and Ethnicity.

Murray, C. J. L. (1994). Quantifying the burden of disease: The technical basis for DALYs. *Bulletin of the World Health Organization, 72*(3), 429–445.

Murray, C. J. L., & Lopez, A. D. (Eds.). (1996). *The global burden of disease.* Cambridge, MA: Harvard University Press.

Murray, C. J. L., Michaud, C. M., McKenna, M. T., & Marks, J. S. (1994). *U.S. patterns of mortality by county and race: 1965–1994.* Cambridge, MA: National Center for Chronic Disease Prevention and Health Promotion, Atlanta and Harvard Center for Population and Development Studies.

Mutare diocese community care program agent of community change. (2001). *Catholic Relief Services.* Retrieved February 27, 2002, http://www.catholicrelief.org/where/zimbab/partner/cfm

Nam, C. B., Rogers, R. G., & Hummer, R. A. (1996). Impact of future cigarette smoking scenarios on mortality of the adult population in the U.S.: 2000–2050. *Social Biology, 43*(3–4), 155–168.

Narayan, D. (2000). *Voices of the poor: Can anyone hear us?* New York: Oxford University Press.

Nathanson, C. A. (1984). Sex differences in mortality. *Annual Review of Sociology, 10,* 191–213.

Nathanson, C. A., & Lopez, A. D. (1987). The future of sex mortality differentials in industrialized societies: A structural hypothesis. *Population Research and Policy Review, 6*(1), 123–136.

Neff, J. (2001). *The unbalanced mind.* New York: Columbia University Press.

Nigeria: Making a bad cop good. (2000, May 13). *The Economist,* p. 46.

A night of madness. (1991, August 12). *Time 138*(6), p. 43.

Noland, M., Robinson, S., & Wang, T. (1999). Famine in North Korea. Retrieved December 18, 2001, www.nautilus.org/pub/ftb/napsnet/specialreports/Famine_In_North-Korea.txt

Omi, S. (2001). Western Pacific. In C. E. Koop, C. E. Pearson, & M. R. Schwarz (Eds.), *Critical issues in global health* (pp. 47–55). San Francisco, CA: Jossey-Bass.

Omran, A. R. (1971). The epidemiological transition. *Milbank Memorial Fund Quarterly, 49,* 509–538.

Pan American Health Organization. (1999). *Brazil: Basic Country Health Profiles, Summaries.* Retrieved December 18, 2001, http://www.paho.org/english/SHA/prfbra.htm

Pan American Health Organization. (2000a). *Health situation analysis: Annual report of the director—2000.* Retrieved March 7, 2002, http://www.paho.org/Project.asp?SEL=HD&LNG+Eng&CD+HTREN

Pan American Health Organization. (2000b). *Health situation analysis in the Americas, 1999–2000.* Retrieved March 7, 2002, http://www.paho.org/English/SHA/be_v21n4-editorial.htm

Pappas, G., Queen, S., Hadden, W., & Fisher, G. (1993). The increasing disparity in mortality between socioeconomic groups in the United States, 1960 and 1986. *New England Journal of Medicine, 329,* 103–109.

Parkes, C. M., Benjamin, B., & Fitzgerald, R. G. (1969). Broken hearts: A statistical study of increased mortality among widowers. *British Medical Journal, 1,* 740–743.

Passell, P. (1993, June 27). Dr. Jeffrey Sachs, shock therapist. *New York Times Magazine, 142*(49375), 20–21, 52–54, 60.

Pérez-Stable, E. J. (1991). Cuba's response to the HIV epidemic. *American Journal of Public Health, 81*(5), 563–567.

Peters, K., Kochanek, K. D., & Murphy, S. L. (1998). Deaths: Final data for 1996. *National Vital Statistics Reports, 47*(9), 1–100.

Polednak, A. P. (1991). Black-white differences in infant mortality in 38 standard metropolitan statistical areas. *American Journal of Public Health, 81,* 1480–1482.

Polednak, A. P. (1993). Poverty, residential segregation, and black/white mortality rates in urban areas. *Journal of Health Care for the Poor and Underserved, 4*(4), 363–373.

Powell, L. H. (1990, October). Emotional arousal as a predictor of long-term mortality and morbidity in post M.I. men. *Circulation, 82*(Suppl. III), 259.

Prescott, N., & Pradhan, M. (1999, February 4–5). *Coping with catastrophic health shocks.* Paper prepared for Inter-American Development Bank (IDB) Conference on Poverty and Social Protection, Washington, DC.

Preston, S. H. (1975). The changing relation between mortality and level of economic development. *Population Studies, 29,* 231–248.

Przeworski, A. (1991). *Democracy and the market: Political and economic reforms in Eastern Europe and Latin America.* Cambridge, UK: Cambridge University Press.

Putnam, R. D. (1993). *Making democracy work: Civic traditions in modern Italy.* Princeton, NJ: Princeton University Press.

Quinton, D., Rutter, M., & Liddle, C. (1984). Institutional rearing, parenting difficulties and marital support. *Psychological Medicine, 14,* 107–124.

Rape war crime verdict welcomed. (2001, February 23). *CNN World News.* Retrieved February 12, 2002, http://cnn.com/2001/WORDD/europe/02/23/hague.trial/

Remmer, K. L. (1986, October). The politics of economic stabilization: IMF standby programs in Latin America, 1954–1984. *Journal of Comparative Politics, 19*(1), 1–24.

Renner, M. (1998). Curbing the proliferation of small arms. *State of the world, 1998* (pp. 131–148). New York: W. W. Norton.

Renner, M. (1999). Ending violent conflict. *State of the world, 1999* (pp. 151–168). New York: W. W. Norton.

Retherford, R. D. (1975). *The changing sex differential in mortality.* Westford, VT: Greenwood Press.

Rhoades, E. R., Hammond, J., Welty, T. K., Handler, A. O., & Amler, R. W. (1987). The Indian burden of illness and future health interventions. *Public Health Reports, 102*(4), 361–368.

Rice, D. P., Kelman, S., & Miller, L. S. (1992). Estimates of economic costs of alcohol and drug abuse and mental illness, 1985 and 1988. *Public Health Reports, 106*(3), 280–292.

Ritter, A. (1992). *Development strategy and structural adjustment in Chile.* Ottawa: North-South Institute.

Robbins, R. (2002). *Global problems and the culture of capitalism* (2nd ed.). Boston: Allyn and Bacon.

Robins, L. N., & Regier, D.A. (Eds.). (1992). *Psychiatric disorders in America: The epidemiologic catchment area study.* New York: Free Press.

Robinson, J. C. (1984). Racial inequality and the probability of occupation-related injury or illness. *Milbank Quarterly, 62,* 567–590.

Robinson, J. C. (1986). Job hazards and job security. *Journal of Health Politics and Policy Law, 11,* 117.

Rodgers, G. B. (1979). Income inequality as determinant of mortality: An international cross-sectional analysis. *Population Studies, 33,* 343–351.

Rogers, R., Hummer, R., & Nam, C. (2000). *Living and dying in the USA: Behavioral, health, and social differentials of adult mortality.* San Diego, CA: Academic Press.

Rogot, E., Sorlie, P. D., Johnson, N. J., & Schmitt, C. (1992). *A mortality study of 1.3 million persons by demographic, social, and economic factors: 1979–85 follow-up* (NIH Publication No. 92–3297). Washington, DC: U.S. Department of Health and Human Services.

Rootman, I., & Hancock, T. (2001). Canada. In C. E. Koop, C. E. Pearson, & M. R. Schwarz (Eds.), *Critical issues in global health* (pp. 101–108). San Francisco, CA: Jossey-Bass.

Rubin, L. B. (1994). *Families on the fault line.* New York: Harper Collins.

Sachs, J. (1999, August 14). Helping the worlds' poorest. *The Economist,* pp. 17–20.

Sandhaus, S. (1998). Migrant health: A harvest of poverty. *American Journal of Nursing, 98,* 52–53.

Sapolsky, R. M. (1993). Endocrinology alfresco: Psychoendocrine studies of wild baboons. *Recent Progress in Hormone Research, 48,* 437–468.

Satcher, D. (2001, April 4). Global mental health: Its time has come. *Journal of the American Medical Association, 285*(1), 1697.

Satcher calls for natio to close disparities in health and care. (1999, Jun 25). *Focus: News from Harvard Medical, Dental and Public Schools.* Retrieved February 14, 200 , http://www.med.harvard.edu/publications/Foc s/1999/June25_1999/class.html

Scheper-Hughes, N. (1992). *Death without weeping: The violence of everyday life in Brazil.* Berkeley, CA: University of California Press.

Schnabel, P. (1992). Down and out: Social marginality and homelessness. *International Journal of Social Psychiatry, 38*(1), 59–67.

Schulman, K. A., Berlin, J. A., Harless, W., Kerner, J. F., Sistrunk, S., Gersh, B. J., Dubé, R., Taleghani, C. K., Burke, J. E., Williams, S., Eisenberg, J. M., Escarce, J. J., & Ayers, W. (1999, February 25). The effect of race and sex on physicians' recommendations for cardiac catheterization. *New England Journal of Medicine, 340*(8), 618–626.

Seaman, J. (1994). Population, food supply, and famine: An ecological or an economic dilemma? In B. Cartledge (Ed.), *Health and the environment* (pp. 29–45). Oxford, UK: Oxford University Press.

Seligman, M. E. (1991). *Learned optimism.* New York: Knopf.

Sen, A., & Sengupta, S. (1983). Malnutrition of rural children and the sex bias. *Economic and Political Weekly, 19*, Annual Number May, 855–864.

Sen, K., & Bonita, R. (2000, August 12). Global health status: Two steps forward, one step back. *Lancet, 356*(9229), 577–582.

Shaiken, H. (1993, August 22). Two Myths about Mexico. *New York Times*, Editorial/Op-Ed.

Shaw, M., Dorling, D., & Smith, G. D. (1999). Poverty, social exclusion, and minorities. In M. Marmot & R. G. Wilkinson (Eds.), *Social determinants of health* (pp. 211–239). New York: Oxford University Press.

Shkolnikov, V., Meslé, F., & Vallin, J. (1996). Recent trends in life expectancy and causes of death in Russia, 1970–1993. In J. L. Bobadilla & C. Costello (Eds.), *Mortality profiles and adult health interventions in the newly independent states.* Washington, DC: National Academy Press.

Sierra Leone's agony. (2000, May 13). *The Economist*, pp. 45–46.

Sinha, S., & Lipton, M. (1999, October). *Damaging fluctuations, risk and poverty: A review.* Background paper for the World Development Report 2000/2001. Brighton, UK: Poverty Research Unit, University of Sussex.

Somerville, C. (1997). Reaction and resistance: Confronting economic crisis, structural adjustment, and devaluation in Dakar, Senegal. In C. Green (Ed.), *Globalization and survival in the black diaspora: The new urban challenge* (pp. 15–41). Albany: State University of New York Press.

Stallings, B., & Kaufman, R. (Eds.). (1989). *Debt and democracy in Latin America.* Boulder, CO: Westview Press.

Stansfeld, S. A. (1999). Social support and social cohesion. In M. Marmot & R. G. Wilkinson (Eds.), *Social determinants of health* (pp. 155–178). New York: Oxford University Press.

Stansfeld, S. A., Fuhrer, R., & Shipley, M. (1998). Types of social support as predictors of psychiatric morbidity in a cohort of British civil servants (Whitehall II Study). *Psychological Medicine, 28*, 881–892.

State woman testifies about strip search humiliation. (2001, August 14). *Milwaukee Journal Sentinel.* Retrieved January 1, 2002, http://www.legis.state. wi.us/senate/sen04/news/ART2001–162.htm

Steinmetz, S., & Straus, N. A. (1974). *Violence in the family.* New York: Dodd, Mead.

Sternberg, S. (1999, September 15). Zimbabwe: Kids forced into manhood. *USA Today.* Retrieved February 27, 2002, http://www.usatoday.com/ life/health/aids/lhaid046.htm

Stokes, R., & Jaffee, D. (1982). Another look at the export of raw materials and economic growth. *American Sociological Review, 47*, 402–407.

Straus, M. A., Gelles, R., & Steinmetz, S. (1980). *Behind closed doors.* New York: Doubleday.

Suh, M. (1998). *Developmental transformation in South Korea: From state-sponsored growth to the quest for quality of life.* Westport, CT: Praeger.

Sutton, R., & Kahn, R. L. (1987). Prediction, understanding and control as antidotes to organizational stress. In J. W. Lorsch (Ed.), *Handbook of organizational behavior* (pp. 272–285). Englewood Cliffs, NJ: Prentice Hall.

Syme, S. L. (1991). Control and health: A personal perspective. *Advances, 7*, 16–27.

Tarlov, A. R., & St. Peter, R. F. (2000). Introduction. In A. R. Tarlov & R. F. St. Peter (Eds.), *The society and population health reader: A state and community perspective* (pp. ix–xxv). New York: New Press.

Tillman, W. A., & Hobbs, G. E. (1949). The accident-prone driver: A study of the psychiatric and social background. *American Journal of Psychiatry, 106*(49), 321–331.

Tremblay, R. E. (1999). When children's social development fails. In D. P. Keating & C. Hertzman (Eds.), *Developmental health and the wealth of nations* (pp. 55–71). New York: Guilford.

Tucker, R. C. (Ed.). (1972). *The Marx-Engels reader.* New York: W. W. Norton.

Tulchin, J. S., & Garland, A. M. (Eds.). (1998). *Argentina: The challenges of modernization.* Wilmington, DE: SR Books.

Tumin, M. M. (1953). Some principles of stratification: A critical analysis. *American Sociological Review, 18,* 387–394.

Twaddle, A. C. (1999). *Health care reform in Sweden, 1980–1994.* Westport, CT: Auburn House.

UNAIDS/WHO Global AIDS Statistics. (December, 2001). *AIDS epidemic update—December 2001.* Retrieved January 23, 2002, http://www.unaids.org/epidemic_update/report_dec01/index.html

UNICEF. (1998). *The state of the world's children, 1998.* Oxford, UK: Oxford University Press.

United Nations. (1991). *The world's women 1970–1990: Trends and statistics.* New York: United Nations.

United Nations Development Programme. (1997). *Human development report 1997.* New York: Oxford University Press.

United States Agency for International Development. (1997). Women—An untapped resource for African growth. *Gender Action, 1*(3), 2–3.

Upbeat Cambodian leader returns home after lucrative meeting. (n.d.). *CNN World News.* Retrieved May 29, 2000, http://www.cnn.com

Vega, W. A., & Amaro, H. (1994). Latino outlook: Good health, uncertain prognosis. *Annual Review of Public Health, 15,* 39–68.

Violence against women: An international health issue. (1997, Winter). *Women's International Network News, 23*(1), 39.

Waldron, I. (1983). Sex differences in human mortality: The role of genetic factors. *Social Science and Medicine, 17*(6), 321–333.

Wallerstein, I. (1974/1980). *The modern world-system, Vols. 1 and 2.* New York: Academic Press.

Wallerstein, I. (1974a). The rise and future demise of the world capitalist system: Concepts for comparative analysis, *Comparative Studies in Society and History, 16,* 387–394, 397–415.

Wallerstein, I. (1974b). Dependence in an interdependent world: The limited possibilities of transformation within the capitalist world-economy. *African Studies Review, 17,* 1–26.

Walsh, J., Feifer, C., Measham, A., & Gertler, P. (1993). Maternal and perinatal health. In D. Jamison, H. Mosley, A. Measham, & J. Bobadilla (Eds.), *Disease control priorities in developing countries* (pp. 363–390). Oxford, UK: Oxford Medical Publications.

Wardlaw, L. A. (2000). Sustaining informal caregivers for persons with AIDS. In A. J. Lemelle, C. Harrington, & A. J. LeBlanc (Eds.), *Readings in the sociology of AIDS* (pp. 119–134). Upper Saddle River, NJ: Prentice Hall.

Waters, M., & Eschbach, K. (1995). Immigration and ethnic and racial inequality in the United States. In J. Hagan & K. S. Cook (Eds.), *Annual review of sociology, 21* (pp. 419–446). Palo Alto, CA: Annual Reviews.

Waters, T. (2001). *Bureaucratizing the Good Samaritan.* Boulder, CO: Westview Press.

Waxler, N. E. (1977). Is outcome for schizophrenia better in nonindustrial societies? The case of Sri Lanka. *Journal of Nervous and Mental Disease, 167,* 144–158.

Weber, M. (1946/1969). Class, status, party. In H. Gerth & C. W. Mills (Trans. and Eds.), *Max Weber: Essays in sociology* (pp. 180–195). New York: Oxford University Press.

Weissman, S. R. (1990). Structural adjustment in Africa: Insights from the experiences of Ghana and Senegal. *World Development, 18*(12), 1621–1635.

Weitz, R. (2000). *The sociology of health, illness, and health care: A critical approach* (2nd ed.). Belmont, CA: Wadsworth/Thompson Learning.

Wenkang, Z., & Schwarz, M. R. (2001). People's Republic of China. In C. E. Koop, C. E. Pearson, & M. R. Schwarz (Eds.), *Critical issues in global health* (pp. 56–61). San Francisco, CA: Jossey-Bass.

Weyland, K. (1997). Growth with equity in Chile's new democracy? *Latin American Research Review, 32*(1), 37–68.

White, P. (1998). Urban life and social stress. In D. Pinder (Ed.), *The New Europe: Economy, society and environment.* Chichester, UK: Wiley.

Wickrama, K., Lorenz, F., Conger, R., & Elder, G. (1997). Linking occupational conditions to physical health through marital, social and interpersonal processes. *Journal of Health and Social Behavior, 38*(4), 363–375.

Wilkinson, R. G. (1994). The epidemiological transition: From material scarcity to social disadvantage? *Daedalus (Journal of the American Academy of Arts and Sciences), 123*(4), 61–77.

Wilkinson, R. G. (1996). *Unhealthy societies: The afflictions of inequality.* London: Routledge.

Wilkinson, R. G. (1997, February 22). Health inequalities: Relative or absolute material standards? *British Medical Journal, 314*(7080), 591–595.

Wilkinson, R. G. (1999). Putting the picture together: prosperity, redistribution, health, and welfare. In M. Marmot & R. G. Wilkinson (Eds.), *Social determinants of health* (pp. 256–274). New York: Oxford University Press.

Wilkinson, R. G. (2000). Social relations, hierarchy, and health. In A. R. Tarlov & R. F. St. Peter (Eds.), *The society and population health reader: A state and community perspective* (pp. 211–235). New York: New Press.

Williams, D. R. (1990). Socioeconomic differentials in health: A review and redirection. *Social Psychology Quarterly, 53*(2), 81–99.

Williams, D. R. (1992). Black-white differences in blood pressure: The role of social factors. *Ethnicity and Disease, 2,* 126–141.

Williams, D. R. (2000). Race and health in Kansas: Data, issues and directions. In A. R. Tarlov & R. F. St. Peter (Eds.), *The society and population health reader: A state and community perspective* (pp. 236–258). New York: New Press.

Williams, D. R., & Collins, C. (1995). U.S. socio-economic and racial differences in health: Patterns and explanations. *Annual Review of Sociology, 21,* 349–386.

Williams, D. R., Lavizzo-Mourey, R., & Warren, R. C. (1994). The concept of race and health status in America. *Public Health Reports, 109,* 26–41.

Williams, D. R., Yu, Y., Jackson, J. S., & Anderson, N. B. (1997). Racial differences in physical and mental health: Socio-economic status, stress and discrimination. *Journal of Health Psychology, 2,* 335–351.

Williams, R. (1989). *The trusting heart: Great news about Type A behavior.* New York: Times Books.

Williams, D., Takeuchi, D., Adair, R. (1992). Socioeconomic status and psychiatric disorder among blacks and whites. *Social Forces, 71,* 179–194.

Wimberly, D. W. (1990). Investment dependence and alternative explanations of Third World mortality: A cross-national study. *American Sociological Review, 55,* 75–91.

Wimberly, D. W. (1991). Transnational corporate investment and food consumption in the Third World: A cross-national analysis. *Rural Sociology, 56,* 406–431.

Wimberly, D. W., & Bello, R. (1992). Effects of foreign investment, exports, and economic growth on third world good consumption. *Social Forces, 70,* 895–921.

Wolf, E. (1982). *Europe and the people without history.* Berkeley: University of California Press.

Women's lives at risk. (1997, September). *Population Reports, 25*(1), 3–7.

World Bank. (1993). *World development report 1993: Investing in health.* New York: Oxford University Press.

World Bank (1994). *World development report 1994.* Washington, DC: World Bank.

World Bank. (1997). *Sector strategy: Health, nutrition, and population.* Washington, DC: World Bank.

World Bank. (1999). *World development report 1999.* Washington, DC: World Bank.

World Bank. (2000). *World development report 1999/2000.* Washington, DC: World Bank.

World Bank. (2001). *World development report 2000/2001: Attacking poverty.* Washington, DC: World Bank.

World Bank, China Country Office. (2000). *China: The health sector.* Retrieved December 18, 2001, http://www.worldbank.org.cn/english/content/347n648939.shtmi

World Health Organization. (1979). *Schizophrenia: An international follow-up study.* Geneva, Switzerland: World Health Organization.

World Health Organization. (1993, May 12). *World health assembly calls for the elimination of harmful traditional practices* [Press release]. Geneva, Switzerland: World Health Organization.

World Health Organization. (1998). *The world health report 1998: Life in the 21st century, a vision for all.* Geneva, Switzerland: World Health Organization.

World Health Organization. (2000). *The world health report 2000 and statistical annex.* Geneva, Switzerland: World Health Organization.

World Health Organization. (2001). *WHO reports on global surveillance of epidemic-prone infectious diseases.* Retrieved February 22, 2001, http://www.whoint/emc-documents/surveillance/docs/whocdscsrisr2001.html/hiv_aids/hiv_aids.htm# Trends

World Health Organization, International Consortium in Psychiatric Epidemiology. (2000). Cross-national comparisons of the prevalences and correlates of mental disorders. *Bulletin of the World Health Organization: The International Journal of Public Health 78*(4), 413–426.

World Health Organization, South East Asia Regional Office. (2001a, June). *Health country profile: India.* Retrieved November 21, 2001 http://www.whosea.org/cntryhealth/india/index.htm

World Health Organization, South East Asia Regional Office. (2001b, June). *Health situation.* Retrieved November 24, 2001, http://www.whosea.org/health_situt_94–97/htm

World Health Organization, Western Pacific Regional Office. (2001). *Health country profile: China.* Retrieved December 18, 2001, http://www.

wpro.who.int/chips/chip01/ctry.cfm?ctrycode=chn&body=chn.htm&flag=chn.gif&ctry=CHINA,%20PEOPLE'S%20REPUBLIC%20OF

World's poor need more money for health. (2002, January 4). *Toronto Star*, p. A22.

Wright, E. O. (1978). *Class, crisis, and the state*. London: New Left Books.

Yeh, E. K., et al. (1987). Social changes and prevalence of specific mental disorders. *Chinese Journal of Mental Health 3*, 31–42.

Yllo, K. (1999). Sexual equality and violence against wives in American states. In I. Kawachi, B. P. Ken-nedy, & R. G. Wilkinson (Eds.), *The Society and Population Health Reader: Volume 1, Income Inequality and Health* (pp. 449–464). New York: New Press.

York, T. (1996, September 20). It's truly a brave new plastic-surgery world. *Silicon Valley/San Jose Business Journal*. Retrieved February 20, 2002, http://sanjose.bizjournals.com/sanjose/stories/1996/09/23/editorial1.html

Yunus, M. (1999). *Banker to the poor: Micro-lending and the battle against world poverty*. New York: Public Affairs.

Index